Haciendas and Plantations in Latin American History

Edited by Robert G. Keith

HM

HOLMES & MEIER PUBLISHERS, INC.

New York   London

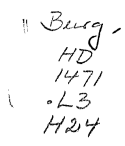

Published in the United States of America 1977 by
Holmes & Meier Publishers, Inc.
101 Fifth Avenue
New York, New York 10003

Great Britain:
Holmes & Meier Publishers, Ltd.
Hillview House
1, Hallswelle Parade, Finchley Road
London NW11 ODL

Copyright © Holmes & Meier Publishers, Inc. 1977

LIBRARY OF CONGRESS CATALOGING IN PUBLICATION DATA

Main entry under title:

Haciendas and plantations in Latin American history.

  Bibliography: p.
  1. Haciendas—Latin America—History. 2. Plantations—Latin America—History. I. Keith, Robert G.
HD1471.L3H24   338.1'098   77-7587
ISBN 0-8419-0319-0

PRINTED IN THE UNITED STATES OF AMERICA

Contents

iv

Acknowledgments

"Haciendas and Plantations" by Eric R. Wolf and Sidney W. Mintz, reprinted from *Social and Economic Studies,* 6 (1957) by permission of the Institute of Social and Economic Studies of the University of the West Indies and the authors.

"The Early Brazilian Sugar Economy," from *The Economic Growth of Brazil: A Survey from Colonial to Modern Times,* translated by Ricardo W. de Aguiar and Eric Charles Drysdale. Copyright © 1963 by the Regents of the University of California; reprinted by permission of the University of California Press.

"The Rise of the Cuban Central," from *Sugar and Society in the Caribbean: An Economic History of Cuban Agriculture,* translated by Marjory M. Urquidi. Reprinted by permission of Yale University Press.

"Masters and Slaves in Southern Brazil," reprinted by permission of the author and publisher from *Vassouras: A Brazilian Coffee County, 1850-1900* by Stanley Stein. Copyright © 1957 by the President and Fellows of Harvard College.

"Spanish Land Grants and the Hacienda in Mexico," from *Land and Society in Colonial Mexico: The Great Hacienda* by François Chevalier, translated by Alvin Eustis. Copyright © 1963 by the Regents of the University of California; reprinted by permission of the University of California Press.

"Masters and Slaves in the Brazilian Northeast," from *The Masters and the Slaves: A Study in the Development of Brazilian Civilization* by Gilberto Freyre, translated by Samuel Putnam 2nd edition, revised. Copyright 1946, © 1956 by Alfred A. Knopf. Reprinted by permission.

"A Land-Grabbing Hacendado," from *Broad and Alien is the World* by Ciro Alegría, translated by Harriet de Onís. Copyright 1941 by Farrar & Rinehart. Reprinted by permission of Holt, Rinehart & Winston.

"The Problem of Hacienda Markets," from *Precios del maíz y crisis agrícolas en México (1708-1810)* by Enrique Florescano. Copyright 1969 by El Colegio de México. Translated and printed by permission of the publishers.

"The Hacienda as an Investment," from *Miners and Merchants in Bourbon Mexico* by David A. Brading. Published in 1971 by the Syndics of the Cambridge University Press. Reprinted by permission of Cambridge University Press.

"Patron and Peon on an Andean Hacienda," from *The Villagers (Huasipungo)* by Jorge Icaza, translated by Bernard M. Dulsey. Copyright © 1964 by Southern Illinois University Press. Reprinted by permission of Southern Illinois University Press.

"A Chilean Fundo" from *Chile: Land and Society* by George M. McBride. Copyright 1936 by the American Geographical Society of New York. Reprinted by permission of the publishers.

"Hacienda Labor in the Valley of Mexico," reprinted from *The Aztecs under Spanish Rule: A History of the Indians of the Valley of Mexico, 1519-1810* with the permission of the publishers, Stanford University Press. Copyright © 1964 by the Board of Trustees of the Leland Stanford Junior University.

"Sharecropping on the Peruvian Coast," from *La hacienda en el Perú* by Henri Favre, Claude Collin Delavaud, and José Matos Mar. Published in 1967 by the Instituto de Estudios Peruanos. Translated and printed by permission of the author.

"The North Mexican Ranch," by François Chevalier, from *The New World Looks at its History,* edited by Archibald R. Lewis and Thomas F. McGann. Copyright © 1963 by the University of Texas Press; reprinted by permission of the publishers.

"The Brazilian Sertanejo," from *Rebellion in the Backlands* by Euclides da Cunha, translated by Samuel Putnam. Copyright 1944. Copyright under International Copyright Union by the University of Chicago. All rights reserved. Reprinted by permission of the University of Chicago Press.

Introduction

Robert G. Keith

European settlement in the western hemisphere gave rise to two distinct types of agrarian systems. In the temperate north, the land was divided into medium-sized farms cultivated mainly by the owners and their families. To the south, on the other hand, the prevailing pattern was one of large aristocratic estates worked by landless laborers or slaves. Such estates were known in English and French as plantations, in Spanish as *haciendas,* and in Portuguese as *fazendas.* In Latin America, this traditional system of large estates, which we may call the hacienda system, has survived in many areas down to the present day, though it has increasingly come to be seen as an obstacle to modernization.

What exactly was a hacienda? It is usually described as a large estate, and this it clearly was in a social sense, since aristocratic status and the ownership of haciendas were closely associated in Latin American history. In an economic sense, on the other hand, the two terms are not exactly equivalent. The primary meaning of "estate" in English is property, something that belongs to someone. Thus a landed estate could be—and often has been—no more than an elaborate country residence surrounded by parks and gardens. "Hacienda," on the other hand (the term is derived from the Spanish verb *hacer,* to do, has the primary meaning of a profit-making or income-producing enterprise. In the past it was not always an agricultural enterprise; there were mining haciendas, lumbering haciendas, and even glass-making haciendas, for instance. And it may be remembered that the treasury, that is the organization which collected the king's taxes and provided his income, was known as the "royal hacienda." From this point of view it would seem more accurate to call agricultural haciendas large farms or latifundia than great estates. This brings its own difficulties, however. For if haciendas were simply large farms, they

1

must be distinguished from small farms which were not haciendas. This cannot be done on the basis of size alone, since the value and importance of haciendas was not always proportional to their size. The small haciendas of the southern coast of Peru or the Chalco region near Mexico City, for instance, tended to be worth considerably more than much larger haciendas in more remote areas.

The traditional hacienda, then, was basically two things: it was an estate which belonged to a recognized member of a privileged elite, and it was a commercial farm which provided an income sufficient to support the conspicuous consumption which demonstrated aristocratic status. Ideally this income did not depend on the owner's direct involvement in the enterprise, since in the traditional view aristocrats were not expected to engage in manual labor or commercial activities. Aristocratic income, in other words, was theoretically unearned income. But though this concept of aristocracy greatly influenced the development of Latin American society, it could not be rigidly enforced. Thus members of the elite could allow themselves to earn money from government jobs, and wealthy landowners, finding that excessive dependence on hired administrators decreased their income, often had to involve themselves to a considerable extent in the management of their estates. The avoidance of manual labor generally remained, of course, to distinguish the elite from the masses. Thus the question of whether a farm was to be called a hacienda or not came to depend less on size than on whether the owner and his family had to perform the required physical labor themselves.

This social distinction was not, of course, unrelated to the size of farms. Other things being equal, the larger a farm was the better it was able to provide the income and support the labor force which made it unnecessary for the owner to work himself. But other things were not always equal. In regions where agriculture was exceptionally profitable rather small farms might meet these requirements. And where land was poor and markets far away, much larger landholdings might be completely unable to do so. There were many regions within Spanish America where the early settlers acquired huge amounts of land for themselves, but because of the lack of adequate markets were forced to exploit this land essentially on a subsistence basis. Under such circumstances an aristocratic society could not develop until agriculture began to generate enough income to support it. Thus in Central America, for instance, most of the Spaniards who moved to the countryside in the seventeenth century did not build up manorial estates but "retired to a rather squalid self-sufficiency on their chacras and bohíos, supported by a few mules and a handful of peons."[1] Here a true hacienda system would not arise until the eighteenth-century indigo boom.

Within the boundaries set by this broad definition of the hacienda there was room for a great deal of variation. In traditional usage, a hacienda was not a particular kind of estate which could be defined in abstract terms but rather any kind of estate, so long as it belonged to an aristocrat and produced a satisfactory income. The term has sometimes been used in a narrower sense, however. Thus Wolf and Mintz define the hacienda as "an agricultural estate, operated by a dominant owner . . . and a dependent labor force, organized to supply a small-scale market by means of scarce capital, in which the factors of production are employed not only for capital accumulation but also to support the status aspirations of the owner." This hacienda is to be distinguished from the plantation (also a hacienda in the traditional sense), which they define as "an agricultural estate, operated by dominant owners (usually organized into a corporation) and a dependent labor force, organized to supply a large-scale market by means of abundant capital, in which the factors of production are employed primarily to further capital accumulation without reference to the status needs of the owners."[2] A systematic comparison of these two types of estates is found in reading 1.

Wolf and Mintz are primarily concerned with the contemporary situation, but their hacienda and plantation types provide a useful tool for understanding older social and economic patterns. The remainder of this essay analyzes the traditional hacienda system of Latin America in terms of this plantation-hacienda dichotomy, first looking at the circumstances under which landed estates arose, and then examining the variations among them, particularly with respect to economic organization, land tenure, labor systems, and social organization.

Our discussion is based on the assumption that the traditional agrarian structure of Latin America was essentially a stable one which was not altered in any fundamental way before the last years of the nineteenth century. This does not mean that change was impossible within it; we will see that considerable change could occur without upsetting the structure as a whole. Nor does it imply that the landowning aristocracy was itself stable; in fact, overall social stability in Latin America seems not to have been inconsistent with a rather high turnover among individual landowners.

This assumption of stability does not of course hold true for the recent past, but we cannot deal adequately here with the often radical changes the traditional agrarian structure has undergone in the twentieth century; in any case these have been quite fully discussed elsewhere.[3] At this point we can only note several modern developments which have tended to produce instability and change in the traditional structure. The most obvious of these is perhaps the rise of revolutionary movements seeking the radical redistribution of land and wealth, and in a few cases achieving it. Another has been the growth of the industrial sector of Latin American economies and the corresponding reduction in the importance of the agricultural sector. This has led to the appearance of new groups whose power and wealth do not depend on the ownership of land and has forced the old landowning elite to diversify its interests to maintain its position. A third development is the rapid increase in direct foreign investment in Latin America, which has tended to introduce a new and less sensitive element into the local power structure and interfered with the adjustments needed to maintain stability. Largely self-contained from a social and political point of view, the traditional agrarian system was once able to perpetuate itself without much difficulty; now it has become increasingly unable to do so and outside intervention to maintain stability is common.

A final development is the growth of the state itself. The traditional system depended to a large extent on the weakness of the central government, on its inability to intervene decisively in the affairs of the countryside in opposition to the interests of the landowners. The steady expansion of the role of the government in recent years—which has taken place in regimes both of the right and the left—has given the state a capacity for intervention in rural areas that it never possessed before and has thus fundamentally altered the balance of power, even where the predominance of large estates has endured. This suggests that the social and economic patterns with which this book is concerned are now being altered very rapidly, though their influence will doubtless continue to be felt for a long time to come.

The Rise of the Hacienda System

There were no market economies or commercial estates in the New World before the coming of the Europeans in the sixteenth and seventeenth centuries. Most of the hemisphere was inhabited by nomadic hunters and gatherers or by shifting cultivators, neither of whom recognized individual ownership of land. Even in the peasant societies of Middle America and the Andes, most land was considered as belonging to local communities rather than to the individuals who cultivated it. There were no landed aristocracies, though there are signs that they were beginning to develop, at least within the Aztec and Inca empires. The development of the hacienda system was clearly, therefore, a consequence of European colonization. It was not, however, an inevitable consequence of such colonization, as the appearance of more egalitarian colonial societies based on small family farms in North America clearly demonstrates. Thus we must examine the particular circumstances which encouraged—or in some cases discouraged—the rise of landed estates in Latin America.

There are several influential explanations for the predominance of large estates in Latin America. One theory suggests that because of their history and traditions, the Spaniards and Portuguese were more strongly predisposed than, say, the English to the establishment of such estates. Another argues that the development of huge estates was primarily a consequence of the extension of the European market economy to the New World, while a third suggests that it reflected climatic factors, occurring mainly in tropical colonies where the settlers came to seek wealth, not in the temperate colonies where they came to build a new life for themselves. The common element in all these explanations is their emphasis on the European social and economic environment; they assume that the hacienda was essentially a foreign institution imposed on the New World. The most interesting research on Latin American estates in recent years, however, has concentrated on their relationship to the American environment, and this is what will be emphasized here.

The main impulse behind the development of profit-making enterprises in the colonial areas of the New World was the desire of the settlers to import European goods, a desire which could only be satisfied if one possessed a monetary income with which to buy them. Thus the settlers expected that their colonies would remain tied to Europe through commerce; they did not come to America to live cut off from all contact with the Old World, deprived of the material goods which reminded them of their earlier life. Merchant ships would visit a settlement only when it could generate enough income to attract them, however. When it could not, as was the case in many Spanish colonies around the Caribbean in the later sixteenth century, it might not see European ships for years at a time, thus approaching, in its isolation and impoverishment, the state of Robinson Crusoe's island.[4]

In the initial stages of colonization, most income was not generated by commercial enterprises that produced exportable goods. Rather, the settlers obtained such goods by trade, either with local Indians or with existing European colonies in the area, or else they conquered the Indians and forced them to provide the goods they wanted as tribute. The former pattern prevailed in most of the Portuguese, French, and English settlements. Here the local Indians—when they survived—could not be effectively exploited to generate income and remained largely outside the colonial economic system. The latter, therefore, had to be constructed from the ground up, and developing colonial enterprises depended heavily on the European economy, which provided their markets, their capital, and through the African slave trade, their labor.

The tribute pattern, found in most of the Spanish colonies, produced a more complicated situation. In the early years Spanish settlement was based on the institution known as the *encomienda,* an administrative institution which diverted a share of the surpluses produced by the conquered Indian society from traditional recipients (chieftains, rulers, or priests, for example) into the hands of the Spaniards. In many of the Indian societies, however, this "tribute" was perceived less as a tax than as part of a complex pattern of reciprocity, being often provided in the form of labor services rather than goods. Even in such a highly developed political system as that of the Inca empire, tribute payers did not individually grow maize for government warehouses on their own land, but did so collectively on community land set aside for the purpose. Initially the conquest changed this pattern very little, merely substituting a new group of recipients; thus Indians wove cloth, cultivated maize fields, or mined gold for their encomenderos as they had for their traditional rulers. From this point of view, the early encomenderos were more like rentiers than entrepreneurs bent on turning their control over Indian labor to a profit. It is true that later on, under the pressure of depopulation and economic difficulties, many of them had to turn entrepreneur and build up profit-making enterprises. But at the beginning their income came from tribute provided by their Indians in amounts and forms which had long been established by tradition and could be changed only to a limited extent. This is why the encomienda was successful only where a tribute system of some kind had existed before the conquest, that is, where a surplus was already being produced and concentrated in the hands of a non-productive class. It did not work with poorer and more nomadic peoples like the Caribs of the West Indies, the Chichimecas of northern Mexico, or the Araucanians of southern Chile.

The principal tribute products in the indigenous societies of Spanish America were goods like maize or cloth which could not by themselves generate income, since the demand for them was essentially local. In some regions, however, the Indians had produced small quantities of precious metals, though for ornamental rather than monetary purposes; thus mining became the original source of most Spanish income.

The early encomienda economies were primarily based on gold, which by itself accounted for well over half the value of Spanish American exports down to the 1550s.[5] In this case, the income of the settlers seems to have depended on previous Indian exploitation of the gold workings; where this was absent, the gold was generally not discovered until much later. Despite more than a century of searching, the Portuguese did not find the rich gold deposits of Minas Gerais in Brazil until the end of the seventeenth century, and the Spaniards never discovered the large California deposits at all.

In most cases dependence on Indian tributes did not last very long. Within a century of the conquest the encomienda had lost its ability to generate sufficient income for the settlers and was largely replaced by the hacienda, which provided an income derived from commercial farming. This was by no means an automatic result of the conquest. The later tribute-based systems of British India and Dutch Indonesia, for instance, underwent no such transformation, and the typical European in these colonies tended to remain an official or tax collector rather than a landed aristocrat.

One reason for the failure of the early encomienda systems was their dependence on an exhaustible resource; when gold deposits eventually gave out—as they usually did within half a century—there was often little else available to export. Another reason was the massive depopulation (in many cases well over 90 percent) which affected the Indian societies of the New World following their initial contact with Old World diseases like smallpox, typhus, malaria, and yellow fever to which they had no immunity. The Indian population of the early gold colony of Española (Santo Domingo) declined from over three million to a few hundred within the space of about thirty years, according to recent investigations.[6] In the process the encomienda first turned into a gang of slaves whose size could only be maintained by kidnapping Indians from other parts of the Caribbean, then failed altogether. In Mexico a population of 25 or 30 million at the time of the conquest declined to less than a million and a half by the middle of the seventeenth century. The scale of depopulation in the Andean region seems to have been similar, though there is evidence that Indians who lived at high elevations (as in the Titicaca basin of southern Peru) may have escaped with less damage. In most of Spanish America the place of the vanished Indians within the ecological system was taken by European livestock, which multiplied with extreme rapidity after their introduction, often becoming wild in the process. But livestock could not pay tribute, and the American demographic catastrophe thus necessarily involved the collapse of the early encomienda systems, which soon became incapable, even in the more populated regions, of performing what was expected of them.

By the end of the sixteenth century, the encomienda had proved unable to support the Spanish colonial system in the New World, though it continued to play a major role in peripheral regions like Paraguay, and for a time, Venezuela. This compelled the settlers, whether or not they personally held encomiendas, to look for alternative sources of income. The result was a gradual change from the redistributive pattern of the early years, in which the majority of settlers were supported in the households of the encomenderos who received the tribute, to a market system in which they supported themselves by selling goods or services. Such a change could not have occurred without the economic revolution produced by the discovery of the great silver mines of Peru and Mexico (Potosí in 1545; Zacatecas and Guanajuato in 1548) and from the introduction of the new mercury amalgamation process for refining silver ore in the 1560s and 1570s. While the early settlers had depended on the export of gold, their descendents would rely on that of silver, which from the 1560s to the end of the colonial period consistently accounted for ninety percent or more of the value of legal bullion exports to Spain.

This change from gold to silver had considerable economic significance. In the first place, silver mining proved able to generate much more wealth than gold mining had ever done. Thus from approximately thirteen million ducats in the 1540s, the value of legal bullion exports from Spanish America rose to thirty million ducats in the 1560s and then to eighty-three million in the 1590s. And since silver mining was a larger and more complex industry than gold mining, requiring larger amounts of capital and more specialized skills, this wealth received wider local distribution. Thus the silver economies not only generated more wealth, but they tended to retain more of it for internal use; this implies that the increase in local purchasing power associated with the shift from gold to silver was even greater than the bullion export figures suggest.

What were the effects of this increase in demand? In Spain it is well known that the influx of bullion in the sixteenth century produced inflation and economic decline, partly because it coincided with a period of population growth, and partly because there were structural obstacles which prevented the Spanish economy from responding adequately to the additional demand. This did not happen in the American colonies, where the population was rapidly shrinking and where the collapse of the traditional indigenous economies removed the major barriers to social and economic change. Thus increasing demand led to the establishment and growth of new enterprises which could meet that demand, or to what we would call economic growth. It stimulated the extension of a widespread market network over the settled regions of Middle America and the Andes, including not only the mining centers but administrative and commercial centers as well. It was this network which was to provide the basis for the hacienda system in these regions down to the nineteenth century.

The network of silver markets did not extend to all of the Spanish colonies, however. There were large areas, including most of the Caribbean region, Chile, and the basin of the Río de la Plata, which remained on the periphery of the developed silver economies. The failure of the encomienda here could not easily be counteracted by developing new income-producing enterprises because there were few good markets, and these regions therefore developed more slowly.

Spanish settlement endured, however, because the spread of European livestock meant that subsistence was not difficult, even if—for the time being—there was little income to be made. Instead of being parasitic on the Indian societies, as they were under the encomienda system, the settlers became parasitic on herds of semi-wild cattle, which were hunted down to provide food and clothing, and occasionally hides to sell. But the demand for hides was usually limited, and Spanish settlements in these peripheral regions remained poor and isolated, their very administration often paid for by subsidies from the viceregal capitals.

These peripheral colonies had two main development strategies open to them. They could try to sell their products in the markets of the silver economies; this usually meant they had to engage in stock raising, since agricultural produce generally could not bear the high costs of transport for the distances involved, though Ecuador and Venezuela were able to send their cacao to Mexico City in the seventeenth century and Chile shipped considerable amounts of wheat to Lima in the eighteenth. The alternative, particularly in the Caribbean region, was to grow tropical crops for export to Europe, following the example set by the Portuguese in Brazil.

There were difficulties with the second approach, however. The Spanish commercial system was not designed to encourage the development of agricultural export economies but to keep the leakage of bullion to a minimum, so that the crown could be sure of receiving its proper share. This latter goal required that trade normally be carried in a small number of large ships which sailed at regular intervals, a pattern which was not totally unreasonable since trade with the main silver-producing regions primarily involved bullion and manufactured products, whose value was high in proportion to their bulk. Trade with the agricultural export economies, on the other hand, mainly involved merchandise whose value was low in proportion to its bulk, such as produce and slaves; here an efficient pattern of trade implied the use of a large number of relatively small ships which were allowed to sail at irregular intervals. But even had the commercial system been designed to handle agricultural exports, the Spanish settlers would have still been at a disadvantage. For the best markets for tropical produce were found in the European northwest, and Spanish merchants, cut off by the religious conflicts of the sixteenth century, had no way of exploiting them. Furtado (reading 2) points out the contrast with the situation of the Portuguese, whose ties with Flemish and Dutch merchants, established in the era of the spice trade, made possible the successful marketing of Brazilian sugar in northwestern Europe.

Under these circumstances, it is easy to see why the Spanish Caribbean islands did not become large centers of sugar production until the nineteenth century, in spite of the fact that sugar was grown on Española as early as 1520. Nor is it surprising that the more prosperous settlements in the region tended to become major centers of contraband trade. Thus the tobacco and cacao planters of seventeenth-century Venezuela depended heavily on Dutch merchants operating out of Curaçao, and the indigo planters of Central America later on would sell their crops to British merchants sailing from Jamaica. The Spanish authorities could complain about the way trade regulations were being violated, but since the legal commercial system could not handle these products very well, they could not effectively enforce them without destroying whatever prosperity had been achieved. In the long run this combination of restrictive commercial policy with dependence on foreign merchants tended to undermine the whole colonial system, encouraging the producers to reject Spanish authority in order to legalize their direct ties with foreign markets.

Markets, Capital, and Profits

Hacienda and plantation, then, represented two different solutions to the problem of settler income, solutions which developed in quite different historical circumstances. The former was characteristic of those regions where the presence of a dense and well-organized indigenous population encouraged early reliance on the encomienda, and where the failure of the encomienda system was counteracted by the rise of a market economy depending primarily on the wealth generated by mining. The latter, on the other hand, was characteristic of those regions where the encomienda system had been weak or had never existed, and where mining failed to generate enough wealth to support a network of regional markets; thus the demand which stimulated development came largely from Europe itself. In the long run, of course, this distinction between plantation and hacienda regions tended to become blurred. Plantation regions might, like Brazil, find they also had minerals to export, and hacienda regions sometimes discovered export markets. In addition plantations generated some local demand themselves, and while this was initially limited it became increasingly important as time went on.

As Wolf and Mintz suggest, many of the differences between haciendas and plantations can be understood in terms of their market patterns. The European markets in which the early plantations sold their produce were larger and more reliable than the regional markets in which haciendas had to sell theirs. This was partly because population density and per capita income both tended to be lower in Latin America than in Europe, but also because a large part of the agricultural population in the former region was effectively excluded from participation in the market economy.

Export markets were characterized not only by their greater size, but also by the greater elasticity of demand within them, a fact which encouraged the establishment of complex marketing systems to sell an increasing quantity of plantation products at decreasing prices. Most of the tropical exports of Latin America from sugar down to coffee and bananas achieved their early success due to the rapid expansion of overseas markets, usually associated with a decline in prices, though this did not necessarily reflect deliberate policy on the part of the producers. In Brazil, for instance, Furtado argues that Dutch merchants took advantage of the sixteenth-century decline in sugar prices to stimulate a rapid increase in European sugar consumption, greatly to the benefit of the Brazilian planters who were the cheapest producers at the time (see reading 2). Plantations thus tended to be highly competitive enterprises, though historically this competition was most obvious among regions rather than individual plantations. The history of Latin America contains numerous examples of the meteoric rise and subsequent decline of wealthy planter classes.

In contrast, the relative inelasticity of demand in local and regional markets within Latin America gave haciendas little inducement to keep their prices down; rather as Florescano suggests in reading 10, the primary concern of most hacendados was to limit production in order to avoid the precipitous decline in prices which typically followed a good harvest. Thus haciendas tended to be essentially monopolistic, keeping their prices artificially high and using their political influence and control of land to discourage competition.

A second advantage of export markets was that they gave the planters who sold in them access to foreign capital. This came mainly in the form of credit for the purchase of equipment and slaves, advanced by merchants or factors who handled the distribution of plantation produce abroad. Thus Dutch merchants provided much of the capital employed in the development of the Brazilian sugar economy and played a similar role later on in the British West Indies, where they had some part in persuading the earliest sugar planters to try the crop. The indebtedness of planters to those who marketed their produce for them was typical of plantation regions, in fact, and seems to have occurred even where the latter were contraband traders who could not count on the state to enforce the debts. Direct foreign investment, on the other hand, did not become common until the latter part of the nineteenth century, when large foreign-owned corporations such as the United Fruit Company began to develop or purchase plantations.

Haciendas had few direct ties with overseas markets and foreigners seldom had much interest in financing or investing in them, except where they did so as a means of gaining admittance to the local landed elite. As a result their owners necessarily relied on the limited supplies of local capital that were available, though most of this capital was traditionally directed into mining and commerce, activities in which the return was higher than in agriculture. Thus the colonial haciendas of many regions acquired the larger part of their operating capital from the Church, which in medieval fashion was often content to employ its accumulated funds in the purchase of fixed rents instead of seeking more profitable investments that would have required more involvement to realize. This difference in the availability of capital was reflected in the level of technology. Plantations employed machinery and equipment which was relatively sophisticated and expensive, particularly in the processing phase of production. The technology of the hacienda, on the other hand, was not very different from that used by peasant cultivators.

Under these circumstances plantations naturally tended to be more profitable than haciendas, at least as long as they retained their ability to compete in the large export markets. Furtado argues (reading 2) that the per capita income of the settlers in the early Brazilian sugar economy was very high even by contemporary European standards, let alone those of the New World, and adds that this income was heavily concentrated in the hands of the small minority of sugar planters. Similarly, in eighteenth-century England, the wealth of West Indian sugar planters was legendary, allowing many of them to return home, buy up country estates and parliamentary seats (the sugar planters' lobby was a particularly effective one), and to stir up considerable dislike among established groups jealous of their exceptional wealth and influence. More recently the concentrated wealth and political influence of the owners of Peru's coastal plantations was one of the factors which led the military to seize power and carry out an agrarian reform which deprived them of their estates.

In contrast, most haciendas do not seem to have been very profitable. Thus in reading 11, Brading argues that even during the prosperous eighteenth century, when the mining industry was at its productive peak, Mexican haciendas provided a rather small return on the capital invested in them, and the same seems to have been true of many other areas. It is true that haciendas were sometimes owned by wealthy men, but these were usually men whose fortunes had come from mining or commerce rather than agriculture. If they invested in haciendas it was not because they were particulary profitable, but rather because they provided a regular income which did not depend on their direct involvement in the day-to-day management of the enterprise. Ironically, Brading's evidence suggests that because of the low rate of return most haciendas provided, they often proved incapable of supporting a growing aristocratic family for very long; thus they were likely to be sold off after two or three generations unless new wealth could be brought into the family from outside, usually by marriage. In this sense, he argues, haciendas consumed wealth rather than creating it.[7]

Finally, the plantation was better organized and more efficiently run than the hacienda. For while the latter bore a close resemblance to the medieval European manor, with its serfs tied to the soil and forced to work on the demesne, the plantation, with its disciplined and closely supervised labor force often detailed to specialized tasks, was a kind of agricultural factory. During the seventeenth century, in fact, there were few individually owned business enterprises in the New World or in Europe itself which were larger and more complex than a big sugar plantation. At the beginning of the eighteenth century, Antonil could characterize the Brazilian sugar planter (*senhor de engenho*) as a businessman whose success depended primarily on his capital resources and managerial ability (see reading 4). In Brazil, his account suggests, simply being a landowner guaranteed neither wealth nor status; to obtain these benefits one had to operate one's plantation efficiently. Nor could this overall responsibility for management be easily delegated. While planters might become absentee landowners and leave the operation of their estates to hired administrators, this tended to bring economic difficulties. In the British West Indies during the eighteenth century, for instance, absentee owners often had to go out in person to halt the deterioration of plantations run by administrators.[8]

The typical hacienda, on the other hand, though it might own more land, was a less complex enterprise and had less need to maintain a high level of efficiency. Thus it was often able to operate without the personal management of the owner. Spanish American hacendados usually lived in the city, visiting their estates only occasionally and leaving their management to hired administrators or even renting them out.

Haciendas and plantations were not always so clearly differentiated as the preceding comparison would suggest. In the case of the plantation, the pattern described here corresponds most closely with that found on the more dynamic enterprises, which retained their ability to compete in the overseas export markets. Where they had lost this ability—as frequently happened—their character was somewhat different. Facing a reduced demand, they became increasingly monopolistic, concentrating on gaining protection within a restricted market. This was how many British West Indian planters survived, for instance, in the face of competition from the French planters of Saint Domingue. As production and profits declined, such plantations found it more and more difficult to obtain capital and underwent a gradual process of disinvestment as slaves and capital failed to be replaced. This process, which can perhaps be most clearly seen in the case of the Brazilian Northeast, in the long run left plantations which possessed many of the characteristics of haciendas.

In the case of the hacienda, the pattern described here corresponds most closely with the manorial type which was found in the more isolated highland areas of Middle America and the Andes. This was a mixed agricultural and stock-raising enterprise with a labor force of dependent peons tied more or less formally to the land they cultivated. There were other kinds of haciendas, however. One of these may be called the *fundo* (earlier known as the *chacra* or *labor*), and was a predominately agricultural hacienda worked by peons, day laborers, and in some cases, slaves. It was most commonly found in irrigated zones well-placed to supply the largest centers of European population, where wealth and demand were heavily concentrated. In

Mexico, large numbers of fundos were found in the Valley of Mexico (particularly the Chalco region), around Puebla, and later in the Bajío; to the south they were common on the Peruvian coast (particularly in the center and south), in the Cochabamba and Sucre Valleys of Upper Peru (Bolivia), and later on in the Chilean Central Valley. The fundo, then, might be described as a hacienda which tended toward the plantation type; and some fundos—those that produced sugar, for instance—have usually been considered plantations.

Another type was the stock-raising hacienda or ranch, which had its own distinctive characteristics. Though ranches were found in the central regions of European settlement, mainly on land which was too dry or otherwise unsuitable for cultivation, they were most typical of the vast frontier zones, where market demand was extremely low and the distances too great to make the raising of cash crops profitable. Such regions included the north of Mexico (though here the presence of mines somewhat distorted the picture), the plains of the Orinoco basin in Venezuela, the dry interior of the Brazilian Northeast, and the pampas of the Río de la Plata. Traditional ranches required little capital, since the animals they raised needed little care and reproduced on their own, but their profits were correspondingly low. In fact, the early livestock economies of Latin America were often not far from subsistence economies. And though there were hacendados who possessed huge estates and immense power, the wealth they derived from ranching was usually limited.

Land

Of all the things which attracted European settlers to Latin America between the sixteenth and the nineteenth centuries, the most important was the availability of cheap land which resulted from the generally low density of population within the region. Much of the western hemisphere had never been densely populated, being occupied by nomadic groups of hunters and gatherers. And though dense agricultural populations had existed in a few areas before the conquest, the epidemics of the sixteenth century reduced them to a small fraction of their former size, leaving large amounts of land open to European occupation. Throughout the centuries of European migration, Latin America would possess a very high ratio of land area to population; even today, though the number of its inhabitants is rapidly increasing, it cannot on the whole be considered over-populated in the sense that India or Southeast Asia are.

But if land was cheap, there were still obstacles which prevented it from being freely occupied by the European settlers. These obstacles may be classed as human on the one hand and physical and economic on the other. In the plantation regions, the human obstacles were relatively unimportant. Plantations most commonly developed in tropical lowland areas previously occupied by semi-nomadic groups like the Tupi of Brazil or the Caribs who gave their name to the Caribbean; these groups were divided into small bands which supported themselves by hunting (or fishing) and shifting cultivation. Though difficult to pacify because of their lack of a hierarchical system of authority and because European settlement tended to drive them into hostility by upsetting the ecological balance on which their traditional way of life depended, these bands were usually not large or well-organized enough to provide much resistance to large-scale European settlement. Thus they were killed off (with the help of the great epidemics, which usually did more damage in lowland than highland areas), driven out, or else settled down in mission villages and reservations. This pattern was reinforced by the law, which in general did not recognize indigenous rights to uncultivated land, since it was considered that men became "civilized" only when they settled down as sedentary farmers in permanent towns.

The physical and economic obstacles to European occupation of land in the plantation regions, on the other hand, were much more important. As tropical lowlands, most of these regions were covered with dense forests when the settlers arrived, so that the land had to be cleared at considerable cost and effort before it could be cultivated. In addition, plantations had to ship their crops out by sea; thus they were located in coastal zones or close to navigable rivers, at least until the coming of railroads in the nineteenth century. The development of plantations was also restricted by the special soil and climatic conditions which many of the successful export crops required. For all of these reasons plantation areas tended to be limited in size, though within them a relatively high proportion of the land was occupied and exploited by the settlers. They were essentially "islands" of settlement, even when—as in the case of Brazil—they were physically located on the mainland.

Within these areas, what were the main factors which determined the amount of land occupied by a plantation? We have often pointed to the influence of the European tradition of large estates and a governmental policy of giving out large land grants. In fact, however, there is little evidence that the size of the original land grants had very much to do with the ultimate size of plantations. In Barbados, for instance, where the original grants (mainly intended for tobacco farms) were small, sugar planters combined them into larger holdings. In the Brazilian Northeast, on the other hand, where the Indian danger and the initial need for capital (Dutch capital came in only after the potential of the sugar industry had been established) produced a feudal pattern in which land grants were sometimes very large, these early holdings were usually broken up into smaller plantations.[9]

Such changes are not difficult to understand. As a competitive enterprise, the plantation was under pressure to meet certain standards of efficiency; thus the amount of land it occupied tended to bear a direct relation to the size of its labor force. This was particularly true since the value of land in the plantation economies was relatively high, and planters who possessed more than they could exploit therefore had a strong incentive to sell or rent it to others. According to Dunn, the norm in the fully developed plantation system on Barbados was one slave for every two acres of cane land, and it would be interesting to compare this ratio with those which prevailed in other areas and for other crops.[10] If plantations occupied large amounts of land, then, it was basically because they were large enterprises.

But why were they large enterprises? Some have pointed to economies of scale as the important factor; but while these clearly existed in the case of sugar they did not in the case of most other plantation crops. Tobacco, cacao, coffee, and bananas, for instance, have all been successfully produced on small holdings. Even with sugar, economies of scale occurred only in the processing phase, and cane could perfectly well be grown on small holdings, as it was by Brazilian *lavradores* and Cuban *colonos,* and then carried to centralized mills for processing.

A more important factor may have been the small size of the agricultural population in relation to the demand. Given a fixed demand, the presence of a large number of potential agricultural producers would lead to the development of relatively small farms. If the potential producers were few, on the other hand, their profits would be higher, thus making it possible to enlarge their holdings and bring in labor from other regions to exploit them. Since in most plantation regions the agricultural population consisted mainly of European immigrants, one would therefore expect the size of plantations to bear an inverse relationship to the density of the European population. On the island of Barbados, for instance, which initially attracted a very large number of immigrants for its size, seventeenth-century sugar plantations were seldom larger than about two hundred acres.[11]

At the same time there were several factors which tended to limit the size of plantations. One of these was the problem of transport. Harvested crops had to be carried to a central location for processing and packing, and if a plantation was too large, it became uneconomic to carry the crops in from the most distant fields. This difficulty became less important when the building of railroads in the nineteenth century reduced transport costs on larger plantations (see reading 5). Another factor was related to the problem of administration. The growth of plantations was always limited by the difficulty of managing large enterprises effectively. Thus there seem to have been few traditional plantations which operated successfully with a labor force of more than five hundred workers, and this tended to keep them from becoming much larger than 1,000 or 1,500 acres. In the present century, of course, it has become possible to manage much larger enterprises and this managerial limitation on size has lost most of its importance.

In the hacienda regions the situation with regard to the occupation of land was quite different. Here the physical and economic obstacles were much less important. Agriculture was not restricted to coastal areas and there were no forests to hold back the occupation of the land, which could be exploited either for stock raising or agriculture without the preliminary labor of clearing away the trees. It was this more than anything else which explains the ease with which the Spanish population dispersed over such wide areas in the New World.

The human obstacles to the occupation of land in the hacienda regions, on the other hand, were much greater. The highland areas in particular had been inhabited before the conquest by dense peasant populations living in permanent agricultural communities, and the Indians of these communities could not simply be eliminated or driven off their land. Spanish domination in these areas ultimately depended on the Indians' passive acceptance of the new order, and this presumably would not have survived any systematic attempt to deprive them of the land needed to support themselves. Thus Spaniards assumed at the beginning that the land would remain large-ly in Indian possession and settlers would not be landlords but rather receivers of tribute.

The collapse of the encomienda system and the abandonment of large amounts of Indian land necessarily altered this assumption, however. Faced with the increasing inadequacy of tribute, the author-ities could not very well prevent the settlers from taking over land which was no longer cultivated in order to develop new agricultural enterprises to support themselves. Thus they concentrated instead on regulating the process of transfer—which took place mainly by land grant and purchase—and insuring that the Indian communities re-tained enough land to meet their immediate subsistence needs. Such guarantees were not invariably effective, but on the whole the theft of land from Indians who were actually using it does not seem to have had the importance usually assigned to it in the develop-ment of the hacienda system. In most areas, European occupation of land largely coincided with the demographic decline, occurring most rapidly in the sixteenth and seventeenth centuries and slowing down thereafter as the Indian population stabilized.

Here as in the plantation regions, then, the theory that the predomi-nance of large estates was a consequence of the excessive size of land grants is not supported by the evidence. Both in Mexico and Peru, the vast majority of agricultural land grants were for less than five hundred acres, and these were turned into large estates mainly through the acquisition of additional land, either from Indians or from other Spaniards (see reading 8). The rise of the hacienda cannot be blamed on the crown and its officials—who were not at all anxious to create a powerful landed aristocracy in the New World—but rather reflects the low level of agricultural profits, which made it difficult for the ordinary settler to make an adequate income from farming and left most of the land for the wealthy minority.[12]

In the case of grazing land the obstacles to European occupation were smaller. The highland regions contained considerable amounts of land which was not well suited for agriculture and which had never been cultivated or else had gone out of cultivation soon after the conquest. Though local Indians might consider such land as be-longing to them, we have seen that the law generally did not recog-nize their rights to it. Originally, in fact, the Spanish crown refused to recognize private ownership of uncultivated land at all; thus it was decreed that grazing land was not to be divided up among private landowners but was rather to be considered the common property of all, as once had been the case in Spain. The early land grants usually insisted on cultivation within a specified period of time as a condition of ownership.

The policy of common pastures proved unworkable, however, because the market demand for agricultural crops was so limited. The authorities therefore found it necessary to make grants of land for stock-raising purposes. As Chevalier has shown (reading 8), these early stock-raising grants did not represent much of a concession to the desire for private ownership. They did not, strictly speaking, confer ownership at all, but rather defined an area—often in fairly general terms—within which the grantee could erect his buildings and pens while preventing anyone else from doing the same. The conversion of this grazing land to agricultural purposes was legally forbidden. Nevertheless, the government was unable in the long run to enforce the limitations written into these grants, and the private ownership of grazing land came to be accepted. The amount of land which could be acquired by means of stock-raising grants was much larger than in the case of the agricultural grants. In Mexico, for instance, one could legally obtain more than four thousand acres to raise cattle or a little under two thousand for sheep, and in remote areas much larger grants were sometimes made. Still, it is not clear that such grants can be described as excessive at the time they were made, since their value and the income that could be expected from the land was very low. In this case also, the size of the great haciendas was primarily a consequence of the extremely low value of land at the time they were first established.

If the circumstances of the post-Conquest period favored the rise of large haciendas, the economic conditions prevailing in later years combined with the weight of tradition to keep them that way. Though land values gradually rose, they rose less than in the plantation areas, and hacendados therefore had less incentive to sell land they could not cultivate. In fact, there were powerful reasons to hold on to such land. For one thing, this kept it out of the hands of potential competitors (either Indian or Spanish) who might cut into the hacienda's already uncertain profits. And for another, the monopolization of land helped to alleviate the hacienda's perennial problem of labor.

We have seen that the early Spanish settlers in the New World established an aristocratic and feudal society based on the encomienda, and that when the latter failed them they were driven to base their position on the ownership of land. But as the English colonial theorist Edward Gibbon Wakefield would point out in the nineteenth century, the situation of a large landowner in an underpopulated region tends to be a difficult one, since as long as men possess or can acquire land of their own they cannot easily be persuaded to labor on the farms of others.[13] The problem, as Wakefield saw it, could be met in two ways: by resorting to some kind of forced labor or preferably by arranging matters so that a substantial part of the population could not obtain enough land to support themselves and thus had to work for wages. In Australia, he argued that this should be done by raising the price of public land to an artificial level set high enough to insure that new immigrants generally could not acquire their own farms before they had spent some time working for others.

Wakefield's analysis of the Australian situation has considerable relevance to our discussion. In Latin America, Spanish landowners at first relied on forced labor taken from the Indian communities under a draft system known as the *repartimiento*. With the decline of the Indian population, however, this system proved incapable of meeting their needs, and they increasingly turned to a permanent labor force of Indian peons who moved out of the communities and onto the haciendas. During the years of depopulation, this movement of Indians was primarily a consequence of excessive Spanish demands for tribute and draft labor (excessive because they were not lowered proportionally to the decline of the population) and of the ability of the hacendados to offer some protection against these demands. After the population began to recover, on the other hand, Indians left their communities because there was no longer enough land for them; and since the surplus land abandoned earlier had largely been claimed by the hacendados, the latter were able to attract workers by offering the use of land in return for labor. The monopolization of land by the hacienda, then, served both to perpetuate the shortage of Indian land and to provide a means of attracting labor without paying wages.

The hacendados did not always wait for these generalized pressures to drive Indians to them. Like Ciro Alegría's fictional hacendado Don Alvaro Amenábar (see reading 9), they sometimes employed force or fraud to deprive their Indian neighbors of land they were actually cultivating. But though such land-grabbing has been documented from the earliest days of the hacienda system, it may be questioned whether it was as typical of the mature system as is sometimes thought. One would normally expect that a small landowning aristocracy living in the midst of a large peasant population would tend to insist on the traditional character and permanence of the existing distribution of land and wealth rather than attempting to alter it. On this assumption, the practice of land grabbing would not have been a basic feature of the traditional hacienda system but rather an element of instability within it. Thus rapid economic development tended to encourage it, as in Mexico during the last quarter of the nineteenth century or in Peru during the early years of the twentieth. It is significant in this respect that Don Alvaro Amenábar is portrayed not as a member of a long-established landowning family—the hacienda had been founded by his father only a few years earlier—but rather as an entrepreneur still in the process of building his fortune who perceives the existing distribution of property as a barrier to his advancement rather than a means of protecting his inherited status.

To conclude this section we must examine the distinct land-tenure patterns of the fundo and the ranch. As we have seen, the economic organization of the fundo reflected the better markets, the greater availability of capital, and the higher level of agricultural profits which were characteristic of the areas of more concentrated demand, conditions which served to increase the value of land and thus encouraged the development of smaller and more intensively exploited farms. Within Latin America this tendency was perhaps most pronounced in the irrigated valleys of the southern coast of Peru, where the land came to be divided among large numbers of Spanish winegrowers and where relatively small farms predominate even today. During the colonial period, this region seems to have supported a larger rural Spanish population for its size than any comparable region in South America.[14]

Where settlement was originally based on stock-raising (as in Chile or the Mexican Bajío, for instance), and where cultivating the soil became profitable only after the distribution of land was over, fundos tended to be larger and more valuable. In such regions the development of commercial agriculture sometimes led to the subdivision of estates; the Chilean fundo described in reading 13, for instance, had earlier been part of a much larger hacienda. In the Bajío and on some parts of the Peruvian coast, on the other hand, development seems to have encouraged hacendados to turn their land over to renters or sharecroppers, who were entrepreneurs in their own right though not completely independent ones (see reading 16). Land grabbing appears to have been less common in these relatively prosperous regions. This was perhaps a consequence of the higher value of land and the greater amount of capital invested in it, which in combination with the greater ability of the state to protect property rights made it more difficult to get away with simply appropriating land. The boundaries of the fundo, like those of the plantation, were likely to be surveyed and carefully defended. At the same time, the more favorable economic situation of the fundo meant that appropriating land of its neighbors was neither so necessary nor so useful as in more remote areas.

The frontier ranching areas represent the opposite extreme. Here the value of land was very low and there was no need for the precise demarcation of boundaries, since livestock were allowed to wander where they pleased, fencing being almost unknown before the nineteenth century. In some ways a ranch was less a landed estate than a vaguely defined territory, initially almost a kind of private hunting ground. Around Buenos Aires, in fact, the titles to some ranches were actually derived from licenses to hunt wild cattle *(acciones de vaquear)* which were issued to the early residents of the city.[15] Under these circumstances there were even fewer legal barriers to the simple appropriation of land than in the manorial hacienda regions. Chevalier has described how the hacendados of northern Mexico in the seventeenth century would strip Spanish or mestizo towns of their legal status in order to annex their lands. Still, in the long run, clear limits were set to this process, both by the relative scarcity of such towns and by the fact that they were somewhat better able to defend themselves than the Indian communities. By the nineteenth century, indeed, Chevalier suggests that it had even become possible for such towns to establish themselves at the expense of the haciendas.[16]

Labor

If the low population densities which prevailed in Latin America during the years of European migration meant that land was plentiful and cheap, they equally meant that labor was scarce and expensive. This high cost of labor was on the whole the most serious obstacle to the development of commercial agriculture in the New World, and the effort to overcome it led to the adoption of four main patterns of agricultural exploitation in Latin America: 1) a pattern based on migrant labor which was most closely associated with the plantation; 2) a pattern of extensive exploitation and low labor utilization which was most characteristic of the ranch; 3) a pattern based on wage labor, tenant farming, or both, which was most commonly found in the fundo regions; 4) a pattern of enserfment which was particularly associated with the manorial hacienda.

Each of these four patterns had European antecedents. The first had been employed, for instance, in the frontier lands of Eastern Europe during the twelfth and thirteenth centuries, when peasants were brought in from the more densely populated regions of the west to settle on the developing estates. The second had been used in the settlement of the frontier territories of Castile, where land was utilized for raising the merino sheep whose wool became the country's principal export. The third was characteristic of western Europe during the years after the coming of the Black Death, when wages tended to rise and peasants evolved from serfs into free tenant farmers who produced for the market and paid money rents. The fourth was found during these same years in Eastern Europe, where landlords responded to depopulation by legally attaching their peasants to the estates and holding down the cost of labor by force.

First let us examine the migrant labor pattern. This was most likely to be found in the plantation regions because there were few other regions where agricultural profits were high enough to cover the cost of bringing in laborers from elsewhere. Theoretically, free labor would have been more economical, but for most plantations, the local recruitment of such labor would become possible only with the rapid population growth of the twentieth century. And Latin America was seldom very attractive to free laborers from other parts of the world, who if they did migrate, preferred to go where they could acquire their own land instead of working on large estates. Thus labor on traditional Latin American plantations was largely provided by African slaves. And when the slave trade was ended in the nineteenth century, the slaves were commonly replaced with indentured laborers, brought from as far away as India and China under arrangements which were sometimes not very different from slavery.

The character of plantation slavery varied a great deal. Sometimes it was more exploitative, dependent on strict enforcement of discipline and military-like regimentation; in other cases it was milder and more paternalistic. In general the former pattern seems to have been characteristic of the more dynamic plantation economies, and the latter of those which were stagnant or declining. A relatively harsh form of slavery, for instance, prevailed in the coffee-growing area of Vassouras in nineteenth-century Brazil (see reading 6). Here planters bought, depreciated, and replaced their workers as if they were machines. Considering that, on the average, slaves had to be replaced after about fifteen years of work, they provided only a minimal standard of living and made little effort to encourage the formation of families and the raising of children. Since men were usually imported in larger numbers than women, then, the labor force on these planta-tions was typically marked by a predominance of male over female and African-born over American-born slaves.

A milder form of slavery tended to evolve in cases where planters were unable to replace their slaves so frequently, either because of declining profits or the rising cost of new slaves produced by the ending of the slave trade in the nineteenth century. Under these cir-cumstances they presumably had more of an incentive to maintain their slaves adequately and to encourage the formation of stable families which would produce more offspring (though they usually drew the line at giving such families legal recognition). Thus the labor force came to be increasingly dominated by American-born slaves and evolved toward the kind of stable, self-reproducing population found on manorial haciendas. The classic case here, of course, was that of the Brazilian Northeast.[17]

Though slavery was most closely associated with the plantation, it was also found on some of the more successful fundos. On the Peruvian coast, for instance, Africans were imported in large numbers to work on the grain-producing haciendas of the Lima area, the wine haciendas of the southern coast, and the large sugar haciendas scattered through the valleys of the center and north. When slavery was abolished in the nineteenth century here, the local population was still not large enough to supply these haciendas with the labor they needed, and indentured laborers were therefore brought in from China and Japan, as well as from the highlands by labor contractors known as *enganchadores*.

The wage-labor/tenant-farming alternative was the most "capitalis-tic" of the four in the sense that workers were attracted and held primarily by the wages they were paid or the profits they could earn. This alternative was possible mainly because agriculture was substan-tially more profitable in the areas of concentrated demand than elsewhere, so that haciendas could afford to pay wages high enough to attract workers from a fairly wide area. Migration from impoverished zones to the islands of prosperity where such wages were paid has been an important factor in Latin American history since the sixteenth century. The bargaining position of free laborers in these prosperous areas must have been exceptionally good during the years of depopulation, and though it was ultimately weakened by population growth, it usually remained better than elsewhere. In reading 15, Gibson shows that during the eighteenth century in the Valley of Mexico, Indians were often able to insist on large advances as a condition for providing their labor and suggests that in this case the level of indebtedness is an indication of the bargaining power of the workers rather than of the ability of landowners to bind them to their estates.[18]

A similar argument can be made in the case of tenant farming, which was possible only where landowners could allow renters or sharecroppers to keep enough of a profit to give them an incentive to produce for the market. Like wage labor, then, it was found mainly in the more prosperous areas. The best-known case is probably that of the wheat farms of the Argentine pampas in the latter part of the nineteenth century, where the tenants were generally European immigrants. But tenant farming had also been common in the Mexican Bajío, where rising demand during the eighteenth century had led many hacendados to distribute their outlying land to renters or sharecroppers. It was also important on the Peruvian coast, where sharecroppers known as *yanaconas* developed into a relatively well-off group of farmers. Here, in one notable case, a Japanese yanacona who had originally come to Peru as an indentured laborer succeeded in establishing himself during the 1930s as the dominant economic figure in the large Chancay Valley north of Lima, renting and operating no less than six major haciendas.[19]

The enserfment pattern, on the other hand, was most likely to be found in regions without good markets, where the cultivation of crops was a marginal affair. Under such circumstances haciendas could not afford to pay wages high enough to attract the kind of labor they needed. Nor could they rent their land; where the market did not give local Indians an incentive to grow cash crops on their own land there was no reason to suppose that Indian sharecroppers would find it worthwhile to grow such crops on hacienda land. Thus the hacienda had to rely on coercion of one type or another to obtain its labor. In the early years workers were largely drafted out of the Indian communities for set periods of time under the system known as the *repartimiento.* Later on, as we have seen, Indians were forced out of their communities by the growing pressure of tribute and labor demands on the shrinking population; and when the population began to recover, the haciendas used their monopoly of land to keep it out of Indian hands, thus forcing those without land to come to the hacienda for it.

The manorial hacienda often used legal forms of coercion, such as debt peonage, in order to minimize the wages it had to pay its workers. In the extreme case—exemplified here by the Ecuadorean hacienda in Icaza's novel *Huasipungo* (reading 12)—the workers received no effective wages at all, their only compensation being the use of the small plots of land provided for their subsistence and the rations of food traditionally given out in times of scarcity. Where manorial haciendas did pay wages, it was often in kind or in "money" that could be spent only at the hacienda store, which recovered much of the amount by selling goods at artifically high prices. In this case, of course, the workers at least obtained some purchasing power in return for their labor. As might be expected, increasing prosperity—especially when it was associated with population growth—tended to weaken this pattern by decreasing the hacienda's need to hold wages down and making it less dependent on coercion. When this happened the labor system tended to evolve toward the type of free labor system described for, the fundo, though this development was often retarded by the weight of established tradition.

In the frontier ranching economies freer patterns of labor again prevailed. One reason for this may perhaps be found in the mobility conferred by the possession of a horse. But freedom was also implicit in the nature of the cowboy's work, which unlike that of the agricultural peon, required considerable initiative and independence. Thus in the cattle economy of the Brazilian Northeast, large ranches (fazendas) were made up of smaller corrals *(currais),* each managed by a *vaqueiro* operating largely on his own. As reading 18 suggests, the ties of these men with their employers were essentially contractual (though not formalized in writing) and the dealings between them were conducted on a more equal plane.

The ability of the ranch to attract free labor did not fundamentally depend on its ability to pay satisfactory wages, something it was frequently unable to do. Cowboys often had to be paid, as can be seen in the Brazilian case, with a share in the natural increase of the herds they watched over, and the monetary value of such payment must usually have been very low. Life in the stock-raising areas had other advantages, however. Given the plentiful supply of cattle, for instance, one did not seriously have to worry about going hungry. Where cattle were killed primarily for their hides, in fact, the supply of meat greatly exceeded the demand and much of it was simply left to rot. In addition, a cowboy whose remuneration took the form of cattle might ultimately be able to build up enough of a herd to go into business on his own account, either as renter or landowner, a development which was also encouraged by the less aristocratic structure of society. Although some wealthy landowners were to be found in these regions, most ranchers were men who operated on a fairly modest scale, like the gaucho proprietors described by Sarmiento, and their life style usually did not differ radically from that of the cowboys who worked for them. On the whole, this was the characteristic pattern of the least developed ranching economies; where a larger demand brought more prosperity and increased the wealth and power of the big landowners, it underwent some alteration. Thus in northern Mexico, where the mining towns offered good markets which were relatively close, ranches often took on many of the traits we have associated with the manorial hacienda—the use of debt peonage, for example—and the egalitarianism characteristic of the more primitive ranching economies was less pronounced.[20]

Social Organization

Up to this point we have considered haciendas and plantations mainly from an economic point of view, treating them essentially as business enterprises which employed land, labor, and capital to make a profit. But these enterprises were never simply "plants"; they were also communities where people lived, in many cases for all of their lives. It is therefore important to understand their social as well as their economic organization.

Both plantations and haciendas have sometimes been described as "feudal" estates. The term is misleading in two ways, however. In the first place, to describe an estate as feudal usually implies that it was not "capitalistic," and we have seen that plantations and haciendas were essentially profit-making enterprises. Secondly, when the term is used in a sociological sense it is usually taken to mean a system in which ties of political subordination (that is, ties between lords and vassals) are recognized, but the commands of superior authority cannot effectively be enforced. While the encomenderos in Spanish America and the early *donatarios* in Brazil may have been feudal lords in this sense, the planters and hacendados of later years were much less so, except perhaps in the frontier regions where the central government always had a difficult time making its authority effective.

But if traditional plantations and haciendas were not feudal they clearly were paternalistic. In social terms this meant they were organized as if they were large households, with the landowner playing the role of father (patrón) and the peons or slaves that of his children. These estate "households" may perhaps be understood as a more extended variety of the traditional European upper-class household, which had always contained servants. It is not surprising, then, that the patrón usually possessed complete authority over his dependents and was able to whip them or lock them up if their conduct displeased him. Fathers usually possess the right to punish their children. Nor was the patrón who administered such justice on his own necessarily usurping governmental authority; the authority of parents over their children was much older than that of the state over its subjects, and governments have normally been reluctant to interfere with it.

Along with this authority over his dependents, the patrón incurred the obligation to take care of them properly and to "raise" them as civilized Christian human beings. Though this obligation was far from universally respected, it did exert a considerable influence over the conduct of landowners. Antonil's criticism of planters who did not feed or clothe their slaves adequately (reading 4) reflects an attitude which was clearly shared by many of the planters themselves. The recognition of these obligations did not depend solely on the attitude and moral authority of the Church. Antonil also stresses that where the planter was a proper "father" to his slaves, they would more willingly accept his authority, even internalizing it so that they would come of their own accord to confess their misdeeds and seek forgiveness. To the extent that this paternalistic ideal was realized, then, discipline and obedience would have depended less on physical force and more on the patrón's moral authority. This was an important consideration, particularly on the less profitable plantations, since of the two, moral authority tends to be the cheaper to exercise.

From an economic point of view, paternalism might be described as a pattern in which the principal responsibility of the landowner to his employees was to insure their welfare rather than to pay them a fixed wage. Society has always taken some responsibility for supporting those of its members who, temporarily or permanently, find themselves unable to support themselves. In traditional societies this responsibility was usually borne by kinship groups or on a community level; in modern societies much of it has been taken over by the state. The indigenous societies of Latin America had in many cases possessed quite elaborate welfare systems; the Inca empire, for instance, has been described as a kind of socialist state. And the Inca case seems to have been exceptional mainly in the degree to which the welfare system was centralized, though even here local communities probably carried the largest share of the burden. What is important in any case is that under European rule such community-based welfare systems were absent or completely inadequate, either because the population was made up of workers who had been uprooted from their communities or because surviving communities were deprived of the surpluses which would have permitted them to support a welfare system on the scale required. Under the new order, it was the Europeans who received most of the surpluses; thus it was they who tended to end up carrying the welfare burden.

Having examined the nature and functions of paternalism on the hacienda and the plantation, we can go on to analyze the various forms it took. It should be noted at the outset that the modern plantation, as it is described by Wolf and Mintz, is not fundamentally paternalistic, being characterized instead by the impersonality of relations between employers and employees. Here the welfare burden is not borne by the landowner, but rather by worker organizations and by the state; the workers on such modern enterprises have usually been among the first to be unionized and they have benefitted more than other groups from social legislation. On the traditional plantation, of course, such alternatives did not exist, and some degree of paternalism could hardly be avoided.

In general, the importance of paternalism in the social structure of traditional estates seems to have been inversely related to economic success. Where the economy was expanding and profits were high, paternalism tended to be less obvious than where the economy was stagnating and profits were low. Thus on the plantations of Vassouras, planters found it easier to replace individual slaves with new ones than to take responsibility for their long-term welfare (see reading 6). Though paternalism had some force as an ideal here—slaves were able to take advantage of it to ward off punishment, for instance—the worker seems less like a member of an extended family than an enemy who had to be held down by force, and the routine of daily life was basically that of a military camp. The repressive tendencies of Vassouras planters were not simply a product of personal inclinations; the problem of maintaining discipline in a labor force composed predominately of African-born slaves was clearly a difficult one.

The plantations of the depressed Brazilian Northeast, on the other hand, were much more paternalistic. For Freyre (see reading 7), the plantation community in this region was a large extended family ruled by an all-powerful patriarch. Brazilian planters were not usually absentees as their West Indian counterparts often were; they lived in immediate contact with their slaves and often formed their closest and most personal relationships with them. Nor were these relationships purely sexual, since the whites of the big house often had very close ties with their old nurses, or with companions of the same sex such as the *mucamas* and *muleques*. Freyre argues that it was through such personal ties that African elements came to hold such a prominent place in Brazilian culture. It is true that Freyre is mainly concerned with household slaves and that the ties between planters and their field hands were presumably less close; this, however, does not greatly affect our conclusions, since the existence of a household does not depend on whether the "father" treats all his "children" equally. It should also be noted that the presence of paternalistic bonds does not necessarily tell us much about the physical treatment of dependents. Freyre argues that the plantation patriarchs of Brazil were often brutal, not only to their slaves, but even toward their wives and children. From a psychological point of view, however, such brutality may sometimes reflect the closeness of personal relations rather than their absence, a possibility which is also implied by Antonil's comments on the relations between masters and their mulatto slaves in reading 4. What does seem clear is that on these plantations, where slaves were more likely to have been born and raised on the estate, repression was less necessary and labor was held by something more than physical force.

Paternalism also played an important role in the social system of the manorial hacienda, though here the patrón, who typically lived in the city instead of on his estate, was a more remote figure to his dependents. Thus the hacendado in Icaza's *Huasipungo* is the "patrón grande, su mercé," a kind of great white father who calls down divine punishment on the heads of his Indians when they do not obey him. The Indians, effectively paid nothing for their labor, expect only that the patrón will leave them the small plots of land from which they obtain their subsistence and will provide supplementary rations (socorros) to keep them from starving. The importance of the economic component of paternalism is shown very clearly here, since Icaza's hacendado fails to respect these basic obligations, leading the Indians to reject his authority and ultimately to revolt against him. Such revolts within the hacienda were relatively unusual; most traditional hacendados seem to have recognized the need for paternalism and had enough respect for their responsibilities to maintain their authority over their peons. Even in Icaza's novel, the behavior of the hacendado is seen as running counter to tradition, not only by the Indians, but also by the mestizo overseer who is quite willing to exploit the Indians on his own account.

Fundos tended to be less paternalistic, at least if we exclude the plantation-like estates worked by slaves. Where the local labor supply was large enough to make possible the hiring of additional labor whenever it was needed, landowners were likely to find it cheaper in the long run to pay wages than to shoulder paternalistic responsibilities which made it more difficult to dismiss unproductive or unneeded workers. Though most fundos did have a nucleus of peons who lived permanently on the estate and were bound by paternalistic ties, the bulk of the labor was performed by seasonal workers who did not remain long enough for such paternalistic ties to develop. The situation of these seasonal workers varied a good deal. Where they lived in Indian communities which offered them some land and security, as was the case in much of central Mexico for instance, they were relatively well off. In regions like the Mexican Bajío and central Chile, on the other hand, where seasonal workers did not have access to land and where they had neither the security of belonging to a corporate community nor that of possessing a patrón, their situation tended to be much more difficult.

Where fundos divided up their lands among tenant farmers the importance of paternalism tended to decline for somewhat different reasons. The renter or sharecropper was of course a permanent resident of the hacienda in a way that the seasonal laborer was not, but to the extent that he was an independent entrepreneur, living on and operating a farm of his own, he was not really within the haci-household (see reading 16). This tendency was partly counteracted, however, by the fact that most sharecroppers were likely to be chosen from among the more reliable peons, who already possessed strong paternalistic ties to the hacienda, since such ties tended to remain strong, supported by the sharecropper's realization that his position was a relatively privileged one.

The frontier ranch represents an exception to our general rule, since it was neither very prosperous nor very paternalistic. This was a consequence both of the survival of feudal patterns of social organization in the regions where the authority of the state had difficulty reaching and of the independence and mobility of most of the population. In the early nineteenth century, as Sarmiento shows us in reading 19, the government in Buenos Aires could maintain a degree of control over the surrounding countryside only by recognizing the authority of provincial caudillos whose power rested ultimately on military force. The dominant figures in such a society needed men who would fight as well as work for them, and the cowboy thus tended to be more vassal than serf. When he gave his loyalty to someone, it was usually because that person had earned his respect and because he considered it in his interest to do so, not because he needed the psychological and economic security that could be conferred by a patrón. As Euclides da Cunha's description of the life of the Brazilian *vaqueiro* suggests, for the most part cowboys neither required nor received this kind of security. And it was precisely this characteristic self-reliance which set them apart from the dependent peons and slaves of the agricultural estates.

Conclusion

The traditional landed estates of Latin America can best be understood as commercial enterprises, dedicated primarily to making profits from agriculture, stock raising, or both, although the amount of profit they were able to make varied greatly. Haciendas and plantations could develop only where there were markets, however minimal, for their products; and if the more marginal estates came to possess traits that seemed feudal, this was less because their owners lacked the motivation of true capitalists than because the economic situation left few opportunities to be exploited through capitalistic enterprise.

Latin American estates varied tremendously in their patterns of social and economic organization so that analysis of them must start by identifying and describing a few basic types. Such types are of course abstractions which may simplify but also tend to distort the picture. The reality, as always, was more complicated. The following readings, then, are intended to give the reader the opportunity to test and make use of the abstractions while at the same time restoring some of the complexity.

1 Haciendas and Plantations

Eric R. Wolf and Sidney W. Mintz

Though we often talk of the landed estate as if it was a single phenomenon in the history of Latin America, the truth of the matter is that the estates of the region have always been most notable for their diversity. Our understanding of them therefore depends in the first place on our ability to distinguish between the different types of estates that existed. This initial selection, which may serve as a theoretical foundation for the rest, suggests a distinction between two basic types of agricultural estates found in Latin America: the hacienda, characterized by its low capitalization and its dependence on small local and regional markets, and the plantation, characterized by its relatively high level of capitalization and its dependence on large export markets.

Eric Wolf and Sidney Mintz are both social anthropologists who have long been interested in the study of Latin American peasant societies. The former, whose research has been concerned primarily with Mexico, teaches at the City University of New York, and the latter, who has worked mainly on the Caribbean area, teaches at Johns Hopkins University.

Analysis of the Hacienda Type

1. *Capital*

a. *As an initiating condition of the type.* While the plantation requires a large supply of capital, the hacienda operates within a situation of capital scarcity. Several factors are responsible for this. First, with limited markets, capital which can be borrowed for

From Eric R. Wolf and Sidney W. Mintz, "Haciendas and Plantations in Middle America and the Antilles," *Social and Economic Studies* 6 (1957): 386–412.

hacienda operations tends to be generated within a limited region, and is only rarely pooled with the capital resources of other regions. Such capital thus remains relatively scarce. Second, the money-lending institutions which furnish hacienda capital are often tradition-oriented groups, such as instrumentalities of the Church, local merchant groups, or small banks. Such organizations are interested in low but secure returns, rather than in rapid accumulation. In a context of limited markets, moreover, they tend to distribute the risks of lending money by spreading credit in limited amounts among large number of enterprises, rather than by concentrating all their resources in a single enterprise.

b. *As an operational condition of the type.* Just as the supply of capital for hacienda operations remains limited, so the needs of the hacienda for capital are geared to a low capital input. Capital must be obtained to cover the initial cost of land and equipment, to meet current costs of operation, and to replace worn elements of production. But haciendas usually pay little for land, and their labor-intensive technology requires only a small outlay for mechanical equipment. They need only enough capital to maintain them in a state of stability. The hacienda rarely expands its production; it is geared instead to a restricted but stable market. The systems subsumed under the type are thus attuned to low capital intake.

c. *Derived cultural conditions.* Given the low input of capital, the financial requirements of the hacienda are rarely beyond the financial means of a person with the appropriate social, political and economic connections to ensure repayment. The most typical form of ownership of such estates is family ownership, which permits the mobilization of wealth through kinship ties and ties of personal friendship, but retains control in the hands of a consanguine primary group, rather than delegating it to a secondary group formed expressly for the purpose of manipulating capital, such as a corporation.

Another cultural condition, accompanying the operational role of capital in the hacienda type, is the use of the hacienda system to furnish not only returns on capital invested, but also to furnish the funds needed to feed the owner and his family and to support his aspirations for power and prestige. In sharp contrast to the plantation type in which the factors of production are manipulated wholly for maximum profit without reference to the consumption or status needs of the owners, in the hacienda type the factors of production are thus burdened with demands which are economically irrelevant to the

process of production. In the absence of "rational" cost accounting, these costs will remain hidden, though none the less real. These
costs of power and prestige in turn may be necessary to support the
capital structure. Only by maintaining the good name of his family,
and by underlining its social status through conspicuous consumption, can the hacienda owner hope to convince the lenders of capital
of his economic viability.

Furthermore, the hacienda owner cannot rely on an abundance of
capital to articulate the needed factors of production. Lacking sufficient capital to pay labor wholly in the form of wages, he must find
other means to spur his labor force to the required effort. Further, he
is limited in his ability to introduce new technological equipment or
new techniques of cultivation. In contrast to the plantation type,
capital thus does not constitute the main axis around which hacienda
life revolves. Some capital is needed to bring a hacienda into being,
but in its maintenance it plays a minor part, when hacienda systems
are compared with those characteristic of the plantation type.

2. Market

a. *As an initiating condition of the type.* Both haciendas and plantations require a market for their cash produce, as an initiating condition
for their appearance and development. The scope of this market, however, is a specific condition which favors the rise of one or the other
type. Plantations are geared to sales in markets of large scope; haciendas supply markets of small scope. The market of a hacienda may
be limited to the inhabitants of a locality or a region, as in the case
of the *pulque* haciendas of Mexico or the brandy haciendas of Peru.
Or the market may consist of the members of a subculture, such as
an upper class with tastes for a specific luxury product. Such consumers purchased most of the coffee grown on coffee haciendas in
Puerto Rico before the 1928 hurricane.

b. *As an operational condition of the type.* The organization of the
hacienda type is geared to the market it supplies. A hacienda owner
keeps his investment secure by restricting the supply of the desired
product somewhat below consumption expectations. Like his creditors, he shows a distinct preference for a low but safe rate of return.

A hacienda owner may attempt to control his market further by
moves in the social and political field. On the social plane, he may
gain the consent of relatives or friends for specific marketing operations, or he may ask them for information which bears on the state

of the market. On the political plane, he may press for legislation affecting markets through the erection of tariffs, or use his political power to guard his marketing advantages from outside interference. In essence, he tries to create a semi-monopolistic situation to reduce his risks, and his investment will be secure only as long as he can maintain these semi-monopolistic advantages.

c. *Derived cultural conditions.* The plantation produces for a mass market. It subordinates all other considerations to the desire to meet the demands of this market. It devotes all its resources to the production of the desired cash crop. The hacienda is much less single-minded in its economic effort. Its emphasis on the production of one major cash crop rarely excludes the production of other goods, either to feed its resident laboring population or to satisfy its own demands for consumer goods.

The plantation accepts integration into a system of economic and political relationships operating on the national or supranational level of integration. It thus tends to become a subordinate system within a larger system, at the mercy of forces over which it itself can exercise little con' 'l. In permitting alternative pursuits to cash crop production, alth... n strictly within the framework of commercial operation, the hacienda also maintains a second line of defense on which it can fall back if its market grows unstable. Less committed to the demands of a national or supranational market, it has few ties which bind it to units beyond the region or locality. Less geared to capital accumulation and to technological innovation than the plantation, it retains a greater capacity than the plantation for self-regeneration after a slump. The hacienda maintains greater control over the conditions and requisites for its existence, and remains more autonomous and less subject to the play of outside forces.

3. *Land*

a. *As an initiating condition of the type.* Both hacienda and plantation require large land areas to come into being. Yet they differ significantly in their demand for land, and in their use of it once it is acquired.

b. *As an operational condition of the type.* The hacienda must control enough land both to grow its cash produce and to provide its workers with subsistence plots and other perquisites, such as wood or forest resources. Such perquisites take the place of wages which must remain limited due to the scarcity of capital which is characteristic of the hacienda. In contrast to the plantation which acquires only land which it can put to use for maximum profits, either at the moment or in the future, the hacienda also needs land to furnish a non-wage incentive for its labor force.

The hacienda must also attempt to monopolize the supply of land in its immediate vicinity. It needs this land less for purposes of agricultural production than to deprive its laborers of economic alternatives to participation in hacienda operations. It pre-empts the agricultural resources to prevent any independent agricultural activities from being carried out by its potential labor supply; and it attempts to bar its own labor force from seeking economic independence outside the limits of the hacienda by cultivating land not owned or controlled by the hacienda.

c. *Derived cultural conditions.* Once a hacienda has reached its goal of setting narrow limits to the economic alternatives open to its resident laboring population and to the potential labor supply in the communities surrounding it, it will cease to grow. Very often, therefore, a large hacienda or a group of haciendas will be surrounded by marginal land which they dominate indirectly rather than directly through control of the legal title. The inhabitants of these marginal zones will depend on the hacienda for cash wages and other perquisites, but often retain traditional cultural patterns in managing their own internal affairs. It has even been argued that periodic work on the haciendas provides such groups of people with some opportunity, however small, to maintain those aspects of their culture patterns which require some small outlay of surplus cash and goods, and thus tends to preserve traditional norms which might otherwise fall into disuse.

4. *Labor*

a. *As an initiating condition of the type.* Like the plantation, the hacienda requires a large supply of labor at strategic periods during the cycle of production of its chief cash crop. Unlike the plantation, however, the hacienda is limited by its lack of capital in its ability to offer purely economic rewards to its labor force. Some writers have argued that the emergence of haciendas or plantations respectively is primarily a function of the available supply of labor. But it is lack of capital rather than lack of labor which constitutes the specific initiating condition for the emergence of the hacienda. Plantations equipped with sufficient capital, can import the required quantities of labor or put pressure on their government to arrange for its importation. Even where the hacienda may be able to increase in population by internal growth, it will not thereby turn into a plantation without further investment of capital. Similarly, a plantation—retaining all of its workers—may well turn into a hacienda if it loses its capital. Capital, rather than labor, would thus seem to be the strategic initiating condition in the emergence of one or the other type discussed here.

Nevertheless, it is probably true that the hacienda requires a minimum density of population as a necessary initiating condition for its emergence. Since it lacks capital, it must always rely on the labor supply of one locality or region, just as its market consists of the aggregate demand of one locality or region. If the region is but sparsely inhabited by agriculturists who have free access to available land resources, no effective control over labor can be established (see above).

b. *As on operational condition of the type.* The hacienda must thus bind labor by means other than money wages. Where some cash payment of wages is made, they are in no way a measure of labor performed. Its techniques of payment thus usually involve the direct or indirect use of compulsion. Some of the means by which the hacienda binds labor to land in the absence of monetary rewards may be noted here.

First, the hacienda tries to deprive its labor supply of economic alternatives. The chief expression of this is the desire of the hacienda to control all the land in its vicinity, discussed above.

Second, it makes use of part of its land to provide its workers with subsistence plots and other perquisites which take the place of money wages. As we have seen, the provision of a subsistence plot and other perquisites has an important function in maintaining the hacienda financially solvent and in keeping its system intact during periods when the market undergoes a severe decline. Since the labor force is able to fill a substantial part of its own consumption requirements within the framework of the hacienda, it can maintain itself in a state of "suspended animation" until market trends are reversed.

Third, the worker is tied to the hacienda through specific economic mechanisms, such as debts acquired at the hacienda store, or through loans obtained from the hacienda owner. According to Tannenbaum,

> [The Mexican peon] was born into debt because the children inherited the parents' obligations. He acquired a debt in his own right at baptism because

the cost of the *fiesta* it occasioned was advanced by the *hacendado,* and money was borrowed for the priest, for the *aguardiente.* His first clothes—made from the white *manta*—were purchased from the plantation (hacienda) store, the *tienda de raya,* against his future wage. When he was old enough to marry, money for the festivities was borrowed from the plantation (hacienda) owner; when children were born, the same process led to the same end—further debt. The religious holidays were celebrated with borrowed money, sickness was marked by dependence upon the *patrón* for the payment of such medication as was to be had; and when the peon died he was buried with such honor, drink, prayer and festivity as money borrowed from the same source made possible.

Fourth, hacienda worker and hacienda owner are tied together by the performance of mutual services. Exploitative as the debt relationship is from the economic point of view, it must be emphasized that in it the hacienda owner takes over many of the risks incurred by his worker. Such relations sometimes acquire the weight of tradition, and are reinforced through semi-sacred cultural mechanisms such as ritual kinship or other ceremonial ties.

Fifth, all of these relationships may be reinforced through the use of force employed by the hacienda owner against his laborers. Usually, the hacienda possesses its private system of law and order for this purpose (see below).

c.   *Derived cultural conditions.* Due to the demands of the hacienda for a dependable labor supply, it not only tries to convert the population of nearby population clusters into a part of its labor force, but it tends to develop special settlements of dependent laborers (*acasillados* in Mexico; *agregados* in Puerto Rico) on its own terrain. The struggle of the Mexican hacienda owner to build up such settlements and to remove their inhabitants from the rival jurisdictions of Indian communities or the national state has been analyzed by Silvio Zavala. The growth of haciendas thus alters the settlement pattern of any given region through the creation of new population clusters. At the same time, once the hacienda reaches its limits of expansion, it will tend to relinquish direct control over the population living on its borders, integrating them only as migratory laborers during peak seasons of the productive cycle (see above). Under these circumstances, the hacienda sets up a cycle of migration from surrounding settlements to hacienda, or from highlands to lowlands, and back, as in Guatemala, Mexico, or Puerto Rico.

The binding mechanisms described above also tend to set up cultural conditions with important consequences for the people involved in them. By rendering aid, the hacienda often takes over functions which the indigenous social group once rendered for its members within the antecedent social structure. It may thus act to stabilize traditional ideal norms and behavior patterns, often reinforcing the "tradition-oriented" character of the labor force (see above).

On the other hand, unlike the relationships which spring up among the hacienda workers themselves, these aid relationships are ties between social and economic unequals, and are hierarchical in character. They are thus reinforced by the development of appropriate symbols of dominance and submission. It would appear that the nature of the hacienda type emphasizes the operation of certain psychological mechanisms within this hierarchical setting. First, there tends to develop a collective representation of the hacienda owner as a symbolic "father," with the hacienda workers functioning as his symbolic "children." As the locus of power, the hacienda owner emerges as the major source of special favors as well as an allocator of perquisites. He may be judge, employer, military leader, and possibly fictive or blood relative to his workers. Since the personal relationship between owner and worker takes shape within a hierarchical system based on an intrinsic division of labor between both, they produce feelings of reciprocal dependence which are yet charged emotionally in different ways for the participants. The hacienda owner must always act to maintain his dominance. Yet he must also use his personal attributes to bind his labor supply through affective ties. These affective ties may reflect father-child relationships, or other relationships characteristic of the family.

It follows that these affective ties will not only be ties of love and affection, but also of hostility. They are reinforced by the fact that they are characterized by the rendering of services which are usually tied to basic needs, such as health and subsistence, rather than by money. If the owner renders such a service, the worker will be expected to respond likewise. Thus, for instance, a worker may agree to perform additional labor in exchange for the right to collect more wood, or feel obliged to cast his vote in favor of the hacienda owner's political candidate in exchange for the right to graze animals on the hacienda pasture. No matter how exploitative these ties may seem to outsiders, they are often phrased in terms of mutual dependence of the owner and worker by the people themselves. The representation of the owner as a symbolic "father," the close bearing of the reciprocal services performed to fundamental subsistence needs, and the phrasing of mutual dependence, in turn, tend to give rise to cultural patterns which duplicate familial relationships in which oral techniques of mastery predominate. Examples of such patterns may be found in the daily distribution of *pulque, rum,* or *coca* in Mexico, the Antilles, and Peru; or in the annual harvest festivities such as the Puerto Rican *fiesta del acabe* or, formerly, the Jamaican crop-over, in which the owner is obliged to feast the workers.

In the minds of the labor force, the person of the hacienda owner— who mediates between them and the outside world—may also come to represent the hacienda itself; his well-being may seem a validation of their collective effort. At the same time, he will act as the funnel through which the yield of some part of their work effort is returned to them. This redistribution, narrow though it is, partakes of the centralized redistributive economies characteristic of primitive societies.

Once such a system becomes established, its functioning may become essential to the feeling of security of those who must live in terms of it. Disturbances of the system, whether due to changes in the position of the worker or of the owner, tend to be felt as threats to a way of life. [1]

In assessing the cultural conditions of the hacienda as derivatives of its use of labor, special mention must be made of the hacienda store. It represents one of the more obvious binding mechanisms through which the hacienda binds its workers. Work performance is credited in goods at the store, and goods received are often credited against work performance in the future. Yet such a store does more than supply a worker's consumption needs. Often it may force him to buy goods which he might not otherwise buy, thus accustoming him to new consumption behavior which, in turn, he can only satisfy by working for the hacienda. The store also acts to limit the amount a worker can consume; it ensures that his demands will not threaten the surplus produced in the course of hacienda operation.

Because the hacienda accomplishes its ends in binding labor through the variety of economic, social, and psychological mechanisms just discussed, labor is often less scarce than available capital. As a result of this particular relationship between the conditions of production, the hacienda owner can express his status needs more easily by expending labor than by expending wealth. Lavish use of labor power thus tends to become the chief way in which the hacienda owner maintains his privileged position within the social group to which he belongs. In many individual cases, this derived cultural condition may indeed become the dominant *motif* in the life of the owner. Where emphasis is placed on the conspicuous consumption of labor, the ability of a hacienda to generate capital for reinvestment and growth may be affected in turn. One should not lose sight of the fact that the hacienda was organized to produce agricultural goods for a market. Yet one of the functional implications of the type does seem to involve the diversion of the factors of production to non-economic ends. This situation contrasts sharply with that of the plantation where decisions are not made in terms of the prestige or consumption requirements of one owner, but in the expectation of maximum returns on invested capital.

5. Technology

a. *As an initiating condition of the type.* Both haciendas and plantations tend to produce their major cash crops by massing large numbers of workers on a large area of land. Both employ some capital to purchase technical equipment, usually to further rapid and efficient processing of the cash crop produced.

b. *As an operational condition of the type.* The technology of the hacienda bears the imprint of the lack of capital which attends its birth and limits its operations. First, the hacienda rarely exploits all of the land under its control. Usually, it concentrates its massed manpower and equipment only on the best land (called the *casco* of the hacienda in Mexico), leaving the remainder of the land to its labor force as subsistence plots or unattended.

Second, its technology remains labor-intensive; there is not enough capital to develop greater intensity of equipment. It achieves its production by massing labor, not tools. Although there is a relatively low level of productivity per worker, by combining the efforts of many workers, the hacienda produces a surplus sufficient for its economic operations.

Third, lacking capital, the hacienda does not have the wherewithal to purchase new skills and equipment. It must thus rely on the culturally standardized technological behavior available in the area under its control.

Fourth, little capital is available to improve means of transportation. Nor is such improvement necessary since the amount of cash produce to be transported hinges upon the demands of a limited and often easily accessible market. Simple animal transportation, such as can be provided by strings of mules, usually suffices to meet the needs of a hacienda.

c. *Derived cultural conditions.* The traditional technology and transportation of the hacienda react in turn to reinforce and maintain the characteristics of the type. Limited by capital and markets, it remains limited in productive capacity; limited in its capacity to produce, it remains limited in capitalization and market. Low productivity per worker and lack of advanced transportation may even help to maintain the stable price structure for which the hacienda strives. Lack of mobility may also act to limit the ability of hacienda workers to find social or economic alternatives to employment on the hacienda.

Since the technology remains tied to the traditional skills of the laboring population, the hacienda typically does not require the specialized group of technicians and technically trained administrators so characteristic of plantation organization. The supervisor on the hacienda need not possess technical skills which differ significantly in kind from those of the workers under his command. His role is social and political, rather than technical, in that he exercises the delegated authority of the owner, an authority backed by the private system of law and order maintained by the hacienda.

6. Sanctions

a. *As an initiating condition of the type.* We have noted above that the hacienda often operates under conditions such that it must systematically limit or destroy social and economic alternatives to the employment it provides in order to obtain an adequate labor supply. We have also seen that, in the absence of monetary rewards, the hacienda tends to substitute social, psychological or economic binding mechanisms to tie the worker to his place of work. When such mechanisms break down or when the security of the hacienda is challenged by the growth of economic alternatives outside its boundaries, it requires a system of force to deal with possible recalcitrants. Such a private system of law and order can exist only where the state is either too weak to exert control on the local level, or where it supports the delegation of judicial functions to local entrepreneurs. Mexican haciendas used to maintain their own police, judges, and jails.

b. *As an operational condition of the type.* The main purpose of such a private system of sanctions within the context of the hacienda is the maintenance of—primarily—work discipline to ensure that the workers put the requirements of production of the hacienda's bulk product above their own private activities. This pattern of exaction may vary from time to time and from place to place, but is usually standardized. Thus, for instance, on some Mexican and Peruvian haciendas, laborers render a fixed quantity of labor time in return for the use of land for their own consumption needs. On Puerto Rican coffee haciendas, workers drop whatever activities they are engaged in when the signal to begin the coffee harvest is sounded.

The existence of such a private system of sanctions leaves the hacienda owner a free hand when he has to punish infractions of such work discipline. He needs this free hand because the relation between his worker and himself is phrased in personalistic terms. He may have to discipline his worker, but at the same time he must continue this personal relation between himself and the culprit. A plantation can discipline by firing a worker or by refusing to hire him—acts which involve no personal tie between it and the subject of the decision. Where the right to fire or refusal to hire may itself be sufficient sanction in itself to enforce discipline on a plantation, on a hacienda the owner may have to adapt his discipline to the character of each particular case.

c. *Derived cultural conditions.* In meting out punishment, the hacienda owner may have to consider the general situation on the hacienda, rather than a set of absolute rules governing standards of behavior. His procedure will be "situational"; its main function will be to serve as an "example" to his workers. On occasion, he may have recourse to higher political officials who will administer such punishment, but usually he will tend to resist the imposition of any impersonal body of law which would tend to limit the exercise of his personalistic authority. Sanctions used on haciendas often take the form of physical punishment. The psychological function of such punishment may be twofold. On the one hand, it allows the offender to return to the ranks of the labor force after he has expiated his offense. It thus restores the affective tie between owner and workers through the elimination of the threat to the owner's authority. On the other hand, it may simply exercise a terror function calculated to paralyze resistance to authority on the part of the labor force. Under such conditions, needless to say, workers can often be subjected to physical punishment for reasons which under another system of law and order would not justify such severity.

Analysis of the Plantation Type

1. *Capital*

a. *As an initiating condition of the type.* Like the organizers of haciendas, so the plantation entrepreneurs need capital to set up a productive organization capable of meeting the demands of an existing market, or to expand those markets by advertising and selling. The demands of the plantation for capital are very much greater than those of the hacienda since it is usually geared to large-scale markets, often supranational in scope. Such capital rarely can be furnished by an individual entrepreneur operating within a local context. Capital generally is concentrated through a series of financial mechanisms in a corporate group which gauges its investment in a given enterprise or area on the basis of maximum returns on capital advanced. The initial investment must be very large to allow the plantation to acquire the needed factors of production under optimal conditions and to make optimum use of them in its operations.

b. *As an operational condition of the type.* Corporate ownership must not only furnish the large sums which are required to equip a plantation for its start in life, it is also a functional requirement for plantation operation. The plantation must be organized so as to be capable of absorbing large amounts of capital, as well as of repaying capital used with large profits. Corporations function on a scale of operations which makes it cumbersome for them to split their investment into small ventures. Use of land, labor and technology on the plantation thus must be geared to production in bulk with maximum efficiency and utilization. In all these respects, the plantation differs sharply from the hacienda, with its limited intake and output of capital.

c. *Derived cultural conditions.* Only rarely are the funds needed for the operation of a plantation found within the country where the plantation is established. Such countries usually are classed as "underdeveloped," and capital formation among the indigenous population is rarely advanced enough to allow natives to assume the burden of financing such large-scale agriculture. Capital for plantations therefore is usually supplied by foreigners, while labor is either drawn from the inhabitants of the country or, much more commonly, is imported into it. Some of the interests associated with the statuses of workers and owners are potentially in conflict in any country. In plantation areas, such conflicts may become further charged with antagonisms arising from cultural differences between the protagonists.

In large corporations, the functions of financial control and management usually have become differentiated, and are delegated to different groups of specialists. Ordinarily, the financiers set the goals of production, while the managers are concerned with implementing these goals through the judicious use of the factors of production under their control. The division between financiers and managers assumes even greater importance in cases where the financiers reside in the country which exports capital for the enterprise, while the managers exercise their delegated function in the country in which the plantation has been established. Since the corporation is organized to obtain maximum returns on invested capital, the managers are committed to impose these goals on a country and a people whose cultural orientation and interests may be at variance with those of the owners at home. And as the managers are often foreigners themselves, the exercise of their role is governed by the same ideal norms which animate the behavior and thinking of their corporate employers.

The flow of capital, subject to the demands for maximum profits, becomes the motor force which underlies all other major relationships within the plantation type. The plantation enterprise evaluates all social arrangements in the light of pecuniary considerations, and tends to make the demand for maximum returns on such generous investment the major factor in deciding whether a pattern of relationships is to be continued or is to be replaced by another one. The result is a situation in which land, labor and equipment are judged wholly in their capacity as commodities, and the relationships which govern their use are evaluated wholly in the light of "rational" cost accounting. The role of land, labor, and equipment in the traditional culture of the area tends to remain as much a matter of indifference to the financiers and managers as do the cultural consequences of plantation organization for the lives of the native population.

The employment of rational cost accounting further differentiates the plantation from the hacienda. The subsistence and prestige needs of the corporation owners are divorced from the uses to which the capital is put. Such needs can be satisfied by intermittent payment of interest only after the completion of a cycle of production. Most capital is ploughed back into the operation of the enterprise and used for economic ends only. In the employment of capital to these ends, we may again note a tendency to treat factors of production as commodities, regardless of the cultural implications of such treatment.

An important consequence of capital investment in a foreign country is the tendency of the investor to attempt to protect his stake by influencing the political machinery of the country in which he has invested. Because of this, "every plantation region is in politics from its inception." The connection between imperialism and plantation economy is too well documented to require further comment here.

2. Market

a. *As an initiating condition of the type.* The plantation requires not only a very large and steady supply of capital to finance its operations, it also needs a market of large scale into which it can pour its product. Such markets are usually found in a "developed" country or countries, often in the country which supplies the capital to the area where the plantation is located. In such countries, the customers are either industries which need such products as jute, rubber, or sisal, or factories producing consumers' goods such as sugar, tea, cocoa, or coffee. Since the First World War, such markets have been increasingly secured against oversupply through international agreements which regulate production through manipulation of quotas, tariffs, or prices. Such attempts at stabilization seem to be necessary to reduce the high risks attendant on the investment of large amounts of capital. We thus witness, on the international level on the part of the plantation, some of the semi-monopolistic techniques employed by the hacienda in its attempt to control its market on the local or regional level. In contrast to the hacienda, however, production on the plantation must be capable of rapid expansion when there is a significant increase in effective demand through the growth of new industries, population, or popularity of a product.

b. *As an operational condition of the type.* In contrast to the hacienda, which attempts to reduce its risks by habitually undersupplying available demand, plantation production is closely geared to the capacity of its market. Since the plantation is essentially a system for the production of maximum returns on invested capital, the use of land, labor, and technology is continuously reevaluated to enable the system to produce more. Yet production is not speculative. It always remains subject to international agreements, as well as to the national policies of both the producing country and the country which receives the final product.

c. *Derived cultural functions.* In contrast to hacienda production, plantation production tends to be more highly specialized. Each plantation grows only one crop. Unlike the hacienda, the plantation thus reduces its ability to resist sudden changes in the outside market. It ties its fate to the fate of its major cash crop and maintains no second line of defence in case of market failure.[2]

The plantation is thus less autonomous in its operation than is the hacienda. Functioning, as it must, within a wider political and economic system, it is subject to economic forces of a different order. In this sense, the risks associated with capital investment in plantations are very high. At this level of market organization, it is impossible for the owners to exercise personal influence over the market. Whatever the semi-monopolistic or monopolistic arrangements made to ensure the security of the investment, they must be accomplished through manipulation of national or supranational agencies where personal influence is of limited effectiveness. Risk taking thus seems to depend primarily on the changing relationships of strength between the dominant powers exercising control over the plantation areas, or between these powers and their agencies.

3. *Land*

a. *As an initiating condition of the type.* Like the hacienda, the plantation needs sufficient land to allow it to produce large quantities of cash produce. The plantation must make such possession of land consonant with its investment in machinery and transportation. For the plantation, land is thus a commodity like any other, acquired, used, and discarded for purely economic reasons.

b. *As an operational condition of the type.* The plantation not only needs enough land to carry on cash crop production in bulk consonant with its goals of increasing profit, it also must improve its land to maintain or to increase its productivity. Much capital therefore is expended on plantations to drain or irrigate the land, and to condition the soil through the use of commercial fertilizers. The plantation also must control enough productive land to allow it to expand production for expanding markets. Unlike the hacienda, however, it will own little unproductive land. Such land may be owned to facilitate transportation or to conduct agricultural experimentation; but it is not hoarded, as it is on the hacienda, to deprive the labor supply of effective alternatives to employment on the estate or to grant subsistence perquisites to its laborers. Generally speaking, the plantation strives to "streamline" production with as little paternalism towards its laborers as possible. In rare instances, a particular plantation may grant some subsistence plots to its labor force for other than paternalistic reasons. The granting of such perquisites may represent a politically expedient move to assuage local discontent, or may grow out of technical considerations related to the requirements of sound land use for the commercial crop. But the plantation does not use such perquisites to bind labor in the way that the hacienda does.

c. *Derived cultural conditions.* Through its massive occupation of land for purposes of cash production, a plantation soon comes to dominate the social and economic life of the immediate area in which it is located. Its demand for land usually brings it into immediate conflict with the preexisting population, whether that consists of hunters and gatherers who make use of land as a hunting preserve, or agriculturists who carry on some form of subsistence or cash crop agriculture. In occupying land that other people have used for subsistence purposes, it usually undermines subsistence production, driving the indigenous population into wage labor on its newly won lands as an immediate result.

The concentration of plantations in certain regions of a country which are located close to markets and major routes of transportation, moreover, has a tendency to dichotomize the structure of the host nation into a plantation sector, marked by intense economic activity and highly charged with capital, and a "marginal" sector, which remains tradition oriented and undercapitalized. At the same time, the marginal sector is often greatly affected by the operations of the plantation sector through such mechanisms as wage labor, commercial activity, tariffs, etc. The result frequently is a quite uneven development of the geographical regions and social structures associated with plantation activity and non-plantation activity respectively. The contrast between the "marginal" mountainous interior, and the belt of coastal flatland occupied by plantations in Puerto Rico would be an example; the contrast between the coastal plantation belt in Brazil, and the Brazilian hinterland would be another. At the same time, the very massiveness of the plantations themselves tends to discourage the development of alternative or additional economic enterprises of smaller scale in the plantation sector itself. McBride has said that

> In such a social order there is little room for a middle class. The plantation largely markets its own crops; it procures supplies, directly or indirectly for its entire population; hence the trader class is small and usually dependent upon the estate. Economic groups outside of the plantations are also decidedly limited. The professional class is not numerous. Most of the population bears some relation to the plantation and falls into one or the other categories into which its people are divided.

Thus the social, political, and economic life of the host country may become dominated by agricultural enterprises producing one or two crops for export, while its own capacity to produce economic alternatives to the plantations remains severely limited.

4. *Labor*

a. *As an initiating condition of the type.* A labor force large enough to carry on production in bulk at rates low enough to guarantee returns on invested capital is an essential initiating condition of a plantation. Where it is not available in the vicinity of the plantation, or where the local population is unwilling to work in plantation operations, such labor must be imported.

b. *As an operational condition of the type.* The plantation operates on the assumption that labor is plentiful and cheap. As in any "industrial" establishment, low labor costs are one of the guarantees of its financial success. It functions at an optimum where many laborers are competing for the same job, since such competition automatically lowers the price of labor. For instance, in the post-emancipation period of the British West Indies, plantation owners—deprived of labor by the development of a Negro peasantry, and also short of capital funds—succeeded in securing cheap labor by sponsoring heavy immigration from India. This migration did not meet the need for labor fully, but it increased the total population of certain strategic areas sufficiently to lower labor costs. In Peru, coastal sugar plantations count on the seasonal migration of hacienda dwellers and members of Indian communities in the highlands, much as the coastal sugar plantations in Jamaica and Puerto Rico depend in part on the seasonal labor of highland peasants. In Guatemala, a highland Indian population resists permanent wage labor because of its culturally conservative standards of consumption, but is forced by law to undertake wage labor on the coastal plantations. Thus, the plantation thrives on conditions under which labor is in year-round or seasonal oversupply. Where such labor power is absent, or does not voluntarily put itself at the disposal of the plantation, the political apparatus of the larger society often functions to facilitate its provision through laws affecting tenure, taxation, immigration, and other means.

In a situation where many workers are competing for available jobs, the most advantageous method of payment for the plantation is in the form of a money wage. The plantation laborer is typically a "free" laborer in a free labor market. To the extent that work effort is rewarded with cash, labor power can be measured impersonally. Payment by the task, by piece work or by hourly rates plus bonuses are the prevalent manner of payment, due to the repetitive and "industrial" nature of the operation involved. Free housing occasionally may be provided to a few workers to maintain a core of year-round operatives. Unlike the hacienda, however, the plantation does not rely on such capital-saving mechanisms for binding labor as the extension of perquisites, the granting of personal credit, or the institutionalization of personal relationships between employer and employee. Such perquisites run counter to the demands of rational management of extensive land areas for intensive production by decreasing "efficiency" and adding to the cost of administration. Ideally, the plantation would keep a small core of workers attached to it throughout the year to carry on necessary routine labor while relying on heavy in-migration of workers during the peak season of work.

Workers who receive wages for their work, in turn, begin to change their consumption patterns. Increasingly, their needs can only be met by purchases in stores rather than by subsistence production on plots owned or operated by themselves. When their ready cash is spent, they will tend to return to the plantation for additional employment rather than expend their efforts on growing or making things for themselves.

c. *Derived cultural conditions.* Plantation use of labor tends to have immediate effects on the prevailing pattern of settlement of a plantation area. Most striking is the development of entire communities of wage laborers directly dependent on work on the plantations. These are usually spatially as well as culturally separate from the traditional settlement of the inhabitants of the country. Some of them are located on the plantations themselves, but more generally they occupy surrounding marginal lands. Such changes in settlement pattern may ultimately affect entire regions and even countries.

Striking also is the pattern of seasonal migration set up as a result of seasonal demands for labor on the part of the plantation. Such migration may link the interior of a country with its plantation belt, as in Guatemala or Puerto Rico. It may also take form across national boundaries, as in the case of Haitian migrants to the Dominican Republic. Such seasonal migration may be expected to have strong effects on the unity, prevailing division of labor, and distribution of authority within the worker family, and on other aspects of worker culture.

Employment for wages also introduces new and decisive factors into a plantation area. Wage payment makes superfluous any personal relationship between the employed and the organizers of production. The laborer retains no relationship with the enterprise other than through the intermittent sale of his labor power. In contrast to the hacienda, and often in contrast also to the traditional cultural patterns of the group to which the worker belongs, personal relationships are not the means through which labor is organized and used.

Not only do the means of earning a livelihood differ sharply from those prevalent on haciendas, but wage payment also alters the patterns of consumption of the labor force. The hacienda worker is paid in goods and perquisites of a nonmonetary nature. The hacienda which provides these services in kind is thus able to impose an upper limit on the consumption of its labor force, a limit which is rarely subject to revision. The plantation worker receives money wages which must be spent at stores. He thus becomes to a much greater degree than the hacienda worker a consumer of goods which are not produced by him or others like him, and which are not produced within the confines of the locality where he lives. Money wages thus condition a continuous flow of store-bought goods into the plantation area, introduced either by company stores or by the stores of small merchants. The consumption habits of the plantation labor force may indeed be patterned on antecedent cultural norms, but the goods introduced set up a continuous flow of cultural alternatives into the worker community. The plantation worker, unlike the hacienda worker, is continuously confronted by consumption choices which he must resolve.

The new goods introduced from outside, in turn, are not isolated elements which diffuse without further cultural implications. A pair of store-bought, two-tone shoes, or sunglasses, or canned goods are not merely new culture traits. They also represent participation in a larger social and economic system in which invidious comparisons are drawn between individuals, in terms of their capacity to consume. The money wages of the plantation worker not only confront him with a choice of items of consumption but also with new social relationships symbolized by these items of consumption. This tends to modify the initial cultural values of the labor force, and to widen its social and cultural horizons. The increase in consumption choices is sometimes furthered by increases in money wages, as in Puerto Rico after 1940; such increases are made possible by the enormous productivity per worker within the plantation system. Although such increases in *per capita* rewards are rarely proportionate to this productivity, they allow the plantation workers to participate far more completely than the hacienda workers in the expansion of the consumption frontiers of capitalist society.

In the case of the hacienda, the owner himself draws revenues for purposes of subsistence and prestige from the operation of his estate. In contrast, the owners of a plantation hardly look upon the enterprise as a source of livelihood for themselves. This is especially evident where the plantation is merely one of a number of enterprises owned by a corporation. In such a case the accumulation of capital is the primary purpose of the enterprise, and all means are geared to this end. There is thus little chance that the cultural patterns based on common understandings of the consumption process, such as are characteristic of the hacienda, will tend to develop on the plantation.

Wage payment of work performed on the plantation has additional consequences for the culture patterns which develop around it. The fact that each worker receives equal wages for similar standardized units of work allows each man to buy as much or as little with his wages as the next man. This equality of rewards operates as a strong leveling influence, placing each man on a roughly equal plane with his neighbor. The experience of similar rewards for similar work performed becomes a powerful factor in making plantation workers conscious of the similarity of their chances in life. Such "consciousness of kind" receives further reinforcement through the frequency with which men are laid off because of fluctuations in the market for the product of the plantation or increased mechanization of operations. The plantation worker lacks the ability of the hacienda worker to fall back on the produce of his subsistence plot and other nonmonetary perquisites when faced with a crisis in the market. In his case, loss of job immediately poses a serious problem for him in terms of biological survival. Since, in the eyes of the organizers of production, on the plantation one man is as good as the next and one man can easily take the place of another, all men tend to be confronted by a similar fate.

Faced with the same life situation, plantation workers tend to develop social relationships to counteract the instability of their individual positions. These relationships may follow a variety of patterns. They may be relations of ritual kinship, patterned on the bonds within the familial grouping but extended to non-kin persons in order to include large numbers of men in quasi-familial ties. These ties may prove effective in lending greater solidarity to segments of the worker community but often are not flexible enough to unite a major part of the total labor force. This is frequently accomplished more effectively through unionization, which represents an attempt to create local scarcity of labor within a total societal situation of chronic labor abundance. Unionization, however, often founders on the very problem that brings it into being: too many men competing for too few opportunities to work. It thus rarely remains purely on the economic plane but tends to develop political ends. If the labor union can gain enough strength to influence policies on the national level, it can work for an increase of institutionalized services provided by the government or forced on the plantations through government intervention. This political role of unions of plantation workers is especially important in societies which are politically and economically dependent on dominant powers. The union may have opportunities to ally itself with groups operating on the national level to restrict the power of the dominant country. Agitation against foreign-owned and foreign-operated plantations may form part of such a political effort, and political success of anticolonial political groups may result in an extension of services to the plantation population.

Finally, the plantation also tends to effect the cultural and ethnic composition of the population under its control. As a result of labor immigration or imports, plantation areas are generally characterized by much cultural and physical heterogeneity. The equality of life chances and the development of a common "consciousness of kind" among the plantation workers may be instrumental in breaking down such cultural and ethnic barriers, resulting in considerable acculturation and interbreeding between different ethnic groups.

5. Technology

a. *As an initiating condition of the type.* In contrast to the hacienda, the plantation requires a substantial investment in machinery, in transportation, equipment and facilities, and in technological skills. Machinery is usually needed for processing but is also applied to field operations as new techniques for such application are worked out. Generally machinery is imported from the industrial country which also furnishes the capital and managerial skills for plantation enterprise. Its benefits to the plantation country are thus only indirect, and consist primarily of that part of wages which reflects increased productivity.

Improvements in transportation are a necessary accompaniment of the plantation system, both in external transport, to allow the product of the plantations to be shipped to overseas markets, and in internal transport, to permit rapid and efficient communication between the plantations and their marketing outlets. Such improvements may be made by the plantation entrepreneurs alone, or by the entrepreneurs in conjunction with local governments. Often, the establishment of a transportation network and the introduction or improvement of transportation facilities may benefit a number of parties to such construction programs: the government, for instance, may improve thereby its ability to tax, to investigate local affairs, to draft personnel for the armed services, and so forth. From the point of view of the plantation, however, an improvement in transportation primarily represents an increase in the efficiency of its operations.

The plantation also requires a body of skilled personnel for the execution of administrative and technical functions. Such personnel is rarely available within the plantation area, and usually must be imported from outside or trained to fulfil the necessary requirements.

b. *As an operational condition of the type.* In sharp contrast to the hacienda, the plantation can afford to spend large amounts to improve its technology. Its mechanization of phases of both processing and cultivation; its systematic use of fertilizer, herbicides, and irrigation; its ability to experiment and to introduce new varieties of the staple crop; its ability to subsidize government research or to further the development of new technological skills in local schools; all these contrast sharply with the labor-intensive character of the hacienda. The introduction of such new devices and skills are, of course, subject to the same yardstick of "rational cost accounting" used in all phases of plantation operation. In any given situation, the form which plantation organization takes will depend on the amounts of available capital, the degree to which manual labor may prove to be cheaper or more efficient than machines, the degree of technological progress achieved in improving the quality of the product in the industry in general, and so forth. Similar considerations will also animate the introduction of new means of transportation or of new technical skills. Only expectable returns on capital investment will bring improvements in the flow of product from field to factory, or in the manner of concentrating, distributing, and interchanging labor or machinery.

Given the scale of plantation operations, a technical staff is necessary to supervise work in the field, processing, marketing, and other phases of production or distribution. The delegation of such functions to specialized personnel creates a gap between the *de facto* owners of the plantation and the technicians, on the one hand, and between the technicians and the local labor force, on the other. This gap is accentuated where the *de facto* owners of the plantation reside in a country other than the one in which the plantation is located.

Hacienda and plantation again contrast sharply in the ways in which labor is marshaled to perform its appointed tasks within the systems subsumed under each type. The hacienda, with its scarcity of capital and its need to bind labor, retains a labor-intensive technology often based on the tools and techniques traditional in the culture from which the labor force is drawn. In contrast, the plantation laborer is integrated into a system of production wherein his productivity is tapped *via* an increased efficiency of the organization of work, or a multiplication of his productivity *via* scientific agriculture, or both. In addition to the technical improvements provided on the plantation, the plantation laborer's productivity is heightened by the systematization of production. Work effort is customarily divided into a number of fixed operations, each of which may be performed by any worker without regard to his individual capacities. This reduction of work tasks into a number of separate operations, each performable by any worker, seeks to utilize the worker purely in terms of his labor power without reference to other characteristics. It permits the quick training of unskilled labor and allows the ready substitution of one worker for another. This rationalization of the labor force contrasts with the customary rationale of production on the hacienda. [3]

c. *Derived cultural conditions.* The presence of machinery on the plantation implies social as well as occupational distinctions between a relatively small technical staff and the large unskilled labor force. Since the technical staff tends to be drawn from the country which provides the investment capital for the plantation rather than from the country in which the plantation is located, it often views local problems in terms of outside interests rather than in terms of local considerations. Often, such a group identifies strongly with the dominant country, and tends to reinforce this identification through in-group cohesion and group self-consciousness. Such cultural aspects of the managerial role are not necessary attributes of the plantation type, but rather are expectable features of plantations which draw their skilled technicians from the home country. Since both technicians and workers tend to form their separate and often antagonistic in-groups, we may expect further that tensions between them may become the focus of nationalist or racialist sentiments. Often, therefore, we may find the technicians laying claim to distinct racial descent, superior intellectual power, and membership in a politically dominant nation, and the workers reinforcing their own solidarity through the use of contrasting symbols. The political tendencies of workers in plantation areas thus receive considerable added strength.

Such tendencies are also reinforced by other cultural conditions derived from the operation of the plantation. It may be noted, for instance, that with the introduction of a complex division of labor on the plantation, the individual worker can no longer span conceptually or technically the range of production operations. Work loses its "holistic" character, and becomes depersonalized. In areas in which the labor force possesses a culture which traditionally evaluates work in terms which integrate economics and other aspects of life into a closely woven fabric, such change in the character of work may produce "secularization" of traditional cultural norms. A machinewrecker ideology may develop, and merge with developing nationalism and class solidarity.

Such trends are also effected by the growth of advanced transportation in plantation areas. Such an increase of transportation lays open community, region, and nation to further penetration from the outside. It may increase geographical mobility and thus affect the worker subculture. It may permit increased contacts between groups of workers on different plantations and thus reinforce the class solidarity evoked by the operation of the plantation. It may render labor more interchangeable over wider areas and thus reinforce the tendency of the plantation to use each worker as an interchangeable and standardized unit. It may also operate in opposite ways: it enables dissatisfied elements in local communities to move out more easily into other areas or urban centers, and it may decrease the solidarity of the local group by opening up new horizons and opportunities for change and social circulation. In the development of such alternatives, transportation must, of course, be seen only as one element among others, and its role can be understood only through an analysis of the total context surrounding its growth.

6. *Sanctions*

a. *As an initiating condition of the type.* Like the hacienda, the plantation requires a system of sanctions to regulate the distribution of surpluses produced and to discipline labor in its operations.

b. *As an operational condition of the type.* In contrast to the hacienda, where an infraction of labor discipline calls into question the authority of the owner and where punishment is used to restore threatened social relationships, the organizers of production on the plantation can enforce work discipline simply by firing the wrongdoer. This is possible first, because the plantation operates within the context of an oversupply of labor, and, second, because one unskilled worker can easily take the place of another in the performance of the simplified and standardized operations to which the work process has been reduced. Just as the wage payment involves no personal bond between the recipient of the payment and the employer, so the sanctions guarding the enforcement of law and order are wholly impersonal and do not involve the restoration of affective relationships between employer and worker.

c. *Derived cultural conditions.* Such manner of punishment tends to reinforce the tendency towards self-help on the part of the plantation labor force. Unable to have recourse to personal relationships with plantation managers and technicians, the worker against whom sanctions have been used can rely only on the sympathy and aid of

sugar. That experimental development was to acquire enormous importance. Besides providing a solution to technical problems related with sugar production, it was to spur the development of the Portuguese sugar-mill equipment industry. In view of the difficulties prevailing at the time for the acquiring of any kind of production know-how, as well as of the prohibitive burdens hampering the export of equipment of any kind, the success of the Brazilian enterprise would have been far more difficult to attain or much longer in coming if it had not been for the technical progress achieved by the Portuguese in this sector.

The greatest repercussions of the experimental work in the Atlantic islands were probably those felt in the commercial sector. All indications are that at the outset Portuguese sugar must have been routed over the traditional channels controlled by the merchants of the Italian seafaring cities. The fall in prices which occured in the last quarter of the fifteenth century would, however, lead to the supposition that those trade channels had not been broadened to the extent required by the expansion of sugar production. The problem of surpluses which made itself felt at that time seems to show that within the mercantile setup traditionally established by the Italian commercial cities, sugar production could find only relatively limited markets. Nevertheless, one of the main consequences of the flow of Portuguese production into the European market was the disruption of the monopoly of access to sugar-producing areas heretofore exercised by the Venetians. Since early days, Portuguese products were shipped in vast quantities to the harbors of Flanders. When in 1496 the Portuguese government, under pressure from the decline in prices, decided to curtail production, one-third of the output was already being customarily routed to the Flemish ports.

From the second half of the sixteenth century, Portuguese sugar production was being amalgamated to an increasing extent with Flemish and Dutch interests, first with those of Antwerp and later with those of Amsterdam. The production phase was in the hands of the Portuguese, whereas the Flemish would load the crude product in Lisbon, to be refined at home for distribution throughout Europe, especially in the Baltic area, France, and England.

The Low Countries' contribution—chiefly that of the Dutch —to the great expansion of the sugar market in the latter half of the sixteenth century may be viewed as a basic cause of the success of agricultural settlement in Brazil. Experts in the inter-European trade—a large part of which was financed by the Dutch—they were at that time the only nation with an available commercial organization capable of providing a huge market for such a new product as sugar. In view of the immense difficulties faced at the outset in marketing the small output of the island of Madeira, as well as the stupendous subsequent expansion of the market which absorbed at steady prices the great Brazilian production, the importance of the commercial phase for the success of the entire sugar enterprise at the time is clearly manifest.

It was not only through their trading experience that the Dutch engaged in the sugar business. A large part of the financing required by the undertaking had come from the Netherlands. There are many indications that Dutch capitalists did not restrict themselves to the financing of sugar refining and marketing, but that Flemish capital also shared in the financing of production facilities in Brazil and in the importing of slave manpower. Once the feasibility of the enterprise had been demonstrated, and its high profitability proved, financing of further expansion would not be faced with any major hindrance. Powerful Dutch financial groups, involved as they were in the sales promotion of the Brazilian product, would indeed be expected to have no objection to meeting the credit required for expansion of productive capacity.

Still, neither Portuguese production skill nor the commercial ability and financial power of the Dutch was sufficient to guarantee the success of the agricultural colonization venture in Brazilian lands. Moreover, there was the manpower problem. The transportation of the necessary number of settlers from Europe would have required too large an investment, probably rendering the entire undertaking unprofitable. Working conditions overseas were such that only by paying much higher wages than those prevailing in Europe would there be any possibility of enticing manpower from the Old World. The alternative of reducing costs by providing land grants to pay for the settler's work over a number of years had no attraction for him nor was it practicable, because without large amounts of capital the land was of no real economic value. Finally, the scarcity of manpower in Portugal, owing chiefly to the highly flourishing condition of the East Indies, had to be considered. Here too another circumstance arose that made solution of the problem much easier. At this juncture the Portuguese had already acquired a fairly thorough knowledge of the African slave traffic. Brigandage operations for the capture of Negroes, begun almost a century earlier in the days of Portuguese Prince Dom Henrique the Navigator (1394-1460), had evolved into a well-organized and prosperous trade for supplying slave manpower for some European areas. Once sufficient resources could be mustered, it would always be possible to expand this business and guide the transfer of low-cost manpower to the new agricultural settlement—without which the undertaking would have no economic feasibility.

Each of the aforementioned problems—production skills, market development, financing, and manpower—had found a timely solution, independent of a general preconceived plan. Most importantly, there was a series of favorable circumstances, without which the undertaking could not have been blessed by the enormous success it achieved. Behind the entire enterprise undoubtedly were the desire and struggle of the Portuguese government to keep possession of its lands in the Western Hemisphere, with the ever-present hope that some day gold would be extracted from them. Nevertheless, this desire could only be transformed into a working policy if some concrete support were forthcoming. If defense of the new lands had continued to be a heavy financial burden on the small kingdom, it would surely have been slackened. The success of the great agricultural enterprise of the sixteenth century—which was unique at the time—was therefore the reason for the continuing Portuguese hold over large parts of the Western Hemisphere. In the following century, when there was a change in the balance of power in Europe, with the hegemony of nations excluded from the Treaty of Tordesillas, Portugal had already gone far toward the effective occupation of its share.

The economic decline of Spain created havoc in her Western Hemisphere colonies. Apart from mining operations, no major economic enterprise whatsoever had even been started. Agricultural exports from the immense territory at no time reached any meaningful figure for three entire centuries. The supply of manufactured goods for the great masses of the native populations was at all times based on local handicrafts, postponing any change in the already existing subsistence economies. Without the regression of the Spanish economy, which was greatly aggravated in the seventeenth century, exports of manufactures from the home country to the colonies would necessarily have been made. This in turn would have led to economic ties far more complex than the mere periodic transfer of a production surplus in the form of precious metals.

Consumption of European manufactures by the swarming populations of the Mexican meseta and the Andean altiplano would have created the need for a counterpart in local production exports for Spanish consumption or reëxport. Such interchange would have necessarily introduced some transformations into the archaic structures of the native economies, permitting greater penetration by European capital and know-how.

If Spanish colonization had evolved in such a direction, the difficulties facing the Portuguese undertakings would have been much more difficult to overcome. It is likely that the Spanish could have dominated the entire tropical produce market, especially that of sugar, from the sixteenth century on. Much of the finest sugar-growing land lay in their hands, it was far closer to Europe, and they had cheap native manpower better acquainted with advanced farming practices, as well as enormous financial resources under Spanish control. The main reason this did not happen was most probably the decline of the Spanish economy itself. Inasmuch as there was no political factor in the background—as in Portugal—the development of Spanish lines of export for Western Hemisphere products had to be established by powerful economic groups interested in sales of their own products in colonial markets. As could be expected, leadership in such moves was to be taken by the manufacturers themselves, but for the deterioration of the manufacturing sector during the phase of vast imports of precious metals and concentration of income in the hands of the Spanish state. Therefore, one of the reasons for the success of the Portuguese agricultural colonizing enterprises was the very decline of the Spanish economy, largely because of the early discoveries of precious metals.

Once the initial difficulties had been overcome, the sugar settlements underwent rapid development. By the end of the sixteenth century, sugar production probably exceeded two million arrobas a year (approximately sixty-five million pounds), at least twenty times as much as the production quota established a century before by the Protuguese government for the Atlantic islands. Expansion was particularly rapid during the last quarter of the century, when a tenfold increase occured.

The amount of capital invested in the new settlement was already considerable by that time. Assuming that only 120 sugar mills were in existence at the end of the sixteenth century, with an average value of £15,000 per mill, the total amount of capital invested in the production phase of the industry would be equivalent to £1,800,000. On the other hand, the number of African slaves in the colony at the time is estimated to have been about 20,000. Surmising that three-quarters of the Africans were used in the sugar industry, and ascribing to them an average value of £25 each, investment in manpower may be assumed to have amounted to £375,000. Comparing data on total investments, it may be inferred that capital invested in slave manpower amounted to about 20 percent of the total fixed assets of the business, a substantial part of which was comprised of imported equipment.

As to the amount of income generated by that economy, there seems to be no possibility of making much more than vague conjectures. The total value of the sugar exported in a favorable year probably amounted to about £2.5 million. Considering 60 percent of this amount as the net income produced in the colony by sugar working, and assuming that the sugar sector accounted for three-quarters of the total income, the latter would approach £2 million. Taking into account the fact that the European population was not more than 30,000 persons, the small sugar colony must have been exceptionally rich.[1]

Income produced in the colony was strongly concentrated in the hands of the sugar-mill and plantation owners. Of the value of sugar ready for shipment at port, only an insignificant part (not more than 5 percent) came from services rendered outside the mills, such as transportation and warehousing. Plantations and mills undoubtedly maintained a number of salaried workers: sundry craftsmen and slave overseers. Even assuming that there was one salaried worker for each ten slaves—totaling 1,500 wage earners in the entire sugar industry—and ascribing to each worker an annual monetary salary of £15,[2] the total would be £22,500 or less than 2 percent of the income produced in the sugar sector. Finally, it must be borne in mind that the mills and plantations involved a certain amount of monetary expenditure, mainly for the purchase of draft cattle and firewood (for the furnaces). These purchases were the main link between the sugar economy and other settlement nuclei in the country. It is estimated that the total number of oxen on plantations and mills may have been equivalent to the number of slaves. Further, the value of an ox is surmised to have been one-fifth of that of a slave, whereas the animal had a working life of only three years. Hence the investment in draft oxen would be about £75,000, with replacement costs amounting to £25,000 a year. Even ascribing to expenditures on firewood and other lesser items twice this figure, the payments made by the sugar economy to other population groups did not amount to much more than 3 percent of the total income. Thus everything seems to indicate that at least 90 percent of the income generated by the sugar economy within Brazil was concentrated in the hands of the sugar-mill and plantation owners.

The utilization of such a vast sum of income concentrated in so few hands seems to be a problem difficult to solve. The aforementioned data testify to the fact that income from productive investments—that is, the part in the hands of the sugar-mill and plantation-owner class—amounted to more than one million pounds in a favorable year in the early part of the seventeenth century. The proportion of such income spent on imports of consumption goods —mainly luxury articles—was indeed considerable. Data supplied by the Dutch administration, for instance, indicate that in 1639 about £160,000 was collected in import duties, one-third of which was levied on wines. Assuming an ad valorem duty of about 20 percent, it may be inferred that the total imports amounted to no less than £800,000. In that same year the value of sugar exported by Dutch Brazil was about £1.2 million. Due account must, however, be taken of the fact that consumption spending was increased considerably at the Dutch conquest, either by the need for keeping strong garrisons or by reason of government pomp and pageantry during the administration of Prince Moritz of Nassau (1637-1644). It can hardly be supposed that the Portuguese colonists, confined to their estates and deprived of any kind of urban conviviality, could afford such consumption expenditures. Assuming, at a generous estimate, that their consumption expenditures may have been as high as £600,000, there remained in the hands of the landlords at least that much more unspent in the colony. These figures stress the wide capitalization margin afforded by the sugar economy, and at the same time explain how production could be increased tenfold in the last quarters of the sixteenth century as noted above.

The data in the previous paragraph suggests that the sugar industry was profitable enough to self-finance a doubling of productive capacity every two years,[3] which was apparently the rate of growth during the most thriving phases. The fact that such financial potentiality had been utilized only on exceptional occasions shows that the growth of the sugar industry was determined by the absorption capacity of the buying markets. Since there was no repetition of the trying experience of the Atlantic islands, with their surpluses, this fact seems to indicate that many precautions were taken in the marketing stage, and further that from the latter the basic decisions regarding the entire sugar business issued.

But if the full self-financing capacity of the industry was not being utilized, what was happening to the remaining financial resources? Obviously they were not being utilized within the colony, where economic activities other than sugar did not require large amounts of capital. Nor is there any record of investments elsewhere by sugar-cane planters or sugar-mill owners. The most plausible explanation is perhaps that a substantial part of the capital derived from sugar production eventually found its way into the hands of the merchants. Thus a part of the income ascribed above to the sugar-mill and plantation owners may have been what is now called nonresidents' income, remaining outside the colony. Hence the close connection between the production and marketing phases might easily be explained. Such coördination would prevent the natural tendency toward surpluses.

The political and economic framework that favored the rise and fast growth of the agricultural enterprise, which was the foundation of settlement operations in Brazil, underwent a far-reaching change when Portugal was taken over by Spain. The war waged against Spain by the Dutch from 1580 to 1640 had profound repercussions on Portuguese South America. From the beginning until the middle of the seventeenth century, the Dutch controlled nearly all the maritime trade of Europe. Sugar marketing in Europe without the cooperation of Dutch merchants was clearly impracticable. They, in turn, were by no means prepared to give up their substantial share in the thriving sugar business, whose success had largely been due to their own efforts. Thus the struggle for control of the sugar trade became one of the main reasons for the relentless warfare carried on by the Dutch against Spain. One of the episodes of this war was the Dutch occupation of the Brazilian sugar-producing regions for a quarter of a century (1630-1654). Nevertheless, the consequences of the breakdown in the coöperative system which had previously been in existence were far more enduring than military occupation itself. While they occupied northeastern Brazil the invaders acquainted themselves with every angle, both technical and organizational, of the sugar industry. This know-how was to serve as a basis for installing and developing a large-scale competitive sugar industry in the Caribbean region. From that time onward the monopoly which had by then existed for three-quarters of a century, based on identity of interests between Portuguese producers and Dutch financial groups controlling European trade, was broken. In the third quarter of the seventeenth century, prices of sugar fell to half their former level, and remained at this relatively low figure throughout the next century.

The period of maximum profitability for the Portuguese agricultural colonial enterprise had passed. In the second half of the seventeenth century, the volume of average annual exports attained barely 50 percent of the highest points reached about 1650. And even those dwindling exports were to be sold at prices less than half as high as those prevailing in the previous phase. Real income from sugar production declined to a quarter of what it had been at its best. The depreciation of the Portuguese currency in relation to gold, as recorded at that time, was in nearly the same proportion, clearly revealing the enormous importance of Brazilian sugar in the Portuguese balance of payment. Portugal had been the chief source of supply for Brazil, and such a depreciation might have entailed massive transfer of real income to the benefit of the colony. However, the same manufactures which comprised the bulk of the commodities brought to Brazil by the Portuguese were also produced elsewhere in Europe. Moreover, as commodities of domestic production exported by Portugal to Brazil were commonly the same as those exported to other countries, most probably their prices would have been established in terms of gold. Hence, income transfers resulting from the depreciation of the currency would revert mainly to the benefit of the Portuguese metropolitan exporters.

3   The Banana Industry in Costa Rica

Frederick Palmer

The rapid growth of demand, high level of profits, and depen-
dence on outside capital and labor which we have seen were
characteristic of the early Brazilian sugar economy were also
found in other plantation economies: that of the British West
Indies in the seventeenth century, for instance, or of Cuba
and southern Brazil in the nineteenth. The last of the classic
plantation crops to be "discovered" was the banana, which
though previously known, began to be exported in large quanti-
ties only during the latter part of the nineteenth century.
Here the commercial role played by the Dutch in Brazil was
taken by the large North American fruit companies, which pro-
vided the capital needed to construct rail transport systems and
storage facilities and brought in black labor from Jamaica.

Frederick Palmer (1873-1958) was an American journalist
and war correspondent. This selection is from a book written
after a trip to investigate political and economic conditions in
the countries of Central America which was taken under the
sponsorship of the Chicago Tribune.

Wherever coffee grows the nights are cool and the air bracing. But
the banana seems to thrive best as the consort of miasma and malarial
mosquitoes. When the train from San José to Puerto Limón leaves the
last scattered coffee fields behind, it descends into the heart of the
lowlands and runs among the banana plantations, where the white
man is inclined to hammocks and to supervising an acclimatized

From Frederick Palmer, *Central America and its Problems: An Account of a*
Journey from the Rio Grande to Panama, with Introductory Chapters on
Mexico and her Relations to her Neighbors (New York, Moffat, Yard & Co.,
1910), pp. 215-220.

race. The banana asks for hot rains and muck in which to set its roots. No skilled labor is required. Set out a sprout and let it grow and wait for the bunch, gathered with a sweep of the *machete,* and taken in pairs on strong black shoulders to the car or boat.

"Yes, young man," Mr. Merry, the veteran American minister to Costa Rica, tells his inquirers, "yes, it is quite true that you can make from 25 to 30 percent on your capital if you start a banana plantation. There is no trick behind the company's offer. It can well afford to take your product at a price which assures such a profit. However, young man, I shouldn't be fair if I did not tell you something else. You must consider that if you are not dead at the end of five years, you may be such a physical wreck from malaria that your fortune will do you no good."

The yellowing bunch in front of the country store and the blackening "four for five" in the pushcart of the city form the most potent American trade influence in Central American affairs. The romance of wheat is commonplace beside this far traveler from the swelter of Caribbean coasts, ripening as it goes, which passes through northern blizzards to our tables.

As an industry in its larger sense, this one is more recent than steel and its growth as rapid. Twenty years ago the United States ate five million bunches a year; ten years ago, fifteen million, and in 1969, sixty million. In every Central American country, after the doleful tales of misgovernment and decay on the west coast, you hear of prosperity on the east coast, which the ever-increasing banana export created.

The Caribbean Islands share the bounty. Jamaica, her sugar plantations in ruins, was saved from economic despair by the banana trade. England has trebled her consumption in the last five years. Germany and France are beginning to receive importations in quantity.

The growth in consumption, primarily due to the recognition of the banana as a food, would have been impossible without improved means of transportation. The problem from the first has been to deliver the banana in edible condition at the purchaser's door. Fast steamers, with their holds kept at the right temperature, which is only 48 degrees Fahrenheit, now run direct to Liverpool and Hamburg. Too much heat means that the banana will ripen too fast.

There are warming houses in big railroad centers of our northern states, where, in winter, the chill is taken off the fruit before the journey is continued. When picked it is green and unedible and not filled out. Sucking the strength of the stem, the fingers swell as they ripen. But no one who has never been in the tropics knows what a really good banana is—a banana which is not cut until its skin sets tight on the plump flesh. And the best are not the big ones which are exported, but the pineapple type, scarcely larger than a man's thumb, found in the height of its excellence, to my mind, in the Philippines. The big banana, like the big strawberry, is the product of cultivation and hardening for market purposes.

A banana belt runs all along both coasts of Central America. But the land on the west coast lies fallow, awaiting a market. That of the east coast extends all the way from the Guatemalan border, a strip from 20 to 200 miles in breadth, with some breaks, to Brazil, while most of the islands of the Caribbean may be included in a field which might produce ten times our present consumption.

The history of the wheat lands is, in one sense, the history of the banana lands. Those which were richest and most accessible were the first to be developed. Political conditions, besides, played a part. No one would think of starting a plantation in the black republics of Haiti or Santo Domingo or in overtaxed, revolutionary, corrupt Guatemala and Nicaragua, when equally good and cheap ground could be had under British rule in Jamaica or in the orderly republic of Costa Rica—which was the loss of the backward and the gain of the forward countries. The best quality of bananas is grown in the republic of Panama; the most prolific soil is in Costa Rica.

Of the whole business of import into the United States the United Fruit Company controls from three-fourths to four-fifths. The company escapes prosecution for its trust methods, the courts having held that, as it controls a product grown outside the United States, it falls outside the pale of the law. By adroit and masterful management, by all the economies and methods of competition known to other corporations, this great example has built up its business in the last twenty years.

It combines freight with passenger traffic. Although American shipping is at its lowest ebb, the company is able to build new ships. With no interest in government except to develop business one way and another, it manages, always with dividends in view, pretty well to gain its political ends. By force of necessity, prosperity and order must prevail more or less in every port which it dominates.

The "banana railroad," a narrow gauge which taps the plantations, bringing on to the wharf trains of cars piled high with bunches of fruit, is the land tentacle of the corporation.

The company does not stop with the ownership of railroads, steamers and piers. It owns vast tracts of banana land, developed and undeveloped. Forty percent of the plantations of Costa Rica are in its possession, and in other regions an equally large or even larger percentage.

Beside the steel trust, which faces the exhaustion of ore, and the Standard Oil trust, which must some day be without oil, the banana trust is in the situation of a flour trust owning 40 percent of the Western wheat country. It has control of the soil, that permanent, unfailing source of wealth which, by comparison, in the long run makes the mining business fitful and beggarly.

Between the stools of home consumption and exclusive foreign production, the banana trust has fallen into a comfortable seat. Criticism of its methods in Costa Rica and Jamaica has as yet carried little weight because of the market which the company has created by its facilities for transportation. It has fed impoverished treasuries and brought silk in place of cotton bandannas to Negro heads and lace curtains to the windows of tumbledown huts. For the banana man is the Jamaican black.

The picture of him with a bunch of bananas on his shoulder running up a steamer's gangway is the one most inseparably characteristic of the Caribbean. Malaria and heat and mire do not disturb him. The company has also brought fortune to many planters, native and American, who have managed to escape without an incurable case of malaria. Our knowledge of the mosquito and of sanitation gained on the Isthmus insure a healthier future.

Most of the planters in Costa Rica are Americans. The Costa Ricans themselves are too happy growing coffee in the cool highlands to undergo the punishing climate of the lowlands, where endurance and killing time are really the chief requisites. A little supervision and the rivers and the Jamaicans do the rest. The sediment washed from the hills by the freshets provides annual fertilization.

Every bunch has from seven to twelve hands; the company refuses the sevens. Though they have more than a hundred bananas, they are not worthwhile in the careful calculation of labor, time, and interest charges. It pays 31 cents for all bunches of nine hands or over and 25 cents for eights. At that rate the young man who fights the malaria will make 25 percent on his money, if he knows anything about banana raising and banana soil.

The company gets an average of $1.70 a bunch, averaging 150 to 175 bananas, in the States, which represents the cost of handling and transportation, while we know what the retailer receives. The business pays because of its magnitude, and pays well. Day after day, under the frying sun, year in and year out, the little engines of the "banana railroads," running in and out among the plantations, sing their chuk-chuk in the still, hot air among the motionless leaves, onward to the pier, where the Jamaican yells and sings and giggles as he starts the bunches on their journey to the pushcarts and the country grocery.

4   The Brazilian Sugar Planter

Antonil

The traditional plantation was a large and complex business organization which required considerable administrative ability to run. In eighteenth-century Brazil, as the following selection makes clear, the large sugar planter or senhor de engenho had in him something of the feudal lord, particularly in his relations with his slaves; but to be successful, he also had to have capital, a practical knowledge of business and agriculture, and the ability to manage and coordinate the activity of many individual workers, both slave and free.

Antonil (Giovanni Antonio Andreoni) was an Italian Jesuit who lived in Brazil—mainly in Bahía where he held several high posts in the Jesuit order—from 1681 until his death in 1716. The book from which this excerpt was taken was published in 1711 in Lisbon, but most copies were subsequently seized and destroyed by the government on the grounds that it made too much economic information on Brazil readily available to foreigners.

Of the Capital a Senhor de Engenho Should Have

The status of *senhor de engenho* is one to which many aspire, because it brings with it the service, obedience, and respect of large numbers of people. And when its possessor is—as he should be—a man of capital and a good manager, this status can be valued as highly in Brazil as titles of nobility are among the *fidalgos* of Portugal. There

Translated by the editor from André João Antonil, *Cultura e opulencia do Brasil por suas drogas e minas,* text of the 1711 edition with a French translation and critical commentary by Andrée Mansuy, Travaux et Mémoires de l'Institut des Hautes Études de l'Amerique Latine, XXI (Paris, 1968), pp. 84-94, 120-132.

are plantations *(engenhos)* in Bahía which annually produce four thousand loaves (about 210,000 kilograms or 232 tons) of sugar, including that made from the obligated cane, half or more of which is kept by the mill.[1] Like the fidalgos, the senhores de engenho have dependents in the *lacradores* who rent parcels of land on the large plantations. A senhor who is powerful and has the necessary resources attracts many lavradores, even among those whose cane is not obligated to the mill either by old obligations or by advances of money.

Beside the field hands and house slaves, the senhor de engenho employs blacks in various positions: as household slaves, boatmen, canoemen, caulkers, carpenters, carters, potters, cowboys, shepherds, and fishermen. He must also hire a number of salaried employees: the *mestre de açucar* and his assistants, the *banqueiro* and *contra-banqueiro,* the *purgador,* a *caixeiro* on the plantation and another in the city, a *feitor-mor* for the whole plantation and subordinate *feitores* for the cane sections and *roças,* and finally, for the spiritual side, a priest.[2]

All the slaves, of whom there are more than 150 or 200 on the larger plantations, must be provided with food, clothing, and medical care when they are sick; thus many hills of manioc muct be planted. The ships must have sisal, cables, rope, and tar. The furnaces, which burn day and night for seven or eight months of the year, require huge amounts of wood; two sailboats must be sent out to buy it in the ports, going one after the other without stopping. For the cane fields there must be boats and carts with double teams of oxen, as well as hoes and scythes. The sawmills need hatchets and saws, and the mill, spare pieces of good hardwood and much iron and steel. The carpentry shop needs strong, carefully selected wood to be used for posts, beams, windmill arms, and water wheels, as well as the usual tools, like saws, augers, bits, compasses, rules, chisels, adzes, gouges, hatchets, hammers, planes, and nails. In the boiling house, kettles, caldrons, boilers, basins, and many smaller utensils, all of copper, are required; these cost more than 8,000 *cruzados,* even when they are sold more cheaply than they are at present. In addition to the slave huts, the plantation must also have houses for the chaplain, feitores, mestre de açucar, purgador, banqueiro, and caixeiro, plus a decent chapel with ornaments and all the altar equipment, as well as the house for the senhor himself, with its separate room for the guests who come so frequently in Brazil due to the scarcity of inns. Finally there are the buildings of the sugar plant, spacious and strongly built, along with the rest of the offices, the purging house, the office of the caixeiro, and other things which are too unimportant to be mentioned here but will be spoken of in their place.

Considering all of this, as well as the fact that there are men with sufficient capital and good judgement who would rather be large lavradores, employing 30 or 40 slaves to produce a thousand loaves of sugar on one or two parcels of land, than to be senhores de engenho, with all the work and effort entailed by the management of a large plantation, it is astonishing how many now dare to establish small plantations with their own mills *(engenhocas)* as soon as they have acquired a few slaves and can find someone to loan them a little money. For they thus commit themselves to an undertaking for which they have neither the administrative ability nor the diligence required, and they often become so burdened with debt in the first harvest that with the second or third they declare themselves bankrupt. This causes those who loaned them money or gave them credit to fail also, and leads others to jeer at their ill-founded presumption, which so speedily transformed the first growth of deceptive hope into dry straw.

Engenhos are not always royal engenhos (plantations with water-powered mills), nor do all of them have such heavy expenses as we have described here; nevertheless, it is well understood that costs tend to increase more than one expects due to the death or flight of slaves, the loss of horses and oxen, the droughts which suddenly squeeze and wither the cane, and other disasters which can occur at every stage. It is also recognized that masons, carpenters, and other craftsmen, desiring to make a profit at someone else's expense, will promise everything in such a manner that to build an engenho sounds the same as to build a slave hut. Thus when the materials and tools are assembled, one finds that all has already been spent before stone is put on stone, leaving nothing to cover salaries or the other expenses, which, like flooding rivers, rise to unforseen levels.

If a planter does not have the ability, deportment, and diligence required for the good disposition and management of his affairs, as exhibited in his selection of feitores and craftsmen, in his relations with the lavradores, in the handling of his slaves, in the conservation and cultivation of his lands, and in the trustworthiness and punctuality he shows with merchants and others he deals with in the market place, then he will find confusion and ignominy in the title of senhor de engenho instead of the esteem and respect he was anticipating. Therefore, having spoken of the capital a senhor de engenho should have, I will go on to discuss how he should manage his plantation, first treating the purchase and conservation of land and its rental to lavradores; then the selection of paid employees for his service, pointing out the duties and salaries of each in accordance with the practice in the royal engenhos of Bahía; and finally the domestic government of his family, children, and slaves, his hospitality to guests, and his punctuality in giving satisfaction to his creditors, on which depends the maintenance of his reputation, the best capital of those who consider themselves honorable.

How the Senhor de Engenho Should Conduct Himself in the Purchase, Conservation, and Rental of Land

If the senhor de engenho does not recognize the different qualities of land, he will buy *salões* for *massapes* and *apicús* for *salões.*[3] Therefore he should avail himself of the knowledge of his most experienced lavradores, taking account not only of the price but also of how well the land meets the needs of a fazenda: whether it has soil suitable for cane fields, pastures, and roças as well as water and forests, or in the absence of the latter, whether it is possible to get firewood nearby; and this can help him avoid other mistakes which the old men can point out, since they are the masters to whom time and experience have taught the things youths do not know.

Many planters sell their lands because these are worn out or short of wood; others do so because, like Job, they can no longer bear listening to the news of so many calamities: of burned cane fields, of oxen stuck in the mud, of slaves dead, of sugar lost. Still others, obliged to sell against their will by the demands of creditors, may offer land that is new and fertile, but then the purchaser runs the risk of buying eternal lawsuits because of the obligations and mortgages with which their estates have repeatedly been burdened. In this case the purchaser should speak with his lawyers and find out what the legitimate claims of the creditors are; if necessary he should have them called before a judge to testify under oath what is owed them. In addition, he should not conclude the purchase before seeing with his own eyes what he is buying and what titles the seller possesses, determining whether the land is entailed or free and whether orphanages, monasteries, or churches own any part of it, so that no necessary condition or formality is left out when the bill of sale is drawn up. He should also inspect the boundaries of the land, determining whether these have been officially measured and if the markers are in place or have to be set up again. Finally, he should make inquiries about the character of the neighbors, finding out if they are friends of justice, truth, and peace, or on the contrary, dishonest, restless, and violent, for there is no worse plague than a bad neighbor.

After the purchase, he should not go back on his word but punctually pay what he owes. And with respect to the conservation and improvement of his purchase, he should diligently maintain the boundary markers and defend his right to the water needed for the operation of the mill. And he should show the said markers to his sons and the overseers, so that they will know what belongs to the estate and can avoid lawsuits, which are a perpetual aggravation to the soul and drain rivers of money into the houses of the lawyers, solicitors, and notaries, bringing little profit to those who carry them on, even when, after many expenses and disappointments, they come to a favorable conclusion. Also he should avoid leaving his important papers in the senhora's chest or on a table exposed to dust, air, and insects. Then he will not have to order the saying of many masses to Saint Anthony in order to come up with some document which disappeared when it was necessary to show it. For it can happen that some household servant will take two or three pieces of paper from the senhora's chest in order to wrap something, or the planter's youngest son will take them from the table to draw pictures or make paper boats for flies and crickets to sail in, or perhaps the wind will make them fly out the door like birds without feathers.

In order to have lavradores who are obliged to bring their cane to the mill, it is necessary to rent them the land in which they can plant. This is customarily done for nine years plus an extra one for departure, with the obligation of leaving planted a certain amount of cane; it can also be done for eighteen or more years, with the obligations and amount of cane agreed on in accordance with the custom of the country. One must be certain that those who come to rent this land will farm it productively and not destructively, so that renting it brings profit rather than harm. The necessary conditions should also be inserted in the rental contract: for instance that the renter shall not cut down royal trees or allow others to take their place on the rneted land without the consent of the owner, as well as other conditions judged necessary to keep some trusted lavrador from turning himself into the owner of the land. And for this reason it is a good precaution to have a paper drawn up by an experienced lawyer with a declaration establishing what will be done about the improvements when the lavrador leaves; in this way the end of the rental period will not turn out to be the beginning of perpetual lawsuits.

How the Senhor de Engenho Should Conduct Himself with his Slaves

The slaves are the hands and feet of the senhor de engenho, because in Brazil one cannot make, keep, or enlarge a plantation nor have a functioning sugar mill without them. And the way they perform in his service depends on his manner of conducting himself with them. Every year the planter must purchase some slaves and distribute them among the cane sections, roças, sawmills, and boats. And because these are commonly of different tribes, some being more uncultured and rude than others, and of different degrees of strength, they must be assigned with care and forethought and not blindly. Slaves come to Brazil from the Gold Coast, the Congo, São Tomé, Angola, Cape Verde, and in some cases from Mozambique, whence they are brought by the ships from India. The strongest are those from the Gold Coast, and the weakest are those from Cape Verde and São Tomé. The slaves from Angola, raised in Luanda, are more capable of learning a craft than those from other places. Among the Congo slaves there are also some who are industrious and suitable, not only for work in the cane fields, but also for employment as craftsmen and in the house.

Some slaves arrive in Brazil very rude and unteachable and continue thus throughout their lives. Others prove within a few years to be adaptable and intelligent, both in learning Christian doctrine and in finding ways to adjust to their situation in life; and they can be entrusted with boats, sent on errands, or given any other task which needs doing. The women use the hoe and scythe like the men, but in the forests only the men use the axe. The *caldeireiros, tacheiros,*[4] carpenters, caulkers, boatmen, and sailors are selected from among the more intelligent slaves, because these occupations require more attention. Slaves who have lived on a fazenda since their childhood should not be taken from it against their will, because they easily become upset and die. Those born in Brazil or raised from childhood in a household of whites become fond of their masters and give a good account of themselves; if they have a good situation any one of them is worth four slaves fresh from Africa.

As craftsmen, the mulattoes are even better; but many of them, taking advantage of the favor of their masters, become proud and corrupt, priding themselves on being daredevils ready to challenge anyone who affronts them. Nevertheless, the mulattoes, both male and female, ordinarily have the best of it in Brazil, because with that part of the white blood—perhaps even the blood of their own masters—which flows in their veins, they so bewitch the latter that some will suffer them to do anything and always pardon them. Indeed it seems they dare not reprimand but only spoil them. It is not easy to determine whether it is the masters or the mistresses who are more at fault in this respect, since there are not lacking some of both sexes who allow themselves to be dominated by bad mulattoes, thus confirming the saying that Brazil is hell for blacks, purgatory for whites, and paradise for mulattoes, except when suspicion or jealousy turns love to hatred and changes indulgent masters into cruel tyrants. It is good to make use of the abilities of the mulattoes when they want to use them well, as some do; but there is no need to give them so much that they take everything, and from slaves turn themselves into masters. To allow restless mulatto women to purchase their freedom is a manifest sin, because the money rarely comes from any other mine than their own bodies, being acquired through repeated transgressions; and after they are free they continue to be the ruin of many.

Some masters oppose the marriage of their slaves and not only pay little attention to their living together out of wedlock, but almost encourage and initiate it, saying to a slave: "in due time you will marry such and such," and then letting them live as if they had been received as man and wife. They say they do not let their slaves marry because they are afraid they will tire of the marriage and kill each other with poison or witchcraft, worthy masters of this art not being absent among them. Others separate them, after the slaves have been married, so that for years they remain as if single, something that cannot in good conscience be done. Others care so little for the salvation of their slaves that they hold them for a long time in the canefields or the engenho without baptism. And of those who are baptized, many do not know who the creator is, what they should believe, what laws they should respect, how to commend themselves to God, why Christians go to Church, why they worship the sacred host, what they should say to the priest in confession, whether they have a soul and if it dies and where it goes when it is separated from the body. And though the least civilized slaves know their names, and who their master is, and how many hills of manioc they have to plant in a day, and how much cane they have to cut, and how many loads of wood they have to bring, and other things pertaining to their everyday work; and though they know how to ask their master's pardon when they do wrong, and how to throw themselves on his mercy with promise of amendment so that he will not punish them, still the masters say their lack of education makes them incapable of learning to confess or seek pardon from God, of mastering the rosary or the ten commandments. In this they fail to consider the accounting they will have to give to God, since as Saint Paul says, being Christians and neglecting their slaves, they will be dealt with worse than if they were infidels. And they do not make their slaves go to mass on holidays, but rather keep them so busy that they have no time for it; nor do they consider it as part of the chaplain's job to indoctrinate them, giving him, if necessary, a larger stipend for this work.

With regard to food, clothing, and the limitation of work, it is clear that the master should not deny these things to his slaves, because justice dictates that he should provide those who serve him with sufficient food, with medicines when they are ill, and with the means to dress themselves in a manner consonant with their status, so that they do not appear almost naked in the streets. And if he wants them to survive, he should also limit the work demanded of them so that it does not exceed their capacities. In Brazil there is a saying that the slave needs three p's: *pau, pão,* and *pano* (the stick, bread, and clothing). And granted that this begins badly, starting off with punishment as represented by the stick, it would be pleasing to God if food and clothing were provided as abundantly as punishment, which is given for any offense hardly proved or checked out, and is inflicted with techniques of such extreme brutality that they are not used on animals, even when their offenses are certain, some masters having more concern for one horse than half a dozen slaves, for the horse is cared for by servants and has his forage provided for him, as well as cloth to wipe off his sweat and a golden saddle and bit.

New slaves must be better taken care of, since they have not developed a satisfactory mode of life, like those who have their own roças; the latter, however, should not be called on for labor but then forgotten when they are ill or clothing is distributed. They normally have Sundays and holidays off, and when their master makes them work as on weekdays they become upset and call down a thousand curses on him. Some masters are accustomed to allow their slaves one day a week to plant for themselves, sometimes sending the overseer with them to see that they do not neglect the work, and this serves to keep them from starving or from approaching the big house every day for a ration of manioc meal. But if the master niether gives them the manioc meal nor allows them the time to grow their own food, and in addition makes them work from sunrise to sunset in the fields, and day and night in the engenho with little rest, how can he be admitted before God's tribunal without being punished? For if it is a denial of Christ to refuse alms to one who asks for them in great need, as it says in the Gospels, what then will it be to refuse sustenance and clothing to one's own slaves? And what explanation can be given by those who make gifts of silk and satin clothing to those who are the occasion of their damnation and afterwards deny four or five yards of cotton and a few more of cheap cloth to a slave who becomes soaked in sweat for his service, hardly having time to find a root or a crab to satisfy his hunger? And if, on top of this, frequent and excessive punishment is inflicted on the slaves, they will be so angered that they flee to the forest; or they will commit suicide by cutting their throats or hanging themselves; or they will try to take the lives of those who have caused them so much pain, having recourse if necessary to the diabolic arts; or they will complain so loudly to God that he will hear them and do to the masters what he did to the Egyptians when they burdened the Hebrews with excessive labor, sending terrible plagues against their children and property as one can read in the scriptures; or just as he allowed the Hebrews to be born off in captivity to Babylon in punishment for the harsh treatment given their slaves, he will permit some cruel enemy to carry off these masters so they can experience firsthand the arduous life they give to their slaves.

Failure to punish the excesses committed by slaves is no light offense, but their offenses must be verified beforehand in order to avoid punishing the innocent. One must listen to the accusers, and if convinced by them, have the offenders punished with a moderate whipping or by putting them in chains or in the stocks for a while. To chastise them with one's own hand, impetuously and in anger, and with brutal punishments like burning them with fire or hot wax or branding them in the face, should not be tolerated among barbarians much less among Catholic Christians. What is certain is that if the master conducts himself as a father with his slaves, providing what they need to feed and clothe themselves and allowing them some relief from work, then he will also be accepted as their master; thus will consider it natural, when convinced they have committed an offense, that they should receive a just and merited punishment administered with compassion. And if, after erring through weakness, they come on their own to seek forgiveness from the master, or find sponsors *(padrinhos)* to come with them, it is the custom in Brazil to pardon them. And it is well that they should understand the value of the master's mercy, because otherwise they will flee at once to some hiding place in the forest, and if they are caught, they may hang themselves before the master arrives to whip them, or some relative of theirs may take it on himself to exact vengeance by means of witchcraft or poison.

To deny the slaves their enjoyments, which are the only alleviation of their captivity, is to want them disconsolate and melancholy, with little spirit and in poor health. Thus the masters should not object to their customary festivities, allowing them to sing and dance decently for a few hours some days of the year and to divert themselves innocently during the evening on religious holidays. This should not be at the expense of the slaves, but rather of the master, whose liberality on these occasions will give them some reward for their long hours of work for him; in this way the organizers do not have to spend money out of their own pockets, which would be the cause of many improprieties and offenses to God since few of them could lawfully acquire it. The slaves should not be allowed to get drunk on fermented cane juice or rum *(aguardente),* the sweet cane juice, which does them no harm, being enough for them; with this they can also do their bartering for manioc, beans, and sweet potatoes. If it is seen that the master saves some of the leftovers from his table for the small children of the slaves, the latter will serve him more willingly and happily increase their numbers. In contrast, there are some female slaves [belonging to harsher masters] who intentionally abort themselves so that the children of their wombs will not suffer what they suffer.

5   The Rise of the Cuban Central

Ramiro Guerra y Sánchez

Though possessing some of the finest sugar-growing land in the Caribbean, Cuba did not become a major sugar-exporting country until the end of the eighteenth century, when the loosening of Spanish trade restrictions, combined with the collapse of the Haitian sugar economy, gave Cuban planters their chance to dominate the world market. The sugar plantations of this period, however, were not the huge estates which would become common by the end of the nineteenth century, and the following selection examines the question of how and why these great latifundia dominated by the centrales *or processing factories arose.*

The noted historian Ramiro Guerra y Sánchez, for many years a professor at the University of Havana, was one of the intellectuals who helped form the social and economic views of the makers of the Cuban Revolution.

From 1840 to 1860 sugar production increased rapidly in Cuba, and sugar exports rose from 12,867,698 arrobas for the five years from 1841 through 1845 to 23,139,245 arrobas for the period 1856 through 1859, according to Pezuela. This rapid development was assisted by a fall in the price of coffee which almost completely ruined the coffee plantations. Consequently, almost all of the farms, capital, and labor that had been engaged in coffee cultivation were turned to the production of sugar. In other words, the sugar industry was strengthened by the destruction of one of the economy's four pillars—livestock, sugar cane, tobacco, and coffee. Coffee, although

From Ramiro Guerra y Sánchez, *Sugar and Society in the Caribbean: An Economic History of Cuban Agriculture,* translated by Marjory M. Urquidi (New Haven, Yale University Press, 1964), pp. 62-67.

the last to appear, had come to be one of the strongest and most prosperous.

Meanwhile, advances in processing methods and mechanical improvements forced constant renewal of machinery and other factory installations in the sugar mills. They expanded continually and were already enterprises requiring large amounts of capital. It became necessary to abandon the old practice whereby each farmer, no matter how few caballerías he had planted, would set up his own grinding mill for his cane; by 1850 or 1860 the number of mills had leveled off. Future development would occur no longer through an increase in the number of mills but through an increase in the capacity of each. It was no longer possible to be a sugar planter without being a large landowner or capitalist. Small sugar mills, less effective in cane juice extraction and often producing sugar of lower quality, could not meet the competition and, at first barely surviving, began to fail and disappear. Many were destroyed during the Ten Years' War. For example, in 1862 in the Bayamo area there were twenty-four sugar mills, including one steam-driven; in the Manzanillo area there were six steam-driven mills out of a total of eighteen. In 1877 not a single mill was recorded for these areas, and around Holguín they had been reduced from sixteen to only four. The number of sugar mills fell from 2,000 in 1860 to 1,190 in 1877.

One of the first effects of this twofold process—reduction in the number of sugar mills and increase in the manufacturing capacity of those that continued to operate—was the appearance of a new type of producer, the colono, who planted cane but did not own a mill to grind and convert it into sugar. Instead, he had his cane ground at the nearest sugar mill and, paying the owner with part of his product, disposed of the rest as he wished. The colono symbolized the division of the production of sugar into separate growing and processing phases and the decline of the traditional planter who also processed and sold his sugar. Nevertheless, farmers continued to be independent producers. They had their cane ground at the mills under specified conditions and received a share of the sugar to dispose of on whatever terms they could get. Mills that received cane from independent farmers in these circumstances came to be called *centrales* at the end of the Ten Years' War. The existence of the central and the system of colonos date approximately from that time.

This new arrangement came about spontaneously to meet the needs of both the mill owners and the farmer turned colono. In the

1850s and 1860s mill owners were hampered by the lack of the capital they required to modernize and expand their factory machinery and by the size of their mills, which presented enormous problems of organization and administration. The Count of Pozos Dulces and other economists of that period advanced the principle of division of labor as a means for solving the industry's problems: sugar manufacture and agriculture should be kept distinct and separate. By devoting himself exclusively to processing, the manufacturer would reduce the extent of his enterprise and could employ all his capital in improving, enlarging, and operating the mill. He would free himself from the immense expense and burden of seeing to the purchase of lands and the cultivation of cane and its transportation to the factory. The mill owner never completely gave up growing sugar cane but, adapting his financial and administrative problems to the problems of the farmer who could not afford to maintain a mill, he began to grind his neighbors' cane and charge for this service in sugar. This opened a new era in the history of the sugar industry by creating and extending a new social class, the colono, which has slowly but surely become economically dependent on the central.

The establishment of the central and colono system at first did not lead to the appearance of the latifundium, but delayed it instead. If the expanding central had not been supplied by the colono, its stock of cane would have had to be ensured by land purchases and farm administration, in spite of capital shortages and the scarcity of labor after the abolition of slavery. Mills could be and were enlarged, therefore, without additional farm land. Although mills were becoming huge, there was no overall movement in the direction of the latifundium. Subdivision of properties continued at a slower rate, creating "cane colonies," and at the end of the century there was a total of 60,711 farms in cane, representing 30 percent of Cuba's total area. The general obstacles to rapid development have been enumerated and, still existing, they stood in the way of the latifundium.

After 1868 another powerful obstacle was added: the insecure conditions for capital and business, especially outside the cities, during the long and bloody wars of independence. Production developed very slowly and even suffered serious setbacks, for example in the years 1885-90, when it was much lower than in 1870-75.

But before the close of the nineteenth century and the end of Spanish rule in Cuba, a new factor came into play that is mainly responsible for the latifundium: the competition among the mills for their raw material, sugar cane.

Mills had not competed with each other formerly because each was limited to a circumscribed area by the lack of adequate and economical transportation. No mill invaded the lands of its neighbor mill, and more than a hundred small mills might be contained in one municipal district.

As mills grew into centrales they required a much greater supply of cane. Although the supply area was constantly being expanded, its boundaries were set by the high cost of carting; but in 1836 the introduction of the railroad finally resulted in bitter competition among the centrales and eventually brought about the latifundium. Until 1878 the railroads developed slowly all over the world because, in spite of their enormous advantages, they were an expensive and still imperfect means of transportation. But after 1870, when iron rails began to be replaced by steel and the price of steel rails in the United States decreased from $106 per ton in 1870 to $44 in 1878, railroads developed amazingly and came into wide use.

The centrales of Cuba, consuming more and more cane as they grew in size, began to lay down their own narrow gauge tracks, which enabled them to bring cane to the mill at moderate cost from regions previously outside the central area. At the same time, the network of public railways made it feasible to move cane over long distances. In theory, the central could now expand endlessly but, in practice, for long hauls the zone of each factory was circumscribed by the expense of laying lines or by freight charges.

From the moment a central was able to invade another's traditional supply area, rivalry between the two was inevitable. At first there was an increase in the amount of sugar offered the colono in exchange for grinding his cane and, until a few years ago, it was still possible to identify these competing zones by the higher number of arrobas of sugar that the farmer received from the central for his cane. In Havana, Matanzas, and Santa Clara, where there were many centrales and a public railroad promoting their rivalry, the colono was free to sell his cane to the highest bidder and was given more than seven arrobas of sugar for every hundred of cane. In Camagüey, Oriente, and parts of Pinar del Río, where there were no railroads, only four—or at the most, five and a half—were offered.

Competition created a new problem for the centrales: how to guarantee that each would have enough cane for each zafra at the lowest possible cost. This could be accomplished through one of two means: by economic domination of the colono—reducing his independence and making him a vassal of the mill, bound by contract and prevented from freely selling his product—or by purchasing lands and administering them as cane farms or having them sharecropped or rented by colonos dependent on the mill.

The first means twisted the original colono system by changing a class of free farmers into feudal vassals of the central; the second led directly to the latifundium by destroying small and medium-sized rural properties and replacing the old-style colono with either a kind of unpaid employee whose earnings would derive from his farming of lands owned and financed by the mill and under its strict supervision and accounting or, in the case of "administration" farming, with a day laborer.

This marked the beginning of the contest between colono and central. The last decades of the century passed without any appreciable change in the situation because the capital resources of each continued to be fairly evenly matched. But independence created new conditions for industry and, through the Cuban government's lack of foresight, permitted foreign capital to weigh overwhelmingly on the side of the factory.

6   Masters and Slaves in Southern Brazil

Stanley Stein

Slavery is generally described as a particular kind of labor system, but since patterns of slavery could vary radically from region to region, it is perhaps better to consider it as including a number of quite different systems whose common feature was that they treated labor as a form of property. The following selection describes a relatively harsh and exploitative slave system, that of the coffee-producing area of Vassouras in southern Brazil during the mid-nineteenth century. Here planters seem to have worked their slaves hard, treating them essentially like replaceable cogs in a machine and taking little responsibility for their long-term welfare.

Stanley Stein is a professor at Princeton University and has written several books on the economic and social history of Latin America.

"Greater or lesser perfection. . .of discipline determines the greater or lesser degree of prosperity of agricultural establishments." Constant supervision and thorough control through discipline joined to swift, often brutal punishment were considered an absolute necessity on coffee plantations. Proper functioning of a fazenda varied directly with the steady application of the working force; in an epoch of little machinery, slave labor or what Brazilians termed "organized labor," had to be guided carefully and supervised closely.

It seemed that apparently slow-witted slaves had to be driven to produce. In a day's work conscientious planters had to "look for a fugitive slave, consider punishing a second, decide to send a third to help a neighbor—check the weeding. . .complain about the escolha

From Stanley Stein, *Vassouras, a Brazilian Coffee County, 1850-1900* (Cambridge, Harvard University Press, 1957), excerpts from pp. 132-156.

. . .explain each morning in detail to a flock of slaves the nature of extremely simple tasks they were to accomplish, check each evening to see if they have been barely achieved." In their reasoning, the needs of production dovetailed with concepts of slave character. "Only with constantly exercised vigilance under military-like discipline" would slaves work hard and earnestly, was a widespread opinion. The Negro slave was "by nature the enemy of all regular work," the "passive partner" in the transaction that entrusted him to his owner at the time of purchase. His salary? The purchase price and food and clothing provided by his master.

Those Brazilian planters who failed to find in the nature of their plantation economy sufficient justification for slavery could find support in the writings of foreigners, both resident and transient. In 1839 planters were informed, for example, that the Negro was a "man-child" with the mental development of a white man fifteen or sixteen years of age. To the French émigré, Charles Auguste Taunay, the "physical and intellectual inferiority of the Negro race, classified by every physiologist as the lowest of human races, reduces it naturally as soon as it has contact and relations with other races (especially the White race) to the lowest rung and to society's simplest tasks. One searches in vain for examples of Negroes whose intelligence and works merit admiration." He felt that Negroes' inferiority obliged them to live in a state of perpetual tutelage and that therefore it was "indispensable that they be kept in a state of servitude, or near servitude." Another Frenchman assured Brazilian slaveholders that the Negro was intellectually inferior to the white because the Negro's cranium was smaller and therefore he could not develop his "moral intelligence to a comparable degree." In defense of these writers it must be noted that their line of reasoning was akin to that of many Brazilian slaveholders who taught their sons that Negroes were not humans but different beings "forming a link in the chain of animated beings between ourselves and the various species of brute animals." This conception of Negro inferiority was generally universal, although some planters and town residents did not share it. A description of a Parahyba Valley planter published shortly before the abolition of slavery, underscores the prevalence of prejudices, the effect of routinism, and the absence of scientific knowledge. Though a planter might be capable of displaying compassion and pity for whites, toward his slaves he was "harsh and very cruel" for he refused to see in them the "nature and dignity" of men. The slave was little more than an "animated object, a tool, an instrument, a machine."

On isolated fazendas, amid numerous slaves, planters perceived the precariousness of their situation. Many declared openly "The slave is our uncompromising enemy." And the enemy had to be restrained and kept working on schedule through fear of punishment, by vigilance and discipline, by forcing him to sleep in locked quarters, by prohibiting communication with slaves of nearby fazendas, and by removing all arms from his possession. Where fazendeiros judged that one of their number did not maintain adequate firmness toward his slaves, they applied pressure, direct or indirect. Manoel de Azevedo Ramos discovered this when he brought charges against the overseer of a nearby plantation for beating unmercifully one of his slaves. Neighbors testified that Azevedo Ramos enforced little discipline on his establishment, and the case was dropped since witnesses refused to testify in his behalf. To judge by tasks assigned him, the model planter was an omnipotent, omnipresent, beneficent despot, a father to his "flock" of slaves when they were obedient and resigned, a fierce and vengeful lord when transgressed.[1] And, unlike the urban slaveholder whose punishments were somewhat regulated by law, "on the fazendas of the interior the master's will decided and the drivers carried it out." Lightest of punishments might be the threat "Mend your ways or I'll send you to the Cantagallo slave market"; more serious might be the age-old instruments of corporal punishment.

Most visible symbol of the master's authority over the slave, the whip enjoyed several names: there was the literate term *chicote* for what was usually a five-tailed and metal-tipped lash, colloquially known as the "codfish" or "armadillo tail." Probably because Portuguese drivers went armed with such cat-o'-nine-tails, slaves tagged it with the name of the favorite article of Portuguese diet—codfish. It was felt that sometimes it was used too much, sometimes too little, for often masters had the "very poor habit of failing to whip on the spot, and prefer to threaten the vexatious slave with 'Wait, you'll pay for this all at once' or 'The cup is brimming, wait 'til it pours over and *then* we'll see'—and at that time they grab and beat him unmercifully; why? because he paid for his misdeeds *all at once!!!!*" It was difficult to apply legal restraints to the planters' use of the lash. When one of the founding fathers of Vassouras, Ambrozio de Souza Coutinho, proposed, as one of the municipal regulations of 1829, that "Every master who mistreats his slaves with blows and lashes, with repeated and inhuman punishment proven by verbal testimony. . ." be fined, fellow-planters refused to accept it. Not sheer perversity but the desire to drive slaves to work longer and harder motivated liberal use of the lash. "Many inhuman fazendeiros," wrote Cactano de Fonseca, more than thirty years after Souza Coutinho, "force their slaves with the lash to work beyond physical endurance. These wretched slaves, using up their last drops of energy, end their days in a brief time." And, he added, "with great financial damage to their barbarous masters." Indeed there were masters who believed "their greatest happiness was to be considered skillful administrators, men who force from their slaves the greatest amount of work with the smallest possible expense."

Whipping was not done by the senhor himself who "ordered his overseer to beat the slaves." The whipping over, overseers rubbed on the open wounds a "mixture of pepper, salt and vinegar," probably as a cauterizer but interpreted by slaves as "to make it hurt more." An ingenious labor-saving variation of the whip was reported by ex-slaves. This was a water-driven "codfish" by which a whip secured to a revolving water-wheel lashed slaves tied to a bench. So widespread was use of the lash, that terms such as "fulminating apoplexy" and "cerebral congestion" were employed as medical explanation for death induced by whipping. Typical is an eye-witness account of a beating told by an ex-slave. On orders from the master, two drivers bound and beat a slave while the slave folk stood in line, free folk watching from further back. The slave died that night and his corpse, dumped into a wicker basket, was borne by night to the slave cemetery of the plantation and dropped into a hastily dug grave. "Slaves could not complain to the police, only another fazendeiro could do that," explained the eye-witness.

In a society half free and half slave, many Vassouras planters maintained harmonious relations with the individual members of their labor force. Strong attachments based upon affection and mutual respect often obscured the harsh reality of slavery. A notable difference developed between the affluent planters and the proprietors of small holdings with regard to this relationship. While the large planter had to employ intermediaries to direct the activities of his labor force, the sitiante directed his few field hands personally, resided in unpretentious quarters hardly better than those of his slaves, even "maintained his slaves as part of his family and fed them on the same fare."

It appears, however, that slaves bore perennial animosity toward planters as a group. While slaves in general accommodated themselves to the conditions of their existence, few were ever reconciled to them. Range of reaction was wide—from merely verbal acquiescence to masters' orders to violent, organized insurrection.

To defend themselves against masters trained to "absolute dominion" who were always ready to interpret independent thought as insubordination, slaves responded automatically "Sim-Senhor" to any positive command or opinion and "Não-Senhor" to the negative. "slaves never resist outwardly" and although "apparently obsequious and attentive, refusing to argue over an unreasonable order. . .they use any means at their command to defend themselves," Couty observed. Where a command demanded no immediate execution, "the slave considers it a law permitting him to do nothing." Mistresses knew they could not order a cook to perform other household tasks. Slave washerwomen or nurses "refuse to wash floors, or they will do so sloppily, soiling walls and curtains; their retort is ready: 'that's not my work.' " Or, in more subtle form of reaction similar to a slowdown in effect, they forced the master "to repeat several times each new detail."

Not always as subtle or restrained was the reaction to a regime where "fear and coercion" were believed the only techniques for obtaining work. Portuguese overseers, as symbols of authority constantly in the view of slaves, suffered much violence. "A slave of the widow, Dona Joaquina, shot Manoel, overseer of the house and land of the widow, and it is necessary that he be severely punished to avoid repetition of similar acts which are extremely poor examples especially in places where the slave population considerably exceeds the free," was reported in Vassouras in 1837. On the São Roque plantation a slave who "lost control over his feelings when his overseers refused to stop beating his wife, seized a shotgun and shot him." In the last two decades of slavery, attacks on overseers mounted as rumor spread that imprisoned slaves received food and clothing without work. Such ideas could not be extirpated, and the local newspaper advised its readers that "there is an erroneous belief that under the penalty of perpetual 'pena de galés,' which is almost always imposed for slave crimes, slaves' existence is less harsh than that which they bear under private ownership." When a crime was committed, slaves surrendered voluntarily to the police, confessed the crime "with cynical disdain and tranquilly awaited inevitable condemnation." Thus, Faustino, "slave of Dr Antonio José Fernandes, killed his

overseer with a billhook at 8:30 P.M. and then gave himself up,"
recorded the same local newspaper which concluded: "Rare is the
week when such facts are not registered."

Individual slave reactions to discipline could readily be kept within
manageable proportions. It was the haunting fear of mass reaction,
insurrection, that terrorized masters and their families throughout
the period of slavery. Many could recall the revolting slaves of Manoel
Francisco Xavier who formed an organized group more than 300
strong in 1838 and supplied with "all the tools sufficient to form a
new fazenda. . .withstood the musket fire" of local police and planters until troops from Rio under the command of the then Marquez
de Caxías defeated them on the Fazenda Maravilha. The dramatic
impact of this episode brought the adoption of a stringent slave code
in the same year, regulating the movement and assembly of slaves
and their possession of any arms. These measures failed to inhibit
repeated abortive uprisings during the forties, the decade when the
largest number of Africans arrived at Vassouras plantations. What
one aged resident of Vassouras termed a "zum-zum" or threatened
insurrection was noised abroad by slaves in 1848, then quickly
squelched by masters who circulated warning letters to neighbors.
Mindful of the violent slave revolts in Bahía during the 1830's, Vassouras planters dreaded that among the northern slaves sold southward when African importations ceased, unscrupulous planters
would include those who "least suit their owners because of their
evil disposition and incorrigible comportment." The commission of
Vassouras planters formed in 1854 instructed its members to use
every means to convince planters of the "danger of insurrections and
of the need to take measures which hinder and prevent so terrible a
misfortune as soon as possible." "If the fear of a general insurrection
is perhaps still remote, nevertheless the fear of partial uprisings is
always imminent, particularly today when our plantations are being
supplied with slaves from the North who have always enjoyed an
unfortunate reputation. We have had partial insurrections in various
spots, and unfortunately they will not be the last." In following
years isolated references in municipal archives to group resistance
may be largely attributed to the exaggerated fears of planters, to
malicious statements by quarreling slaves eager to settle accounts
with their fellows, or to incitement by a few slave leaders. Despite
planters' fears, Vassouras slaves are reported to have harbored animosity toward the northerners or *Bahianos,* who felt themselves

culturally superior. To this element of division among slaves may be added the activity of slaves who curried favor with their masters by offering to help catch fugitives or by informing on their companions. Slaves are reported to have ostracized the slave tale-bearers *(chaleiras)*, refusing to speak to them or to aid them in their work. Furthermore, when the chaleira could be enticed from under the overseer's eye, a group of slaves might maul him unmercifully.

The interest and planning that planters lavished upon the marriage of their children were absent where slaves were concerned. Married slaves, according to one early manual, were to live apart, meeting briefly at night in the slave quarters. "As for the passing unions, these must remain completely secret and unknown. . .the proprietor of a plantation does not want priests or nuns, but a race of robust, obedient and docile workers; and he should therefore shut his eyes to anything that does not disturb decorum or discipline. The duties and quarters of both sexes should be separated; there must be difficulty but not the impossibility of their meeting; and as the Spartans punished not theft but its discovery, so must planters punish not the action but the scandal thereof." Thirty years later, ten years after the end of the slave trade, another writer stressed the absence of marriage among slaves as a factor in their low reproductive rate. He appealed to planters' self-interest by pointing out that the offspring of married Negroes enriched the planter. And Couty observed that planters permitted their slaves to be together two or three hours each evening with the result that "most of the slave children have only one parent, the mother."

These conditions helped foster among Brazilian Negroes the passing union or *amazia* that replaced the African tradition of polygyny. The pattern of temporary union was reinforced by economic equality between male and female slaves, by the importance of the mother in African polygynous society, and by the disproportion between male and female slaves in Vassouras until the closing decades of slavery. Fights over women were a constant source of friction among male slaves, and undoubtedly were more frequent until the normal reproductive ratio equated the number of female to male slaves.

7 Masters and Slaves in the Brazilian Northeast

Gilberto Freyre

Relations between masters and slaves in the traditional sugar economy of the Brazilian Northeast were quite different from those which prevailed further south. In the following excerpt from a classic study that has greatly influenced modern views of slavery and race relations in the New World, the slave is portrayed not as the enemy but as the intimate friend and confidante of the whites of the Big House; as playmate, as surrogate mother, as mistress. Such intimacy may to some extent reflect the privileged position of the household slave, but even field hands in the Northeast seem to have been rooted to their plantations and brought within the partriarchal households characteristic of these estates in a way the slaves of Vassouras seldom were.

Gilberto Freyre, himself the descendant of sugar planters in the state of Pernambuco, was trained as a sociologist and social historian and has become one of modern Brazil's leading men of letters.

The pleasing figure of the Negro nurse who, in patriarchal times, brought the child up, who suckled him, rocked his hammock or cradle, taught him his first words of broken Portuguese, his first "Our Father" and "Hail Mary," along with his first mistakes in pronunciation and grammar, and who gave him his first taste of *pirão com carne,* or manihot paste with meat, and *molho de ferrugem,* or "rusty gravy" (a thick gravy made with meat juice) as she mashed his food for him with her own hands—the Negro nurse's countenance

From Gilberto Freyre, *The Masters and the Slaves: A Study in the Development of Brazilian Civilization,* translated by Samuel Putnam (2nd ed.; New York, Alfred A. Knopf, 1956), pp. 349-356.

was followed by those of other Negroes in the life of the Brazilian of yesterday. That of the Negro lad, companion of games. That of the aged Negro, the teller of tales. That of the housegirl or *mucama.* That of the Negro cook. A whole series of varied contacts bringing new relations to the environment, to life, to the world. Experiences that were realized through the slave or under his influence as guide, accomplice, empiric healer, or corrupter.

The young Negro playmate of the white lad was both companion and whipping-boy. His functions were those of an obliging puppet, manipulated at will by the infant son of the family; he was squeezed, mistreated, tormented just as if he had been made of sawdust on the inside—of cloth and sawdust, like those Judases on Easter Saturday, rather than of flesh and blood like white children. "As soon as a child begins to crawl," writes Koster, who was so astute an observer of the life of the colonial Big Houses, "a slave of about his own age, and of the same sex, is given to it as a playfellow, or rather as a plaything. They grow up together, and the slave is made the stock upon which the young owner gives vent to passion. The slave is sent upon all errands, and receives the blame for all unfortunate accidents; in fact, the white child is thus encouraged to be overbearing, owing to the false fondness of its parents." "There was not a house where there was not one or more *muleques,* one or more *curumins,* who were the victims specially devoted to the young master's whims." So writes José Verissimo in recalling the days of slavery. "They were horse, whipping-boy, friends, companions, and slaves." And Júlio Bello reminds us of the favorite sport of the plantation lads of a former day: that of mounting horseback on sheep—and lacking sheep, it was the *muleque* who served. Their games were often brutal ones, and the Negro boys served every purpose; they were cart-oxen, saddle horses, beasts for turning the millstone, and burros for carrying litters and heavy burdens. But especially cart horses. To this day, in those rural regions that have been less invaded by the automobile, and where the plantation cabriolet still rolls along over the fertile topsoil, between the fields of sugarcane, there may be seen small white lads playing horse-and-buggy, "with Negro boys and even little Negro girls, the daughters of their nurses," between the shafts. A bit of packing twine serves as the reins and a shoot of the guava tree as a whip.

It is to be presumed that the psychic repercussion upon adults of such a type of childish relationship should be favorable to the development of sadistic and masochistic tendencies. It was chiefly the child of feminine sex that displayed a sadistic bent, owing to the greater fixity and monotony in the relations of mistress and slave girls. It was even to be wondered at, as Koster wrote at the beginning of the nineteenth century, "that so many excellent women should be found among them," and it was "by no means strange that the disposition of some of them should be injured by this unfortunate direction of their infant years." Without contacts with the world that would modify in them, as in boys, the perverted sense of human relationships; with no other perspective than that of the slave hut as seen from the veranda of the Big House, these ladies still preserved, often, the same evil dominion over their housemaids as they had exercised over the little Negro girls who had been their playmates as children. "They are born, bred, and continue surrounded by slaves without receiving any check, with high notions of superiority, without any thought that what they do is wrong." It is again Koster speaking of the Brazilian senhoras. What was more, they frequently flew into fits of rage, shouting and screaming from time to time. Fletcher and Kidder, who were in Brazil in the middle of the nineteenth century, attributed the strident, disagreeable voices of the women of our country to this habit of always shouting out their orders to slaves. For that matter, they might have observed the same thing in the South of the United States, which underwent social and economic influences so similar to those that acted upon Brazil under the regime of slave labor. Even today, owing to the effect of generations of slave-holding ancestors, the young ladies of the Carolinas, of Mississippi and Alabama, are in the habit of shouting just as the daughters and granddaughters of plantation owners do in northeastern Brazil.

As to the mistresses' being more cruel than the masters in their treatment of the slaves, that is a fact generally to be observed in slave-owning societies, and is one that is confirmed by our chroniclers, by foreign travelers, by folklore, and by tradition. There are not two or three but many instances of the cruelty of the ladies of the Big House toward their helpless blacks. There are tales of *sinhá-moças* who had the eyes of pretty *mucamas* gouged out and then had them served to their husbands for dessert, in a jelly dish, floating in blood that was still fresh. Tales of young baronesses of adult age who out of jealousy or spite had fifteen-year-old mulatto girls sold off to old libertines. There were others who kicked out the teeth of their women slaves with their boots, or who had their breasts cut off, their nails drawn, or their faces and ears burned. A whole series of tortures.

And the motive, almost always, was jealousy of the husband. Sexual rancor. The rivalry of woman with woman.

"Among us," wrote Burlamaqui, in the early years of the last century, "the most common phrases, when a woman is suspicious of her husband or her lover, are: 'I'll have her fried, I'll roast her alive, I'll burn her, or I'll cut out such and such a part,' etc. And how many times are these threats even put into execution, and all because of a mere suspicion!" Anselmo da Fonseca, writing half a century later, stresses the cruelty of the "slave-owning Brazilian women" who "take a delight in exercising an iron-handed tyranny over them (the female slaves), under the most afflicting of conditions; for the victims are obliged to be constantly at their mistress's side and to live at the feet of their executioner." As an example, Fonseca cites the case of D. F. de C., who carried her cruelty toward her women slaves to such an extent that legal proceedings were instituted against her, following the death of one of them, Joana by name.

The Arabic isolation in which Brazilian women lived in former years, and, above all, the mistresses of the sugar plantations, with passive slave girls as practically their only companions, and the Mussulman-like submission of the woman to her husband, who was always timidly addressed as "Senhor," afforded, it may be, powerful stimuli to sadism, the *sinhás* revenging themselves on the *mucamas* and *mulecas* in the form of hysterical outbursts. What they were doing was "passing it along," as is done in certain brutal games; for, in the first place, it was the husbands who were sadists in their relations with their wives.

The padre schoolmaster Lopes Gama wondered quite as much as did the Englishman Koster at the fact that Brazilian women, growing up amid "the crudeness, the shamelessness, the licentiousness, and the disordered conduct of the slaves. . .the floggings, the blows that the latter received almost daily from our forebears," should still be as virtuous and as delicate as they were. "It may even be maintained that the Brazilian women are the most inclined of all to the virtues; since having viewed from their childhood so many examples of lubricity, there has still grown up among them so large a number of respectable, truly honorable ladies. What would they be like if they had had a delicate and careful upbringing? "

It is true that there were cases of sexual irregularity between mistresses and their male slaves. There was one said to have occurred in Pernambuco in the middle of the last century, and in the bosom of an important family. We are assured by an old plantation owner that he himself saw a report of the matter in a private document replete with convincing details. But neither rural traditions, nor the accounts of trustworthy foreigners, nor the criticisms, which are frequently nothing more than libels, of cynical gossips of the stamp of Father Lopes Gama, would authorize us to accept the statement of M. Bomfim, in his *América Latina,* to the effect that "not infrequently the young mistress, who has been brought up to rub against the sturdy slave lads (*mulecotes*), yields herself to them when her nerves give way to her irrepressible desires. Then it is that paternal morality intervenes; the Negro or mulatto is castrated with a dull knife, the wound is sprinkled with salt, and he is then buried alive. As for the lass, with an increased dowry, she is married off to a poor cousin. . . ."

It is not that paternal despotism in the days of slavery appears to me to have been incapable of such wickedness as this and even worse crimes; nor am I denying that the *iaiás,* the young ladies of the Big House, were often endowed with a morbid sensibility and lubricious desires; but the very environment in which they were reared rendered such adventures extremely difficult. That "not infrequently" of M. Bomfim sounds to me artificial, or at least exaggerated. We have but to recall the fact that during the day the white girl of whatever age was always under the eye of an older person or a trusted *mucama,* and this vigilance was redoubled during the night. A small room or bedroom was reserved for her in the center of the house, and she was surrounded on all four sides by her elders. It was more of a prison than the apartment of a free being. A kind of sickroom, where everyone had to keep watch. Do not misunderstand me: I am not praising the system; I am merely reminding my readers that it was incompatible with such adventures as those that M. Bomfim relates.

It may be objected that sex is an all-powerful thing, once it is unleashed; and this is something that I would by no means deny. The obstacle that I am recognizing is, rather, a physical one: that of the thick walls, the true convent bars behind which young ladies of the Big Houses were guarded. It was here that their bridegrooms would come for them in marriage when they reached the age of thirteen to fifteen years. There was, accordingly, no time for great passions to develop in the young bodies of these little girls; and what passion they knew was to be quickly satiated, or simply stifled, in the patriarchal marriage chamber. Stifled beneath the caresses of husbands ten, fifteen, twenty years older than their brides and very often utter strangers to them. Husbands who had been chosen solely to suit the parents' convenience. University bachelors, their mustaches glistening with brilliantine, a ruby on their finger, and a political career ahead of them. Or Portuguese merchants, big and fat, with enormous whiskers and huge stones on their shirt bosoms, their wrists, and their fingers. Officials. Physicians. Plantation owners. Yet these marriages made by parents did not invariably result in domestic dramas or unhappiness. Possibly for the reason that the husbands of a riper age and with cool heads envisaged the problem with more realism and better practical sense than romantically impassioned young men would have been able to show.

True, the parents, in their choice of husbands for their daughters, were not always obeyed. There are traditions that tell of cases—rare ones, to be sure—of brides being abducted and of romantic elopements. Sellin asserts that, from the middle of the nineteenth century on, these cases became more numerous. In them there always figured a Negro or *mucama*—an accomplice of either the abductor or the one abducted—whom it was the custom to set free for his or her services. It was through the complicity of an experienced *mucama* that a pretty young daughter of the C. family in Pernambuco eloped in the early 1860s. The elopement occured on the eve of her marriage to a distinguished gentleman of her parents' choice. The parents promptly offered the deceived bridegroom the hand of their other daughter, which was at once accepted, and as a result the marriage ceremony took place quietly enough, with no further incident to mar it.

It is a well-known fact that the *mucamas* attained an enormous prestige in the sentimental life of the *sinhazinhas*. It was through the trusted Negro or mulatto woman that the young girl was initiated into the mysteries of love. In the middle of the nineteenth century the celebrated novelist Joaquim Manuel de Macedo, author of *The Little Brunette,* observed that "the slave girl known as a *mucama,* although a slave, is at the same time more than the young lady's father-confessor or her physician; for the father-confessor knows only her soul, and the physician, in cases where her health had been seriously affected, knows only her ailing body, and that imperfectly; whereas the *mucama* knows her soul as well as the padre and her body better than the doctor."

On hot days the long hours of gentle lassitude would be filled with stories of love and marriage and other less romantic but equally fascinating tales told by the *mucamas* to the *sinhazinhas,* as the latter sat, Moorish fashion, upon a pipiri mat, sewing or engaged in lacework; or else the young lady would lie stretched out in the hammock, her hair down, as the Negro maid snapped her fingernails through it, searching for lice; or perhaps the girl would keep the flies away from her mistress's face with a fan. This made up for the lack of reading in an aristocracy that was practically illiterate. It was with the *mucamas,* too, that the white girls learned to sing the airs of the day, those colonial *modinhas* that were so imbued with the eroticism of the Big Houses and the slave huts—with the passionate longings of the young masters, or *ioiôs,* for the fragrant mulatto maids or for little white cousins—voluptuous songs, of which Eloy Pontes has given us one example that is highly expressive of the love between whites and blacks:

> *My little white charmer,*
> *Sweet master, my brother,*
> *Your captive adores you,*
> *You and none other.*
> *For you say "little sister"*
> *To a black girl like me,*
> *Who trembles with pleasure,*
> *So happy is she.*
> *At nightfall you go fishing,*
> *Little master, so sweet;*
> *You send piau and corvina*
> *For the little black girl to eat.*

8   Spanish Land Grants and the Hacienda in Mexico

François Chevalier

*It was once thought that the rise of the great estate in the
Indian countries of Spanish America was an immediate and
natural consequence of the conquest. Was it not to be expected,
after all, that conquerors should usurp the lands of the conquered? As the following selection shows, however, the story of
the rise of the hacienda system was a much more complicated one.
At first the Spaniards were interested in treasure and tribute-
paying Indians rather than agriculture and land, which were to
be left to the Indians. Thus the hacienda system—unlike the
encomienda system—was not created all at once; the vast estates
of later years would come into existence only gradually, through
a slow process of accretion. And at least during the sixteenth
century, the land policies of the crown tended to hinder rather
than encourage the growth of these estates, though the ability
of local authorities to prevent Spanish appropriation of land
not cultivated by the Indians was always limited.*

*François Chevalier, one of the most eminent French histor-
ians of Latin America, is a professor at the University of Paris
and director of the Casa Velásquez in Madrid.*

[The desire for Spanish foods and the difficulty of getting the Indians
to grow them] led some soldiers and settlers to overcome their initial
reluctance and to take an interest in the land, acquiring and running
estates and even planting orchards and vineyards. Such activities fell
naturally into the framework of the traditional *municipium,* as old as
the Reconquest in Spain but newly implanted in the Indies: Each

From François Chevalier, *Land and Society in Colonial Mexico: The Great
Hacienda,* edited by Lesley B. Simpson and translated by Alvin Eustis (Berkeley
and Los Angeles, University of California Press, 1963), excerpts from pp. 52-92.

member of a new community receives, in addition to commonage, a plot of land commensurate with his rank.

As if to facilitate this first land distribution in the new towns, which were often located in the midst of native population centers, some fields, as we know, had been legally free since the Conquest. "Your Majesty need have no fear to grant Spaniards reasonable areas of land," writes Ramírez de Fuenleal about 1532, "since in every village there are pieces that were worked for the benefit of the idols or Moctezuma." Around the years 1527-1528, in fact, Mexico City's inhabitants were often given orchards or fields "that used to belong to Moctezuma" or to some native chieftain "killed during the late wars," providing no heirs came forth to make a claim. In 1532, the king requested details of the lands in the city's outskirts which the Oaxaca Indians "had consecrated to, bestowed upon, and set aside for their idols and sacrifices" in order to reply to a petition from the Spanish settlers, who wanted them portioned out. Still, they were not entirely allocated by 1538, although numerous local caciques had appropriated them without leave.

Land allotments were traditionally of two kinds: *peonías* and *caballerías*. The former were for foot soldiers and the latter, five times larger, for those who had fought on horseback. As early as July, 1519, the municipal government of Villa Rica de la Vera Cruz requested the magistrates to authorize land allotments, with full title for the possessors at the end of a two-year period. In 1523, the king recommended to Cortés that he grant the Spaniards in the new towns "their allotments—caballerías or peonías—in accordance with their individual rank"; the grants were to become final after royal confirmation and five years of residence.

However strong the pull of legal tradition, the realities of the American environment soon gained the upper hand. The new arrivals, all hidalgos and caballeros in their own estimation, would have none of the peonías, which they identified with inferior rank. (Significantly, the word peón, or foot soldier, was never applied except to Indians.) The fact that some new cities and towns were exempted from the commoner's tax—the *pecho*—proves nothing, since in fact no Spaniard ever paid it within the confines of the viceroyalty. Consequently, peonías (or peonerías) belonging to Spaniards occurred in Mexico only rarely; in 1528, a few did exist in far-off Villareal de Chiapas (San Cristóbal las Casas). Just the same, the judges of the Council of the Indies continued, for fifty years more, to rule on these nearly nonexistent holdings. In 1573, they went so far as to establish down to the last detail the composition of each peonía—so much land for wheat, maize, and fruit trees, so many cows, pigs, sheep, mares, and goats—in a series of laws often quoted by historians, but having no practical application whatever.

During the first ten years, few caballerías were brought under cultivation. On drawing up ordinances for two new towns in Honduras, in 1525, Cortés, with experience in the Islands as well as a grasp of practical matters, made provision for only scattered cattle raising. Even in 1524, when his intent was precisely to develop harvest land and plantations, he continued to follow the encomienda system: Spaniards to whom natives had been consigned must plant a thousand grapevines for every hundred Indians and grow wheat, vegetables, and other Castilian produce. The royal jurists, it is true, quickly put an end to this kind of land appropriation by the encomenderos.

It was at Puebla de los Angeles that holdings were first given out in any numbers. At the time, the crown had reverted to the ideas of Bartolomé de las Casas: The Indies were to be settled by farmers who would be given, not encomiendas, but "a moderate amount of land" that they would work themselves. In the spirit of these early agricultural laws, the Second Audiencia decided to establish a town composed of Spaniards in an uncultivated region near the road to Vera Cruz. (About the same time, an Audiencia judge, Vasco de Quiroga, founded the curious settlement of Santa Fe, part hospital, part village, for free Indian farmers; harvests were held in common, as in Sir Thomas More's *Utopia.*) In 1531-1532, each inhabitant of the new town of Puebla received one or two caballerías, "so that they may be their property and inheritance forever, to clear and to plant them, in conformity with existing and future ordinances passed by the government of this city." The caballería's dimensions not having been fixed for the entire country, each of these allotments measured only "ten fanegadas of grain," that is, six or seven hectares. For once, the holdings were really seeded and planted, notably at Atlixco, a warmer valley slightly to the south. The founding of Puebla had been far from easy: The magistrate Salmerón, bearer of a special commission for the town, had found it impossible to avoid supplying the settlers with Indian laborers, but he was able to limit their number and to set up a new distribution system closely supervised by royal officials.

Barring a few exceptions in Mexico City and elsewhere, the score or so of Spaniards at Puebla were the first farmers in the country.

Their farms were for the most part on a modest scale, and although they did not work in the fields themselves, they did live on their land and supervise its working. Since the very large estate did not do as well in Puebla as elsewhere, the small farmers, as their numbers grew, set the pattern for the settlement of the entire region.

As soon as the judges of the Second Audiencia arrived in Mexico City to defend the crown's interests, they were given, by cédulas dated 1530, 1531, 1533, and 1535, a major role in the distribution of land. The prerogative of making land grants was increasing in importance, and in 1535, as a result of a particular instance, it came to be vested in the viceroy: He was to grant caballerías to those conquistadors and former colonizers who had settled in the country, with the stipulation that they might not make them over to any "church, monastery, or ecclesiastic."

After 1523, by edict, all land grants were theoretically subject to royal approval. In fact, however, the deeds issued by the viceroys were never confirmed by the sovereign except when a grant was made by direct order from Spain. The crown thus held a heavy juridical weapon in reserve against New Spain's landed proprietors, who a century later, had to pay out large sums to legalize their irregular titles.

When Viceroy Mendoza began to grant caballerías, he tried to standardize their measurements, which until then had varied from one town to another. In early 1537 he established the dimensions as 552 x 1,104 varas, or a little less than 43 hectares. (Eighty years later in remote Tabasco, the official dimensions were still unknown and had to be pointed out to the local authorities.)

In accordance with the Castilian custom, stubble fields were by royal decree open to common grazing, "once the harvest is gathered in." From 1565 on, all deeds issued by the viceroys bore this clause. It seems to have been observed in the sixteenth century, inasmuch as landowners were obliged to remove their fences after harvest time. In view of the immense areas readily available for grazing, the regulation had little meaning until considerable land had been brought under cultivation. Whereas in Spain the custom tended to favor the poor and the landless by guaranteeing them grazing rights, in New Spain it opened the natives' fields to the Spaniards' cattle.

In short, the first viceroy distributed gifts of land, called *mercedes*, made up of caballerías (never *peonías*), in His Majesty's name. The legal procedure was never to change. The interested party would make a request specifying what land he wished to cultivate or was already cultivating. If sufficiently powerful, he would back up his request with a royal ćedula ordering the grant's execution. The viceroy would issue a writ, or *mandamiento acordado,* whereby the alcalde mayor or corregidor of the region was empowered to investigate the possibility of making the grant without harm to third parties, particularly Indians. If the final decision was favorable, the petitioner would receive a deed in due form, the merced, which was entered in a register. The alcalde mayor would then give possession of the land, following an ancient ceremony held to be essential. The new owner would be led by the hand around his property, pulling up grass, cutting twigs, or throwing stones as he went. Carrying out these ritual gestures ensured an almost definitive title to the land.

Although the first register of mercedes to be preserved begins in 1542, we find vicercgal deeds to caballerías as early as 1537. Ordinarily, the allotment was given with the proviso that, by the end of the first year, one-quarter or one-fifth of it would be planted in fruit trees or grapevines. Furthermore, it was not to be sold or exchanged for six years; at that time, the grantee entered into permanent possession. The medieval clause prohibiting sale or other disposal for the benefit of "church, monastery, hospital, or other ecclesiastical institution or person," as specified in the royal orders, appears from 1542 onward.

Soon requests were being made for caballerías outside the narrow districts surrounding the Spanish towns, in which all land had been given out at the same time. Encomenderos requested fields near Indian villages where they had their dwelling and some sort of business. There were also miners who needed to grow maize to feed slaves and Indian laborers in regions where that staple was not easily come by. Over a period of years beginning in 1538, for example, the Pérez de Bocanegra family was granted a number of holdings around their encomiendas at Apaseo and Acámbaro, on the northern border of Michoacán, and in 1544, a mine owner, Martín de Pisueta of Sultepec, was given two caballerías alongside his smelter, in the area where he had "cut down a section of forest" and "cleared land in order to sow maize and wheat...to feed his slaves and dependents."

Grants were handed out in many cases for reasons other than economic. A keen concern for the country's development did not prevent some viceroys from following the custom that made the merced a reward for services rendered, especially when those services were military. The conquistadors, who were to be favored in every way possible, had a right to two caballerías each, regardless of their occupation. Even though this sort of reward could not compare with the deed to an encomienda or with an official appointment, like that of corregidor, a few powerful personages and the members of the viceregal household were in an excellent position not only to obtain such rewards but also to develop the land that they thus acquired. (We shall see how they frequently got hold of grants originally distributed to conquistadors' widows, dowerless girls, or impoverished men; also, how well-to-do Spaniards bought up large quantities of land from the Indians.) Except for several sugar refineries, the grants made by the early viceroys were always on a modest scale, as prescribed by royal decrees. By the turn of the century, however, they had become often very large. The spirit of the decrees was further violated in some cases by the simultaneous issuance of land grants and of authorizations for the sale of the granted properties.

Although each caballería contained 43 hectares, the Spaniards very early acquired more than one. By repeated grants, by purchases from other grantees and caciques, or, even more simply, by taking over unoccupied lands, some of them managed to accumulate estates of three, eight, fifteen or more caballerías. At Tepeaca, for example, a six-caballería farm was in 1600 classified as "average." Wheat and sheep raising were often combined in order to utilize the stubble. In that event, the estancia was called *de labor y ganados* (fields and livestock) and had added to its caballerías one or more *sitios,* or grazing areas, of 780 hectares each. When agriculture became more intensive, some *sitios* were partly plowed—with or without the authorities' permission. These were the largest farms, for a single *sitio* contained the same land area as eighteen caballerías. Most of the farms destined to grow into great wheat haciendas were officially recorded as being for grazing rather than crop raising. Out of ten estates around Tepotzotlán which were made up exclusively of harvest land, seven possessed in 1569 title deeds as sheep estancias only. Conversely, through negligence or lack of labor, caballerías were sometimes given over to sheep in defiance of existing regulations.

On the estancias, we know that only a small portion of land was cultivated each year. From 50 to 100 fanegas of grain were sown—sometimes, but rarely, as much as 300 or 400—and a crop harvested of twelve or fifteen times that amount. Irrigation, apparently already known to the Aztecs, was developed on a local scale; canals were dug in the vicinity of Mexico City and Atlixco and in parts of the Bajío.

Excellent crops were also obtained on virgin land and well-watered sections, but the farming done on the plateau was as a rule far less intensive.

Some of the estancias were not even inhabited the year round. A few Indians or Negro slaves lived on the others, and sometimes (but not always) a family of Spaniards. In 1569, there were only sixty permanent residents on eight estates located near Huehuetoca. The same proportion held for the entire zone north of the capital. The farmers of Tepotzotlán, for example, "come and go. . ., because their place of residence is Mexico City; some live on their estates a couple of years or whatever length of time they feel like spending there." If we may believe contemporary statistics, only 200 Spanish farmers dwelt on the 150 estancias of the archbishopric of Mexico City, in comparison wirh 8,000 in the capital itself. Many of the country dwellers were actually stewards, tenant farmers, or sharecroppers, since only the poorest owners lived on their land the year around; one, for example, "is in debt and therefore stays in the country," while another states that he is "confined" to his estancia, "not having the wherewithal to own a house in Mexico City."

This situation was peculiar to the region around the capital, the only big town in the country and a center of attraction. Elsewhere, the proportion of farmers living on their estates was always much higher. Six hundred out of 1,200 white and mestizo proprietors in Michoacán were residents; in the Puebla area, "more than 200 Spaniards" were scattered throughout the Atlixco Valley. The fact that they moved into the Villa de Carrión (now Atlixco) when it was founded in 1579 showed that, even in districts which were perfectly safe, community living was invariably preferred.

Except for a few very large estates and sugar refineries, construction outlays consequently went for town houses, at least until well into the seventeenth century. That is why almost no trace remains of estancia buildings. Usually made of adobe, sometimes of stone, they were almost without exception roofed with straw or shingles. The following contract of 1575 between the Marqués del Valle and a Spaniard from Oaxtepec will give an idea of their value and appearance: For a three-year period, the second party was given the use of two unplowed caballerías, which twenty years before had been bought from the Indians for the considerable sum of 600 pesos. In exchange, he was to "make them into an estate," put the land under cultivation, and build at his expense "a house having an outside gallery and a room 60 by 18 feet; also, a granary with wooden uprights and walls to support it, and a thatch or shingle roof; finally, alongside the threshing floor, a shed 60 by 20 feet and a cattle stockade." This outside gallery, or *portal,* is still typical of many houses in rural Mexico.

Ancient Castilian custom held grass to be a gift of nature; consequently, pastures and untilled fields (*baldíos*) were free and open to all, in the same way as stubble was after the harvest. Called *realengos,* they belonged directly to the crown. When Ferdinand and Isabella conquered the kingdom of Granada, they distributed much land to their soldiers and retainers; but the beneficiaries were forbidden to establish enclosures (*dehesar*) or "block off (*defender*) grass and other products that the soil bears without cultivation."

In the Spanish Peninsula, however, powerful landowners had been much inclined to fence their grazing lands and keep them for their own flocks. In 1531, the citizens of Antequera de Oaxaca petitioned his majesty not to allow this sad state of affairs to obtain in Mexico; in Spain, they said, there were too many barriers, too many pastures reserved for the mighty—nobles and other rich men—with the result that the poor often had to buy grass for their cattle from them. These settlers in the New World wanted all grazing land to be held in common. They were obviously afraid that Cortés, having become Marqués del Valle de Oaxaca, might succeed in gaining exclusive rights like the lords of Old Spain.

As an order of 1497 shows, the crown early opposed any division of grazing land in the Indies. As soon as the king had personal representatives in Mexico City, he determined to settle the question on the basis of all pertinent data. In 1530, the jurists of the Second Audiencia were asked whether it would be advisable to declare all grazing land in New Spain to be commonage, and, barring that, at least the grazing land within a radius of fifteen leagues from each town; "that is the custom and observance in all the cities, towns, and villages of our realms (in Spain)." The replies received were unequivocal. Licenciado Salmerón wrote the next year concerning Puebla and its environs that there as elsewhere pastures, woods, and watercourses should belong to all, "except the properties (*heredades*), commons (*ejidos*), and enclosures which would be allotted to each of said villages." The presiding judge, Fuenleal, was even more categorical: neither individuals nor communities should be granted reserves or zones around towns; everyone should be able to drive flocks wherever desired, since even though enclosures might be beneficial to some, they would be established at the Indians' expense.

Referring as usual to specific cases, a series of royal orders accordingly declared all grazing land in Mexico to be common property. In 1532, His Majesty issued the following instructions: "In the entire district of said city of Antequera and the Oaxaca Valley, on both the King's perserves (unutilized) and private estates, grazing land shall belong to all the inhabitants. . .after the harvest; all may and shall drive their livestock throughout." There was, however, one restriction: "Enclosed pastures, town commons and districts, sheep lanes, and private properties are to be protected by fences." At the same time, and in line with the Audiencia's request, the Marqués del Valle was forbidden the exclusive use of pastures and woods on his estate. In 1538, the right to commonage in the Oaxaca district was reaffirmed for all unenclosed land; this was followed by similar orders in 1538 for the Puebla region and in 1539 for a fifteen-league zone around Mexico City.

As a last step, the viceroy interpreted as open all pasture land and untilled fields in New Spain. The same held for Santo Domingo and Puerto Rico, where by royal decree shepherds were free to install their cabins and folds wherever they pleased (San Juan, 1541 and 1543). On the books at least, the regulation remained in force in Española until 1550, when it was restricted to a ten-league belt surrounding the towns; cattlemen were authorized to stake out enclosures beyond the belt. As a result of this liberal policy, hardly any of the numerous royal cédulas granting land to individuals, prior to the middle of the sixteenth century, concern pasturage. When the conquistadors requested such land, they were given a dilatory answer. On the other hand, the caballería grants contained a clause reserving the right of way for grazing.

It would seem, in summary, that the crown, after hesitating initially, wished to avoid the splitting up of pasture to the benefit of individuals and wished to endow New Spain with a general system of common grazing, similar to the one that must have existed in the Spanish Pennisula before its destruction by the erection of numerous barriers.

Commonage, like many medieval ideas, was not always clearly defined, particularly in the sixteenth century, which was a period of transition. The institution reached full development in the ejido, or municipal pasture for work and draft animals, as well as in all regions where cattlemen could build pens and cabins without special permission, in conformity with a few laws and the views expressed by certain jurists. Except for the ejidos, necessarily limited in area, community ownership of grazing land was anachronistic by the sixteenth century. Local authorities, virtually escaping the crown's control, and finally even the viceroys, were brought to recognize a much more flexible notion of common pasture; this notion would eventually place the soil in the hands of individual cattlemen.

It was the municipal authorities who, lacking royal approval, took the responsibility of sanctioning the early cattle barons' more or less permanent squatting.

Communities did acknowledge certain of their citizens' rights to fixed sites (sitios, asientos), where they could put their sheep and swine out to graze. A new word, *estancia,* was coined in the West Indies and used extensively to designate the point where wanderers and their flocks finally came to rest. Although in the beginning its sense was sometimes vague, it soon came to mean, when used without a modifier, a site for livestock, as Mexico City records show between 1527 and 1530. The word's appearance there coincides with the fixing of several droves, or *hatos,* which until then had grazed freely. Significantly too, the word hato soon disappeared in the central portion of New Spain; but it survived alongside *estancia* in other parts of the New World, such as Panama, where to a certain extent livestock raising and even agriculture remained nomadic in nature.

Stockmen were desirous of having their rights to specific grazing lands—and even their exclusive rights—recognized by town councils; the task was not difficult, since the councils were frequently no more than their mouthpieces. The most important council, Mexico City's, began to grant sites and estancias not only around the capital but sometimes far away, in Michoacán or on the Pacific coast. Instead of preceding the stockmen's moving in, such grants would often come after it; or the grants would confirm purchases (or sham purchases) from the Indians. It could be said that the interested parties were attempting to cloak in legal procedures situations that had no foundation in law.

Municipal authorities were aware it was not their right to give title to pasture land. In 1527, the Mexico City council granted a license for some estancias near Zacatula, but the council made clear to the grantee that it was not vesting in him "either property or seigniorial rights." The same year, a man requested "a site (at Chapultepec) on which he was at present pasturing his sheep." The council acceded to his request "in the manner and form consonant with its powers, as it has done for other inhabitants pending delimitation of its prerogatives." In the years following, the council continued to distribute grazing land, but in each instance with some restrictive clause: "of its own free will," "without title being vested," "no buildings allowed" (the opposite was stated in its title deeds for harvest land), "only the usufruct to be enjoyed." All such grants were revocable, notably if the recipient should absent himself; this latter characteristic assimilates them to the *vecindad,* or rights and duties of the burgher.

In the light of the above restrictions, what real advantages and specific rights could the holders expect to derive from these early estancias granted by the town councils? The answer must lie in certain lost ordinances to which a Mexico City grazing license, dated 1530, refers. Since they are not extant, we are obliged to fill in the gap with information from the West Indies, where several decades earlier similar problems had had to be met, and especially from regulations that Cortés laid down for two Honduras towns in an environment similar to Mexico's at the time.

According to these curious ordinances, citizens wishing to raise livestock were to request authorization from the town government, which would grant them a definite site. The grantee could then prohibit any other stockman from establishing the center of a new estancia less than a league away, for cattle or sheep, or less than half a league, for swine. A crop farmer, however, could be authorized to cultivate fields inside one of these overlapping circles, providing he fenced his fields. But stockmen could not settle closer than half a league from land, Spanish or native, already under cultivation. It was naturally quite impossible to prevent flocks and herds from leaving their own areas and mingling; consequently, each stockman had to brand his livestock and register his brand with the town clerk. The custom already existed in pastoral Spain, but it assumed new importance on the American continent, especially at Mexico City, where it is found as early as 1528.

The only right to the land that such regulations gave was a purely negative one: the right to prevent others from establishing on it cabins and pens for tending livestock. The spaces thus set aside (but not enclosed) were vast, measuring about 75 and 20 square kilometers. Although the grass remained common property, probably because the droves could not be separated or fenced in, here, in embryonic form, is the first example of the cattlemen's gradual seizure of the soil. Inasmuch as grazing experiments in the Islands antedated those on the mainland and there were no Spanish precedents, Hernán Cortés, who had raised cattle in Cuba, almost certainly imitated island customs in his regulations. Rather than legislation created *ab ovo,* these 1525 ordinances appear to reflect a previous set of conditions and a spontaneous response to actual needs. The crown took a long time to recognize the fact.

Circular grants are the rule in the West Indies; they have left few traces in Mexico. In Cuba, the first grant known to us was made by the municipal authorities of Espíritu Santo in 1536; grants went on until the eighteenth century. In Santo Domingo, the king in 1550 allowed, ten leagues outside of each town, the allocation of a circle a league in radius to each drove (hato), under conditions identical with those laid down by Cortés 25 years earlier: common grazing, erection of buildings prohibited for stockmen other than the interested party (but not prohibited for crop farmers).

In New Spain, a land dispute in 1602 revealed that the crown had formerly possessed near Tlaxcala a cattle estancia circular in form, for "by order of Viceroy Antonio de Mendoza no one else was permitted to establish an estancia within a league's distance round about." The pasture was later sold to private individuals; but for a long time it kept its unusual shape. As late as the seventeenth century, we find a map, drawn up by an alcalde mayor, on which appears a group of three adjacent circular estancias; third parties had laid claim to the intervening space (*blanco*). We may conclude that these first estancias had, as in Honduras and the Islands, a monopoly on the fixed accessories of livestock raising in the sector corresponding to municipal grants; that is to say, unless a stockman could obtain his own estancia from a town council, he could erect no buildings. The observation will be true for New Spain until the end of the sixteenth century, and it would be hard to explain otherwise what advantages would accrue from possessing one of those grazing sites.

The estancias distributed by municipalities were neither identical in size to those that Cortés had defined in 1525, nor were all circular. Diversity in the harvest caballerías before 1537 would make us suspect that even if we did not have more direct proof. Prior to 1539, a New Galicia governor granted a square estancia measuring 5,000 paces on each side; in 1543, the viceroy issued a reminder that sites for cattle should not exceed 3,000 paces (square) nor those for sheep 2,000 (square), "in conformity with the ordinance passed by the municipal authorities here in Mexico City."

The Mexico City authorities were the first to regulate the heretofore spontaneous growth of the estancias, just as they had drawn up in 1537 the statutes of the first *mesta* in New Spain, which was simply the official body of the cattle barons, themselves members of the town council. Surprisingly enough, there is no mention of estancias either in this 1537 charter composed of twenty-seven articles or in the royal ordinance of the same year fixing the dimensions of the harvest caballería. The reason is that the documents were important legislative measures; the mesta statutes had to be approved in Spain. (They were confirmed by the viceroy in 1539 and by the king in 1542.) And since the crown still considered the woods and pastures of its overseas possessions to be common and indivisible, the estancias were on the borderline of legality, if not in overt contradiction with it.

A few years later, the ways in which the cattle barons, outdistancing legislation, had already begun to seize hand became apparent. The first viceroy's attitude is significant. Realizing that it was impossible to backtrack, and wishing to keep the situation under control at least, he set to apportioning estancias in His Majesty's name— without a trace of royal authorization. Many such grants were made to stockmen already in possession of their land. In 1542, 1543, and 1544, the first grants of which we are aware are frequently for sites on which the recipients' herds had been grazing "for a long time"—8 12, 15, 16 years, and longer. Such precise quoting of figures would seem to indicate a desire to claim some sort of squatter's rights. At times, the viceroy's title deeds confirmed grants originally made by the municipalities; much more often, however, the deeds were for pasture seized without anyone's leave.

9 A Land-Grabbing Hacendado in the Peruvian Sierra

Ciro Alegría

One of the most characteristic traits of the traditional manorial hacienda was its tendency to monopolize land, even when it could not exploit it very productively. In most regions the haciendas acquired the bulk of their holdings by grant or purchase during the years when population density—and consequently the demand for land—were at their lowest levels. Subsequent population growth then made it possible for them to use their control of land to limit competition and hold down labor costs. But in spite of the large amounts of land they controlled, haciendas often remained greedy for more. Given the unequal distribution of power within Latin American societies, there was always a temptation for large landowners to strengthen their land monopoly, either in outright violation of the law (commonly legalized during the colonial period through the payment of a fee) or by manipulating the law to their own advantage. The following selection from a Peruvian novel of the 1930s suggests how easy this was to do.

Ciro Alegría was born in 1909 on an hacienda in the sierra province of Huamachuco in northern Peru and was educated in Trujillo, where he became an early member of the Aprista party. Exiled to Chile during the 1930s for his political activities, he started writing and became one of Peru's best-known novelists.

Don Alvaro Amenábar y Roldán, lord of Umay, master of lives and lands for twenty leagues around, raged when he heard the news of Bismarck Ruiz's answer, and the high-flown language in which

From Ciro Alegría, *Broad and Alien is the World,* translated by Harriet de Onís (New York, Farrar & Rinehart, 1941), pp. 161-168.©1969 by Holt, Rinehart and Winston. Reprinted by permission.

it was couched. With the letter in his hand he walked out of his office to the broad arch-trimmed porch of the house, shouting to the servants; but almost at once he recovered his composure, assuming the stern air of the important man whom nothing upsets or frightens. But his shouts had been heard, and the servants stood about trembling.

"Saddle Montonero for me and tell Braulio and Tomás they are to come with me. They'd better pick strong horses. Right away."

Montonero was a little skittish, but very strong. Braulio and Tomás, two herders of the many who also acted as bodyguards, lived with their families in the other houses that formed the big white and red rectangle of the Umay ranch house. At the foot of the old eucalyptus in the court, with its broad-seamed trunk and its blue-green and reddish leaves, the servants saddled the horse, and Don Alvaro left with a brief good-bye to his wife and children. At the entrance to the ranch where a gate of stout bars creaked heavily Braulio and Tomás were waiting. The two men were dark and strong; they were mounted and carried rifles. They set out at a gallop along a straight road bordered with pleasant poplars, under the warm, friendly sun. On the slopes of the hills that encircled the plain, smoke was rising from the cabins of some of the tenant farmers beside their scanty fields. And the farmers, seeing the three men galloping along in the distance, said:

"There goes Don Alvaro with two bodyguards."

"What mischief are they up to? "

The rancher had his eyes fixed on the road and his thoughts fixed on the dispute over the boundary. They left the poplar grove and took the winding trail that led to the uplands. His eyes devoured the the trail and his thoughts darkened his white face to a sullen red.

Don Alvaro was the son of Don Gonzalo, a determined person, who got hold of Umay nobody knows exactly how through a lawsuit with a convent. After a thorough consideration of the heiresses to the neighboring ranches, he fell madly in love with Paquita Roldán, an only daughter, and he married her. And the property of both of them increased. Don Gonzalo was hard-working, unscrupulous, and clever. He knew when to spend money freely and when to grasp his rifle firmly.

Umay grew, toward the south, engulfing ranches, villages, and communities. It grew until it reached the boundaries of Morasbamba, the ranch of the Córdovas. Don Gonzalo started a suit over boundaries and attempted to snatch a piece. But it did not work. The

Córdovas were strong, too. When Don Gonzalo rode up with his men, the judge, the subprefect, and a group of mounted police to take possession, they were received with a volley of shots.

The struggle lasted, off and on, for two years. The subprefect, powerless to intervene or even admonish the ranchers, asked the prefect of the department for orders and reinforcements. The prefect was afraid to undertake to bring two such powerful men to heel on his own authority, and asked Lima for instructions. And Lima, where both the litigants had great influence among the ministers, senators, and congressmen, answered never a word. So in the hills between Umay and Morasbamba the fighting and killing went on. The Córdovas imported a first-class shot from Spain, a native of the Pyrenees, and they built a stone fort with loopholes where they stationed men under his command.

Don Gonzalo, who was stubborn but, nevertheless, level-headed, yielded for the time being. The struggle was preventing him from attending to his other duties, and he decided to wait for a more propitious moment to take over possession "of the property which is mine by law." He would make himself more powerful and Lima would have to back him up. So he began to spread out toward the north. But death carried him off, and Don Alvaro inherited, to the last jot and tittle, his ambition, his plans for power, and his rivalry with the Córdovas. Don Alvaro soon showed that he was a man of prey, and the advance continued. Until finally his land extended as far as Rumi, which lay in his path, a defenseless, unsuspecting quarry. Busy with his other conquests, he had paid no attention to it for many years. Now it would seem that its turn had come. Don Alvaro brought suit over the boundaries. . . .

The rancher dismounted before the house of the pettifogging Iñiguez, alias Spider, a perfect example of the small-time lawyer of the provincial capitals. He had been through the third year of law school at the University of Trujillo, and this gave him from the start a prestige which he took good care to back up with an abundance of legal hocus-pocus. In contrast to Bismarck Ruiz, his closest rival, he was small and skinny. He suffered from numerous ailments, and was unable to share in the town's opportunities for enjoyment. He ate gruel, drank medicinal waters, and his wife pined. Iñiguez spent his time in his office surrounded by sheafs of stamped paper, on which he and his two aides scribbled assiduously in the thick fog of the strong tobacco he smoked. His skin was yellow and his drooping mustache and gnarled fingers were still more yellow from tobacco stain. In spite of all this, his head was a formidable arsenal of defense within its fortress of stamped paper.

Stamped paper comes in long wide sheets, sometimes bordered from corner to corner with a red line, and bears in the upper left-hand corner the seal of the Peruvian Republic. A beautiful shield of symbolic nobility, never more vilified than here.

There are sheafs, piles, mountains of this stamped paper all over Peru, in the form of affidavits, proceedings and briefs. In the offices of lawyers and would-be lawyers, in the notaries' offices, in the courts, in the government offices, at the military courts, in the tax bureaus, in the hut of the pauper and the palace of the millionaire. "Draw up your petition on stamped paper," the order always went. From Lima to the most remote corner of the country spread the smothering snow of stamped paper. There might be no bread, but there was always stamped paper. It was the national ill. In law codes, and on stamped paper, part of the tragedy of Peru has been written. The rest is written in guns and blood. The law, the sacred domain of the law! Order, the sacred domain of order! And the country, like a soldier lost in no man's land, was caught between two fires and always vanquished.

Iñiguez, the wire-puller, fired with sly delight from his paper fortress. Don Alvaro was a man who chose wisely. To all the above must be added the circumstance that the pettifogger was the son of a humble landowner who had been robbed of his farm by the Córdovas. When his father was plunged into poverty, he had to give up his studies at the university and return to his province. Therefore Iñiguez put special zeal into his defense of the enemy of his enemies. He knew perfectly well that, even if Amenábar won, he would not restore his property to him. But he would derive satisfaction for his own misfortunes from that of his despoilers, Don Alvaro suspected this, and he lost little time in laying the matter before him. He arrived late in the afternoon and he and the lawyer went into one of the interior rooms of the dusty, silent house.

"Listen, Iñiguez," he said in the tone of a man accustomed to being obeyed, as they sat down facing one another, "our first problem is to get Bismarck Ruiz out of the way. I can't tell you how exasperated I am at his insolence. But you know the Córdovas look out for him, and, even if they didn't they would make a hullaballoo about it in the papers of the capital of the province. What would you advise me to do? ''

"Ha, ha," laughed the lawyer. With his scrawny body sunk between his long legs and his skinny arms he really did look as though he belonged to the spider family. "Maybe Bismarck would find it a good thing to play the fool. You know what he is: a woman chaser, a pleasure hound. . . . We might be able to. . .you understand—"

"Yes, we might be able to. But Ruiz has got it in for me. And you know why? He blames me because he hasn't got ahead. When he began to make a name for himself as a lawyer he wanted to get to the top. He has always been a second-stringer with a lot of ambition. He and my son Oscar—you know what a rattlebrain he is—became friends because they both have a weakness for the bottle. And Ruiz thought this would be a big help to him. But not on your life. I never once invited him to any of our parties nor let him set foot on my place, and the people of my class all did the same. He has hated me ever since then and I just laughed at him. But there's no such thing as a little enemy, now I see it, and here—"

"Ha-ha! You know that he has completely lost his head over that brazen Melba Cortez. She's a friend of the Pimentel girls. So is your son Oscar."

Don Alvaro slapped himself on the brow with the palm of his hand.

"You are absolutely right, my friend. That's the right road. It so happens that Oscar, who hangs around town most of the time, is here. And about the other matter, what are we going to do? ''

"Don Alvaro, sir, I have told you that I think we ought to take over the whole community. What good are those ignorant Indians? We can do it legally. There is a basis for the claim."

"No, I have already said no. We have to make it look as though we were just revindicating our rights, not despoiling the Indians. I think, the same as you, that these ignorant Indians are no good to the country, and that they should be handed over to men of enterprise, the men who make their countries great. But Zenobio García has told me that the part of Rumi I am claiming is the best part. Further up there's nothing but rocks. We are handling this well. They will work for me if I leave them on their land, which is arable land. But I need them in a silver mine I'm working on the other side of the Ocros River. When I get Rumi it will bring me right up to the boundary of the ranch where the mine is. There are plenty of hands to work on it. Either they sell the ranch to me or I'll sue them. If I were to do what you want me to, we'd probably have a scandal on our hands. You know I plan to run for senator and we have to avoid any possibility of a scandal.

"In the capital of the department there's a bunch of those parrots that are always defending the Indians and attacking respectable people like us. They publish a sheet called *La Verdad.* Now they will attack me, but I'll be within the law and I can defend myself. If I were to take over the whole community, even if I did have the law on my side, people would think it was robbery. I have to be careful of appearances because of my candidacy. With the community and this neighboring ranch and the silver mine, I'll be the biggest man in the province and one of the biggest in the department. I'll be senator. And then, my friend, it will be the Córdovas' turn. I never forget. It's a sacred debt I owe my father's memory. Besides, Peru needs men of enterprise who will make people work. What's the good of all this cheap humanitarianism? It's work and more work, and so that there will be work there must be men who will make the masses work."

"Certainly. And your determination seems all the more praiseworthy, considering that you are just one and there are four of the Córdovas."

Don Alvaro, who had grown excited talking about his plans, sank into a gloomy depression as he spoke of his family.

"Yes, I have had no luck. There's my brother Ramiro. From the time he first went to school he was a highbrow, and he has wound up as a woman's doctor. Did you ever hear of such degeneration? And Elías is still worse. Doctor of Literature and Professor of History. Have you ever heard of anything so effeminate? If they wanted to have professions they could have been first-class lawyers, members of the Supreme Court. And my sister Luisa? In Paris. In her last letter to some of her friends she says she's going to marry an Italian prince. I send her three thousand soles a month and she is always complaining about how poor she is. I hope she doesn't get married, for this prince is probably a sponger and they'll want more money. I have my own family pride, but I make a distinction between the man who uses his titles because he's proud of them, and the one who lives off them.

"I have been more fortunate with my children. Aside from Oscar, who is too big to do anything about, Fernando likes the country and my daughters are quiet and I'll marry them off well. And no studying! Five years of primary school, and then the girls get married and the boys go to work. My father made a mistake giving my brothers too much education. We need practical men. I am going to have Pepito, the youngest of the boys, study. He wants to be a lawyer, and there's a lot of room in that profession, a lot of room. . . ."

"A great deal of room," Iñiguez agreed gravely.

"Well, Iñiguez, I've let my tongue run away with me because of the confidence and trust I have in you. Besides I believe in the saying: *Tell your doctor and your lawyer everything.* Anyway, you know I've got backbone, and I don't care if there are four or twenty Córdovas. I'm relying on you."

Don Alvaro clenched his fists and assumed again his determined air.

"I am highly honored, Don Alvaro. Now, allow me to inform you that I am going to need witnesses. We have said that the lands of Umay extend as far as the so-called ravine of Rumi. Now, to explain how the Indians come to be there, we will say that they are unfairly usurping your lands because of a deliberate misinterpretation. That what is really Lombriz Creek is called Rumi Gorge, and as a result of this the community has extended its lands. We'll call in several people from these parts as witnesses. Besides, we'll say that what is now called Lombriz Creek was formerly Culebra Creek and that the real gorge of Rumi is where that little stream that dries up in summer runs between the cliffs that face Muncha. We will ask for the lands as far as what is *now* called the Rumi Gorge which was, and is, described on the deeds as Lombriz Creek."

"That's an excellent idea."

"Besides, we'll have to have the boundary stones that go from Lombriz Creek to El Alto taken away, and say that the community lands are those that lie around Lake Yanañahui. That will be the finishing touch. I've worked up the brief very carefully and that's why it has taken me a while. Now I want the witnesses."

Don Alvaro's big eyes glittered.

"I'll send you Zenobio García and his people, and the Magician, a peddler who has been very useful to me. He has traced over twenty runaway hands for me. To be sure, I have paid him ten soles for each one, but he has been useful and we can count on him. García has been on my side for a long time. Both are already working on the Rumi business. Don't think I've been asleep. I have already arranged the matter of taking possession with the subprefect as soon as the judge—"

"How about the judge? "

"On my side. He owes his job to me. I used my influence and got him appointed even though he was only second on the list of candidates."

Don Alvaro rubbed his hands together and the lawyer asked permission to light up a cigarette. It was generously granted, and he added:

"That's why I told you we ought to win Bismarck Ruiz over. I have put a spy on him, a clerk, with a good handwriting, a young fellow who offered him his services very cheap. I make up the difference—you understand. Don't think the Indians aren't going to smell a rat. The other day one of them came in to tell Ruiz that they suspected you were hand in glove with Zenobio García and the Magician. Ruiz told them not to worry, because he would discredit their testimony by bringing up unsettled charges against them. You see? Besides, he could appeal the judge's verdict. The Indians know nothing about this. All he has to do is keep quiet."

"Those wily Indians! Leave the matter to me, I'll take care of it. And as soon as possible I'll send you García and the Magician and some others, so you can rehearse them in what they are to say."

"That will be fine, Don Alvaro, sir."

"And what about you? How much do you want for your services? " asked Amenábar pulling out his wallet.

"Whatever seems right to you, sir. . .You know I have the expense of that spy for Ruiz, too."

Don Alvaro counted out a thousand soles in broad blue bills which Iñiguez received with a polite smile. They walked to the door talking over the final details. The bodyguards were waiting outside and the rancher mounted and set out for the house he owned in town.

The night was falling slowly, and two Indians were hanging up on the street corners lanterns of tin and glass, patched here and there with strips of paper, which held a reddish candle. A drunkard was weaving down the middle of the street waving his arms and his poncho and cheering for Piérola. He was that vagabond singer and poet known as El Loco Piérola. Don Alvaro almost rode him down, and he went on his way without paying any attention to the insults El Loco hurled after him by way of protest. But one of the two bodyguards, to show his devotion to duty, gave him a good crack with his reins as he rode by. The poet would get his revenge through mortifying verses.

The oldest of the two-storied houses that surrounded the square opened its gates slowly. The bustling of servants could be heard in the halls and the courtyard. Don Alvaro rode in, answering submissive greetings.

10   The Problem of Hacienda Markets

Enrique Florescano

*If the plantations of Brazil and the Caribbean were highly pro-
fitable enterprises, at least so long as they could compete
successfully in world markets, the manorial haciendas and fundos
of the mining economies were much less so. Geography and
Spanish commercial policy combined to cut them off from large
markets, forcing them to depend on regional markets where demand was limited and prices were subject to wild fluctuations.
In periods of scarcity, when famine brought high food prices
and starvation for many, they might do very well; but when
harvests were good and prices low, they often failed to break
even. To survive under these circumstances, hacendados tried to
force prices up, hold their production costs down (especially
the cost of labor), and increase their self-sufficiency—at least in
the short run—so that they could last through the bad years. In
this sense, as the present selection suggests, the "distortions"
which were characteristic of the traditional hacienda in these
regions may be seen as a rational response to the inadequacy of
their markets. It should be noted that the Chalco haciendas
discussed here possessed one of the best markets. in Spanish
America—in our terms they were essentially fundos rather than
manorial haciendas—but the very excellence of this market tended to increase their dependence on it, while the proximity of
the capital and its officials made it more difficult to manipulate
prices and costs.*

*Enrique Florescano is a Mexican economic historian whose
work has been strongly influenced by the French* Annales *school.*

Translated by the editor from Enrique Florescano, *Precios del maíz y crisis
agrícolas en México (1708-1810). Ensayo sobre el movimiento de los precios y
sus consecuencias económicas y sociales* (Mexico, El Colegio de México, 1969),
pp. 182-189.

> In the arithmetic of market value and agri-
> cultural income, the sum of abundance and
> low prices is poverty; the sum of scarcity and
> high prices is misery; but the sum of abun-
> dance and high prices is wealth.
>
> —François Quesnay

Quesnay's maxim sums up the drama of Mexican agricultural history. During the eighteenth century, at least in the Valley of Mexico,
the first two alternatives apply in turn to the commercial production
of grain. Years of scarcity and high prices follow years of abundance
and low prices without ever approaching the ideal alternative of the
celebrated maxim. The combination of abundance with relatively
high prices, dreamed of by governors and hacendados alike, was
never achieved. Throughout the century hacendados, officials, and
publicists never tire of repeating complaints like this: "Until the present we find ourselves between two terrible hazards: if the maize
harvest is bad. . .all is grief, hunger, and misery caused by a general
shortage of food and even of other goods. . . .and if the harvest is
good. . .the hacendados suffer irreparable harm due to the low prices
at which they have to sell their maize."

This constant disequilibrium between production, demand, and
prices, repeated over the whole century, is not a result of meteoro-
logical factors, as in the case of the cyclical movement of prices.
Rather it reflects a structural inconsistency. We cannot, of course,
give a definitive explanation of these problems, which are still obscure, But some revealing facts permit us to suggest a few hypotheses
which are not without foundation.

The great hacienda in danger (1721-1778). The fifty-eight years
included in this period are difficult years for the great hacienda, that
is for commercial agriculture and large-scale production. They are not
years of "general ruin," as the landowners so often proclaim, but
they are years of instability. After each "good period," when crisis
drives prices up, the latter then fall to a minimal level (nine or ten
reales a fanega). Between 1721 and 1754 the average price of maize
is only thirteen reales. After 1755 the situation becomes worse: the
tendency of prices is downward. Between 1763 and 1770 the depression becomes even more severe. Thus in 1772 the farmers of
Chalco protest angrily that their haciendas are in ruins, worth nothing, and that many hacendados find themselves obliged to abandon
"the noblest of the arts" altogether. The cause, they say, "is none
other than the low and unreasonable level of prices. . .which have

prevailed for maize during more than ten years. . .and it is for this reason that politicians advise those responsible for government always to avoid the pernicious principle of cheapness."

It is true that between 1763 and 1770 the weather tended to favor consumers and small landowners. But the repeated fall of prices and the long depression which began in 1754 can better be understood if we examine other factors.

Disequilibrium between production and the market. The history of the great centers of cereal production shows a similar pattern of development throughout the colonial period. After the rapid advance of the early years, the period of vigorous development, come difficult years and at times decline. The case of the Puebla region at the end of the sixteenth century, of the ranchos and haciendas which supplied the northern mining camps at the beginning of the seventeenth century, and of the Valley of Mexico at the end of the same century all show that in a relatively short space of time the hacienda was able to produce enough to satisfy the regional demand. But where this end was achieved before the hacienda had fully developed its productive capacity, the regional market structure, the great distances, the bad roads, the high transport charges, and the commercial policies of the crown all worked to prevent the sale of its surpluses outside regional limits. The hacienda was therefore compelled, if not to reduce its production, at least to hold it stable; if it did not, it faced the risk of an imbalance between supply and demand.

Often this commercial strangulation was aggravated by the rise of new haciendas and centers of production within the region. Thus in the seventeenth century the haciendas of the Bajío offered new competition to the older haciendas supplying the mines, and the haciendas of the Toluca Valley later provided competition for those of the Chalco region in the Valley of Mexico.

From 1721 to 1778 the great haciendas of the Valley of Mexico, and above all those of Chalco, suffer the consequences of this difficult equilibrium.

Everything indicates that from the beginning of the eighteenth century, the production of the Chalco haciendas was sufficient to satisfy the consumption needs of the capital city. We know that at the middle of the century the total consumption of the city reached 160,000 fanegas a year. In 1795, when the population was still larger, a careful investigation revealed that annual consumption did not go over the figure of 200,000 fanegas. We compare these figures with others on the maize production of Chalco haciendas.

In 1709 the hacendados of Chalco sent 97,330 fanegas of maize to the city by way of the canal alone; in 1710, 3,463 canoes carried 155,120 fanegas to the city. The following figures also show that the Chalco region was able to supply the city by itself:

Size of Harvests on the Haciendas of Chalco

Year	Fanegas harvested	Number of haciendas
1741	113,701	57
1744	250,000[1]	46
1759	135,783[2]	43
1773	146,000[2]	37

To the production of the Chalco region was added that of the Valley of Toluca, whose enormous production began to filter into the markets of the valley and city of Mexico from the beginning of the eighteenth century. At the middle of this century, several estimates by city officials suggest that the annual production of maize in Toluca, Chalco, Texcoco, Tianguistengo, Apan, and Istlahuaca was a little over 500,000 fanegas. It was during these years, especially between 1760 and 1770 when prices descended to their lowest level, that the hacendados of Chalco demand that the city authorities cease favoring the Toluca region or else allow them full liberty to sell their crops in other regions.

But this was an empty threat. Reality had taught the Chalco hacendados that they could not sell their grain in other provinces except in times of crisis, when the general failure of harvests and resulting high prices broke down the regional market structures. In normal times they could not compete with the production of the Puebla region and the warm country to the south, nor with the Bajío and the agricultural zones which supplied the mines. Nor could they export their crops to the Spanish islands in the Caribbean, which were always short of cereals, or anywhere else because the commercial policy of the crown "hindered the trade of colonies with each other."

The only solution was to cut back on what they planted, store their harvested grain, and wait for the years of crisis.

Epidemics and demographic recessions. Demography as well did not favor the hacendados in the period we are studying. The epidemics of 1727-28, 1736-39, 1761-64, 1768-69, and 1772-73, to mention only the most important, severely hurt a population which was recovering only with difficulty from the disasters of the preceding centuries. It is true there are no fully reliable censuses before 1790, but the testimony of travellers and the conclusions reached by recent investigations are in complete agreement that the first half of the century was a period of slow demographic recovery which often turned temporarily to decline. The terrible epidemics of typhus and smallpox, which in 1736-39 and 1761-62 alone carried off more than 65,000 of the inhabitants of Mexico City, leave no room for doubt.

These losses, which particularly affected the Indians and *castas* (mixed bloods), the population which consumed maize, doubtless increased the disequilibrium between supply and demand.

The small holding versus the great hacienda. Finally, the years of good and excellent harvests, which were frequent between 1721 and 1778, together with the other depression-producing factors created a true crisis of overproduction (1763-70). We have already seen that the sales of maize in the *alhóndiga* (public granary) fall to their lowest level during these years. All the Indians who have a little land of their own immediately stop buying maize, and along with the sharecroppers and other small landowners, begin selling their surplus maize in competition with the haciendas. And they are unbeatable competitors, since they can sell cheap and are in a hurry. The immediate and continuous supply of grain from these small farmers after a good harvest thus provokes the violent collapse of prices and "the ruin of the hacendados."

The response of the great hacienda. The decline in the number of Chalco haciendas, which falls from fifty-seven in 1741 to thirty-seven in 1773, and the frequent complaints of their owners between 1760 and 1770, appear to confirm, if not the general ruin of all of them, at least the difficulties under which the great hacienda operated during these years. A more detailed study of their development, their costs of production, and their account books will permit us to examine more closely the impact caused by the depressions in the price and population curves. For the present we must limit ourselves to the conclusion that this period helped to fix the characteristic traits and classic deformities of the great hacienda. These years of "immoderately low" prices and the commercial strangulation which hinders its development add up to an experience which the landowners would never forget.

After their birth at the end of the sixteenth century and their slow development during the seventeenth, the cereal-producing haciendas of the valley consolidate their structure during the first half of the eighteenth. During this century they recognize their limitations and accommodate themselves to the economic circumstances of the region.

The low productivity of the great hacienda since that time, considering the amount of land it had available for cultivation, represented a logical response to those closed regional markets, which due to geography and bad roads tended toward self-sufficiency. To avoid the losses which could result from excess supply, the hacienda found it necessary to adjust production to the needs of the local market. The very characteristics of maize, which could be cultivated in all lands and climates, compelled this. Wheat, by contrast, had a more open market. In the Valley of Mexico, for instance, where little wheat was produced and that only of average quality, most of what was consumed came from the Bajío, Puebla, or other distant regions.

On the other hand, the need to counteract the low prices which prevailed in the years of good harvests led landowners to endow their haciendas with the formidable barns which allowed them to store large amounts of grain and wait for the years of high prices. These barns, along with the devices used by the hacendados to encourage scarcity and high prices, are consequences of the economic structures which define the shape of the regional market.

A more important result of these distortions was that a large part of hacienda profits were used to eliminate the cause of the price failures: the small Indian holding. The expansion of the hacienda has generally been explained as a consequence of the "seignorial spirit" of creole and Spanish landowners. But the mechanisms we have seen entering into the play of supply and demand offer an economic explanation which is more solid.

By buying or otherwise acquiring the lands of the Indian and small farmer, the large landowners obtained at least three important benefits. First, they reduced production and consequently the supply of cheap grain. Secondly, they obtained labor for their haciendas. Thirdly, they increased the demand for maize, since the Indians who did not hire themselves out as peons went to the city where they added to the number of consumers.

At the end of the eighteenth century, the continuous expansion of the haciendas and the cyclical crises, which as we have already seen had similar consequences, had brought about all these objectives. The larger part of the land, and the best agricultural land, was in the hands of the great creole and Spanish landowners. In the Valley of Mexico alone there were about 160 large and medium-sized haciendas. And these, as was true throughout almost all of the country, grew most of the grain which was sold. The loss of Indian land had led to the appearance of the peon, the indispensable worker needed for the exploitation of the haciendas. Finally, the combined blows to Indian society from the agricultural crises and the expansion of the great haciendas strongly stimulated emigration from country to city.

Thus the slow price rise from 1721 to 1754 and the depression from 1755 to 1778, accentuating the distortions characteristic of the great hacienda, seem to have contributed to the development of the structural contradictions which were tearing the colonial society apart.

11 The Hacienda as an Investment

David A. Brading

The inadequacy of local and regional markets in the mining economies of Latin America meant that many haciendas were really not very profitable. Hacendados were sometimes rich men, of course; but they were more likely to be hacendados because they were rich than rich because they were hacendados. The great fortunes of Mexico and Peru, unlike those of Brazil and the West Indies, seldom derived from commercial agriculture. The following selection suggests that in eighteenth-century Mexico, haciendas provided only a small return on the capital invested in them; so small, indeed, that in the long run they tended to drain off the wealth of the landowning class instead of building it up. From this point of view, the purchase of a hacienda was less an investment than a form of consumption.

David Brading is an English historian who has written mainly about the colonial economy and society of Spanish America; he is currently director of the Center for Latin American Studies at Cambridge University.

Neither the limited number of professional jobs, the celibacy of the clergy, the *gachupín* (i.e. peninsular Spanish) control of trade, nor the risk-laden nature of silver mining will suffice to explain the social and economic debility of New Spain's native-born elite. For the stronghold, the basis, of the creole class was the land. The immigrant merchants, the wealthy miners, creole and gachupín alike—these men all invested their fortunes in the purchase of haciendas. In a country without joint stock companies or banks, only the land offered rich entrepreneurs the prospect of a well-endowed and secure future for

From David A. Brading, *Miners and Merchants in Bourbon Mexico, 1763-1810,* Cambridge Latin American Studies, no. 10 (Cambridge, Cambridge University Press, 1971), pp. 214-219.

their descendants. Lucas Alamán's theory, therefore, stands or falls upon the economic viability of the Mexican hacienda. If these large estates were profitable, then it is difficult to explain why the families which owned them should have been subject to a continuous process of social replacement. No description of the Mexican elite can be complete without a discussion of the hacienda and its problems.

Whereas the 6,680 ranchos and the 4,680 Indian villages listed in 1809 of necessity mainly lived off their own crops, New Spain's 4,945 haciendas and estancias produced for a market. A hacienda existed to provide its owner with an income. True, many were left deserted as mere parks for semi-wild herds of cattle and sheep, but in such case they served no observable purpose. For in general most landowners preferred to live in a town; they visited their estates for a few months in a year, if at all, and for the rest entrusted their property to the care of a manager. The Mexican hacendados formed an absentee landlord class who relied upon their estates to yield an income sufficient to maintain an upper-class town-dwelling family in style and comfort. Almost no one bought a hacienda to live on it, still less to feed himself. Many large estates frequently had to support two elite families—the owner's and that of his manager.

But as a unit of production the hacienda was notoriously defective. For there was a peculiar disproportion between the number and average size of the Mexican hacienda—some covered over a hundred square miles—and the minuscule market it supplied. Travelers of the period, such as Father Morfi, lamented over the vast tracts of land left derelict by their owners. But to what point cultivation, if the crops could not be sold? Only the sparsely distributed chain of towns and mining camps offered an adequate market. True, certain regions such as the Bajío and the Valley of Mexico presented urban markets situated at an economic distance. But elsewhere most haciendas made use of but a small portion of their land, and rented out the remainder to their peons, vagrant squatters, and neighboring Indian villages. Moreover, the depressed price level of most agricultural produce did not permit landowners, even on favorably situated estates, to make much profit. For example, the one district of Chalco, with some help from Toluca, satisfied Mexico City's demand for maize; yet in 1773 it was estimated that average production per hacienda amounted to no more than 3,000 fanegas a year, which, with maize prices varying from one to two pesos a fanega, provided a return of at most 6,000 pesos, from which the production costs had still to be subtracted.

In general, the Mexican hacienda yielded a poor return upon the large quantity of capital usually invested in its purchase. The Marchioness of Bibanco owned two haciendas, Chapingo situated in Texcoco, and Ojo de Agua located in Sepuala. The latter estate produced puluqe. Her income and average yield upon capital is shown in table 1.

Table 1. Income and return upon capital of two haciendas, 1800–5 (in pesos)

Year	Chapingo	Ojo de Agua
1800	19,825	10,368
1801	4,695	8,844
1802	10,365	9,047
1803	8,217	10,914
1804	6,414	10,250
1805	16,325	10,034
	65,843	59,459
Average annual income	10,940	9,909
Capital value of estates	193,082	140,442
Annual return upon capital	5.6%	7%

The Jesuits enjoyed fame as the most efficient managers of haciendas. Yet M. Berthe, in his study of the order's sugar plantation at Xochimancas, found its profits, especially in the early eighteenth century, to be remarkable low. It can be proved that the vast estates belonging to the Mexico City College of St. Peter and St. Paul and the seminary at Tepotzotlán yielded but a low return upon their capital value. These estates, which comprised 'a substantial fraction of all the land in the northern part of the valley' in 1767 passed into royal administration after the expulsion of the Jesuits, and in 1775 were sold to the Count of Regla. At the time of the sale a scheme of income for the years immediately before and after confiscation was drawn up, which we present in summary in table 2.

*Table 2. Value and income of former Jesuit haciendas purchased
by the Count of Regla, c. 1775. (In pesos)*

	Haciendas					
	Jalpa and subsidiaries	Santa Lucia, San Javier	Gavia	Portales	Molino	Total
Value	575,830	1,151,694	184,440	52,186	2,500	1,966,650
Sale price	—	—	—	—	—	1,020,000
Annual income before occupation	35,000	23,065	5,979	3,594	436	68,074
After occupation: avg. of 8½ yrs. (1767–75)	28,793	16,486	2,733	336	314	48,662
Tithes & excise: annual avg. (only charged after occupation)	—	—	—	—	—	8,317
Avg. return on capital by Jesuits	—	—	—	—	—	3.5%
Return on capital after occupation, including tithes and excise	—	—	—	—	—	2.9%
Return on sale price to Regla	—	—	—	—	—	4.7%

Our eighteenth-century evidence, therefore, supports the estimates of Francisco Pimentel, who, writing in the 1860s, reckoned that in Mexican agriculture the average return upon capital was no higher than 6 percent.

A contributory cause for the colonial hacienda's low income was to be found in the taxes to which its produce was subject. The Crown levied an excise duty of 6 percent, and sometimes 8 percent, on the value of all its sales. In addition the Church collected a tithe of all its produce. The Jesuit estates mentioned above, once confiscated, paid, in both excise and tithe, over 14 percent of their total income. The Church bore heavily upon Mexican agriculture: in the period 1779-89 its tithes in New Spain (excluding Yucatán) averaged 1,835,000 pesos a year.

Moreover, the Church also acted as the colony's land bank. By 1805 it possessed a capital of about 44 million pesos, which was mainly invested in mortgages and loans secured upon urban and, more especially, rural property. This huge sum represented the accumulated product of three centuries of pious donations, testamentary bequests, and invested interest. It comprised the annuities that supported the secular clergy and the endowments that sustained hospitals, asylums, orphanages, and colleges. Thus the Mexican hacienda, upon which largely fell the burden of paying the 5 percent interest accruing from these clerical mortgages and annuities, maintained not merely the fabric and liturgy of the Church, but also the entire charitable, medical, and educational establishment of the colony.

The explanation for this peculiarly heavy burden can be found in the reciprocal needs of the Church and the land-owning class. Most haciendas required credit, and hence tended to accumulate debts. A bad harvest, a drought, a mining or commercial venture, a charitable donation, a daughter's dowry, an annuity for a younger son, mere conspicuous consumption: all these expenses were met by mortgages charged upon haciendas, and although in the first instance such loans were usually only granted for five-year periods, an almost perpetual extension was common. It was not infrequent to encounter haciendas which bore inherited mortgages worth up to 50 percent of their market value. For its part the Church—almost the only source of long-term credit open to the hacendado—clearly deemed haciendas to be far safer prospects than silver mines or an *obraje*; only urban property offered comparable advantages. Moreover, such mortgages yielded an income—at 5 percent—without the labor that outright ownership of an estate entailed. Thus most clerical capital was charged upon the hacienda, invested in land, the colony's only tangible security which provided an income. Naturally this reciprocity of interest between Church and landowner soon led to situations where the impecunious hacendado became little more than a manager for his clerical creditors. The intendant of Puebla reported that the 38 haciendas and 17 ranchos of Cholula were worth 788,442 pesos, of which value 550,504 pesos were held by the Church. Although Cholula was probably atypical, the tendency it represented was universal. By the end of the eighteenth century most haciendas bore a heavy burden of debt.

The Mexican hacienda thus constituted a weak foundation for a stable class of landed families. The cycle which Gómez de Cervantes observed at work in the seventeenth century proved to be a continuous process, equally applicable to the eighteenth century. Apart from a handful of magnates, the owners of entire provinces such as the Rincón Gallardo or the Marquises of San Miguel de Aguayo, the average hacendado family found it difficult to weather the passage of the generations. In general a contemporary student of clerical mortgages declared that few families held their estates for more than three generations. Francisco Pimentel stated that barely a hacienda existed which had not been purchased with capital acquired in mining, industry, or trade. If such be the case then the Mexican hacienda was a sink through which drained without stop the surplus capital accumulated in the export economy. The fortunes created in mining and commerce were invested in land, there to be slowly dissipated or to be gradually transferred into the coffers of the Church. In consequence, a continuous replacement in the hacendado class occured. New Spain's elite was unstable in composition precisely because its chosen economic basis, the hacienda, absorbed and wasted the greater part of the colony's accumulated capital. This instability was not to end until the Mexican Revolution.

12 Patrón and Peon on an Andean Hacienda

Jorge Icaza

The burden placed on haciendas by the smallness and unreliability of regional markets was not borne completely by their owners, since part of it could be passed on to the workers by holding their wages below market level. This shifting of the burden depended in part on the use of coercive mechanisms like debt peonage to hold workers on the estate, but it also reflected the fact that the conditions of life in independent landowning communities were often such as to make it possible for the hacienda to attract laborers by providing a degree of economic security they could no longer find elsewhere. In this sense paternalism, the usual mechanism for providing such security, played an important functional role in the organization of the hacienda. Though he might effectively pay them nothing, a patrón was expected to take ultimate responsibility for the welfare of his peons. The novel Huasipungo (1934) from which the following excerpt is taken, shows us how ingrained these expectations were and suggests that an hacendado who failed to live up to them was likely to drive his peons into revolt.

Like Ciro Alegría, the Ecuadorean writer Jorge Icaza gained an international reputation during the 1930s for his novels of social protest, of which Huasipungo was the first and best known.

After speaking to his neighbors on the slope of the big hill, where hunger and the necessities of life had become more and more urgent—in that area the families of the huasipungueros[1] displaced from the banks of the river were clustered in caves or in improvised huts—the crippled Andrés Chiliquinga climbed down by the short cut. It should be added here that the Indians who had lost their huasipungos and

From Jorge Icaza, *The Villagers*, translated by Bernard M. Dulsey (Carbondale, Southern Illinois University Press, 1964), pp. 148-155.

all the peons of the hacienda, some bitterly and some with naïve illusions, were expecting the socorros—the annual help—that the administrator, the owner, or the tenant on the land had always been accustomed to sharing after the crops had been harvested. "Will it be on the patron saint's day? Will it take place on Sunday? Maybe for the feast of the Holy Mother? Perhaps on. . .? When will it be, pes?"[2] the Indians asked one another as the days kept going by.

In truth, the socorros—one and one-half bushels of corn or barley—with the huasipungo loaned to them and ten cents a day wages (money which the Indians never even got a whiff of because it went to pay for, with no possibility of amortization, the hereditary debt of all living huasipungueros for the advances on the saints' or Virgins' feast days of the taita[3] cura for the sake of the dead huasipungueros) made up the annual payment that the landowner granted to each Indian family for its work. Someone from the valley or from the mountain asserted that the patrón must have forgotten the traditional custom, but the gossip that ran through the village was different: "No. . .He won't give any socorros this year. The Indians have been screwed." "They're screwed. . . ." "He's buying up grain to fill his granaries." "He's buying like crazy. . . ." "He's buying so he can fix his own price later when. . . ." "We'll be screwed also, cholitos."[4] "He won't give a single grain to anyone. Nooo. . ."

When the waiting period could no longer be endured and hunger was an animal barking in their bellies, a goodly number of the Indians, old and young, on Don Alfonso's property swarmed up to the patio of the hacienda in a dark, noisy, and unrestrainable group. Since it was very early, and drizzling besides, each one sought some shelter in the corners until the patrón should awaken and decide he was ready to listen to them. After a long hour of waiting they again solicited the help of the cholo Policarpio, who was going in and out of the house constantly:

"Be kind to us, pes, master mayordomo. Socorritus. . .We have come to ask for socorritus."

"For socorritus."

"The master mayordomo already knows."

The cholo, become more sly and proud because of the Indians' entreaties, spread news of vague hopes:

"Now. . .the patrón is up now, goddamit."

"We only hope so, pes."

"He's drinking his coffee. Don't bother him now."

"Taitiquitu."

"He's angry. . .angry. . ."

"Ave María. God help us."

With a big frown and a whip in his right hand, Don Alfonso showed himself on the porch that faced the patio.

"What's the matter? What do you want? " he cried in a grating voice.

Suddenly the Indians, both men and women, with a magical briskness and in an apparently humble silence gathered at a prudent distance from the porch. In those first few seconds—as they urged one another forward with little pushes and elbowings—not one of them dared to compromise himself by stating their urgent case to the patrón. Impatiently, tapping his boots with the whip, Don Alfonso again shouted:

"What do you want? Are you going to stand there like a bunch of idiots? "

Somewhat unhappily, and with the attitude of a dog fawning on its master, the mayordomo, who also would profit by several bushels from the socorros, spoke up:

"Well, it's like this, patrón. They've come to request a little charity from your worship. . . ."

"Eh?"

"A little charity, pes."

"More? More charity than I already give them, goddamit?" interrupted Don Alfonso icily hoping to eliminate once and for all the daring attitude of the Indians.

He knew. . . .

"The socorritos, pes! The poor Indian is dying of hunger. He has nothing. They've always given socorros, su mercé," dared to request in chorus the Indians who were of the group displaced from the banks of the river. And then as if someone had opened the floodgate of the physical needs of that sullen, dark mass, all suddenly found their tongues to tell of the hunger of their babies, the sickness of their old people, the increasing boldness of the Indian girls, the tragedy of the devastated huasipungos, of the endurable misery of past years, and of the unendurable misery of the present one. It quickly became a threatening clamor, chaotic and rebellious, in which diverse cries would rise and fall:

"Socorrus, taiticu!"

"We've always received them!"

"All-l-l-ways!"

"The baby, too. . ."

"The wife, too. . ."

"Socorrus, a little corn to roast."

"Socorrus, a little barley for porridge."

"Socorrus, a few potatoes for a fiesta."

"Socorruuus!"

Like surging waves the supplications rolled on to the hacienda porch enveloping the increasingly nervous patrón, increasingly bathed in that fetid bitterness of the peons' outcries. But Don Alfonso, shaking his head, was able to shout:

"That's enough, damn it, that's enough."

"Taiticu."

"I've told you over and over that I'm giving you nothing this year. Do you understand me? It's nothing but a barbaric custom!"

"What do you mean, patroncitu? "

"That's what I pay you for. . . .That's why I give you the huasipungos. . . ."

"We need the socorritus, too, pes."

"You're still complaining, goddamit? Get out of here! Get out!"

The complaints stopped at once, but the throng stayed on, motionless, petrified, grim. Meanwhile some miserly calculations went through the landowner's mind: "I must not give in. Four or five tons just to give away to these barbarians. No! They can fetch a good price in Quito. It would bring enough to pay the priest for the use of his trucks. Enough to. . .If I give in to them I won't have enough to do business with the gringos. Oh, they've met their match in me. They'll learn I'm a real man!" Mechanically Pereira took a step, two steps forward until he came to the edge of the first stone step of the porch. Then he arched the flexible whip handle with both hands and, breaking the silence, shouted:

"You're still here? You didn't hear me, goddamit? "

Stolid as a wall, the Indian throng didn't budge. Confronted with such resistance Don Alfonso for a few long seconds didn't know what to say. Perhaps for an instant he felt beaten, swallowed up by what he believed to be an unheard-of rebellion. What could he do with them? What could he do with his pent-up rage? Almost crazed with wrath he went down the three stone steps and, approaching the nearest group, he grabbed a young Indian and shook him like a filthy rag, all the while uttering half-choked oaths. Finally the victim was rolling on the ground. The mayordomo, fearful of what might occur, for he could see how icy was the fury in the eyes of the Indians, helped the fallen Indian to his feet and reproached the crowd in a loud voice so that all of them could hear:

"Don't be so ill-mannered. You shouldn't get the poor patrón so angry. He'll die of rage. He'll just die. What'll happen to you then? Don't you understand or don't you have any hearts? "

Hearing the cholo's words Don Alfonso felt himself to be a martyr to his duty, to his obligation. In a voice hoarse with fatigue he managed to shout:

"These. . .These Indians are driving me to an early grave. . . .Me. . . I'm the one to blame, goddamit. . .for having spoiled them as though they were my own children. . . ."

"Poor patrón," said the mayordomo, and instinctively, in defense against any possible attack from the outraged Indians, mounted his mule.

The landowner, on the other hand, inspired by the example set by the priest, lifted his eyes and hands to heaven and, in a voice that demanded as infernal punishment for his cruel enemies, screeched:

"Oh, my God! My God! You watch us from above. . . .You who have often told me to be harsher with these Indian savages. . . . Protect me now. Defend me! Don't you hear me? Send a punishment for a warning to them. . .Or a voice. . . ."

Don Alfonso's attitude and his request stunned the Indian throng. It was dangerous for them when the priest or the patrón began a dialogue with Taita Dios. Yes, it was. It was something superior to the weak efforts of Indians caught in the trap of the huasipungo, to the feebleness of men dirty, meek, and forsaken. They forgot the socorros, forgot why they were there, forgot everything. A desire to flee overpowered them and, immediately, some covertly, others openly, they began to dissolve.

"Goddamit! Turn the dogs loose on them. The fierce dogs!" the mayordomo then shouted, his kindness and fears abruptly transformed, with a devilish cynicism, into the cries and actions of an executioner.

The angry dogs and the whips of the mayordomo and the Indian servants of the patrón's house angrier still, swept the patio clean in a few minutes. When Policarpio returned to the patrón he said to him with slavering deviousness:

"You'll see, su mercé. Just now when I was chasing the Indians I overheard them swearing to return in the night to take the socorros by hook or crook."

"What's that? "

"They're starving. They could even kill us."

"That they may be able to do with some fool coward, but not with me. Here I am the power and the law."

"You're right, 'of course, pes," murmured the cholo, just to be saying something.

"Go at once to the sheriff and tell him to send me the two peasants who are his deputies. Armed. . . ."

"O.K. patrón."

"Oh, and tell him to telephone Quito and ask the Police Inspector in my name to send us a squad to crush any possible criminal uprising among the Indians. Don't forget: in my name. He knows what to. . . ."

"Sí, certainly, pes."

The mayordomo went off like a shot from a cannon, and Don Alfonso, feeling himself all alone—for the huasicamas were, after all, Indians and could betray him, the cook and the female servants were Indians and would not inform him—was stricken with a strange fear, an infantile, stupid fear. He ran to his room and took the pistol from his night table and, with terror-crazed violence, aimed at the door as he shouted:

"Now, goddamit! Come on, now, you filthy Indians."

When the echo of his threat was his only answer he became somewhat mollified. Nevertheless he advanced a few steps and looked suspiciously in all the corners. "Nobody's here. . .I'm just like a woman. . . ." he said to himself, and he laid the pistol down. Then, exhausted from the nervous fright brought on by the impertinences of the Indians, he flung himself headlong on his bed like a betrayed woman. Of course, he didn't cry: but instead sadistically evoked macabre scenes which proved to him the savagery of the Indians. How did they kill Don Victor Lemus, the owner of Tumbamishqui? By making him walk on a gravel path after first flaying the skin of his hands and feet. And they disposed of Don Jorge Mendieta by tossing him into a caldron of boiling cane syrup at the sugar mill. And Don Ricardo Salas Jijón by abandoning him on the mountain in a pit dug to trap beasts. "All. . .All because of stupidity. . . .Because one doesn't give them what they want. . . .Because one gets their lands or water through some court action. . . .Because the brazen young

Indian girls have been violated at a tender age. . . .Because. . .All little insignificant things. . .Stupid things. . ." Don Alfonso thought.

That night, the presence of the two armed peasants and Policarpio restored his peace of mind. Nevertheless, when he went to bed he said to himself: "These criminals will rebel one of these days. And when that happens we won't be able to choke it off as we did today. . . .Today. . .Then I'll. . ." A charitable voice vibrated hopefully in the great señor of the region: "The hell with those who come after me; I'll be gone by then."

"Yes. To hell with them," Don Alfonso muttered in the darkness, with a smile of diabolic selfishness.

13   A Chilean Fundo

George M. McBride

*The Chilean hacienda described below is very different from
the haciendas of Icaza's Ecuador. Chile had once been a land of
large ranches and manorial haciendas, but the rise of nitrate
mining and the growth of the city of Santiago during the second
half of the nineteenth century, by greatly increasing the local
demand for agricultural products, had brought the fragmentation
of many larger estates into smaller and more intensively cultivated fundos like this one. These fundos generally maintained
the traditional labor system of peonage (peons in Chile were
called* inquilinos*), but in contrast with the situation in the
Andean regions to the north, these resident peons represented
a relatively privileged minority within a rural population composed mainly of landless laborers or* rotos. *One of the problems
facing agrarian reformers in Chile has thus been how to redis-
tribute land in such a way as to benefit the whole rural population and not just the minority of inquilinos.*

*George McBride, a geographer who taught for many years at
the University of California in Los Angeles, was one of the
earliest North American students of patterns of land tenure and
use in Latin America.*

This fine farm is located in the Aconcagua Valley, about forty miles
(ca. 65 kilometers) north of Santiago and up the Aconcagua River
some fifty miles from Valparaíso. It thus lies outside the great longi-
tudinal valley but within the region generally considered as central
Chile. It is one of a hundred or more farms that are found in this
beautiful and productive valley and is a part of the famous great

From George M. McBride, *Chile: Land and Society* (New York, American
Geographical Society, 1936), excerpts from pp. 45-52.

estate known as Panquehue which some years ago was divided into three sections, each of which now forms a magnificent independent property.

At present the Aconcagua Valley is intensively developed. It contains the towns of Los Andes, San Felipe, and Quillota and many of the best farms in the country. The greater part of the valley floor is given over to alfalfa production, though fields of wheat and barley with their rich golden hues are interspersed with the deep green of the grasslands. The main auto or wagon road and the railway, following closely along the south margin of the valley on the first slight elevation, touch and skirt the jutting spurs that descend with considerable regularity from the high bordering hills. Between each pair of promontories that protrude into the valley there sweeps back a long, curving, semicircular cove like the symmetrical scallops of a giant shell, and in each of the smoothly curving recesses piedmont slopes rise gently from the level valley floor. In these wide, sweeping re-entrants, snuggling up against the foot of the hills and protected upstream and down by the points of jutting cliffs, lie the choicest sites for fruit farms and vineyards. In such an alcove, a great natural amphitheater containing nearly a thousand acres (ca. 400 hectares), are situated the farm lands of the estate, with 240 cuadras (960 acres) of fruitful irrigated ground, while back over the mountains behind this slope stretch some two million acres more of hill land also belonging to the estate.

We were met at the railway station by the owner's grown son, who was acting as administrator of the estate. In a good foreign automobile he drove us through the single street of the little town of Palomar, between rows of low adobe houses thatched with straw, then out along a country road lined with Lombardy poplars, now bright yellow in the late May days of autumn. Then, entering the farm through a gate in a high mud wall, we followed through avenues of eucalyptus, poplar, and weeping willow a couple of miles by a roundabout road to the house. Most of the land we saw was in alfalfa, with cattle and horses grazing its short-cropped growth. We passed a few fields of grain and saw well-kept vineyards rising row on row along the foot of the hills as far up the slope as canals could supply them with water. Each individual field was enclosed by rows of tall poplars, the red roots of the trees exposed along the half-filled irrigation ditches. Long lines of weeping willows, too, bordered some of the plots, and their drooping branches were neatly cropped by the cattle into an evenly barbered "bob." Mud walls some four feet (1 1/3 meters) high also separated the fields, built close to the rows of trees. Each of these fields, called potreros and containing some twenty to twenty-five hectares (50 or 60 acres) as an average, bears its own name, we are told. One is called the Field of the Serpents, another the Field of Copper, another that of the Walnut Trees, while several bear the names of persons, possibly former owners of the lands now incorporated into the hacienda. The naming of fields is a common practice on the larger Chilean farms.

Soon after luncheon we were told that horses were ready to take us over the farm. Don Santiago led the way. Through a labyrinth of corrals and farm buildings, dairy barns, granaries, implement sheds, stables, sheep pens, workshops, fruit depositories, and vast wine bodegas he conducted us in a roundabout way to the public road that passes through the farm. This highway was lined much of its length by well-built mud walls, topped with tile or hard-packed earth so high that from our saddles we could just see, as we rode along, the extensive vineyards and orchards that lay between us and the hills. On the other side of the road, reaching down to the wide gravel bed of the river, were fields of grain and rich alfalfa pastures. Some two miles from the house the road passes close to the intake of the large canal, Don Santiago's own canal, that leads his water supply from the river along the base of the hills behind his orchards. Just above this point the river bends to meet the hills, and Don Santiago's land pinches out into a narrow band. Rounding a projecting spur at this point, we turned up over some uncultivated gravelly fields and past an abandoned quarry and a small mine (still on the farm), climbed the slope by zigzag trails, and finally came out on the point of a long ridge, whence we could look over the whole valley above and below the farm.

The hacienda of Panquehue was almost at our feet, but fully three thousand feet (1,000 meters) below us. The poplar-bordered fields lay like a checkerboard on the valley floor. The highway cut the farm into two slightly unequal parts, that on the river side variegated in sharply contrasted grain and alfalfa fields, the other largely orchard and vineyard.

Down the valley we could trace the broad gravel bed of the river, a thin line of silver marking all that was left of its waters. The secret as to what had become of its full upstream supply was revealed by the canals that lay one above another like narrow parallel roads along the foot of the bordering hills on both sides of the valley. Most of the canals gave the distinct impression that they were rising rather than going downstream and recalled to mind the Chilean inquilinos' boastful saying that "the *patrón* can make water run uphill." The highest of these *acequias,* as the irrigation ditches are called in Chile, marked a neatly cleft divide between two types of growth. Above, upon the slopes of the hills could be discerned hardly a vestige of green in the prevailing brown of the chaparral. Below the canals all was the fresh green of the early spring of our middle latitudes. No effort had been made to cultivate any part not reached by these life-giving arteries. Land above was worthless—below it was the best the country affords. Water alone made the difference.

On the Panquehue side of the valley, curving in long sweeps around the upper borders of the cultivated lands, the main irrigation canal of the farm, marked by a line of tall young poplar trees, lay like a contour line upon the slope. Don Santiago's hacienda, like most Chilean estates, has an independent water supply. It has built its own aqueducts, four in number, taking the water from the Aconcagua just above the upper edge of the property and carrying it by gravity flow to all the level or gently sloping parts of the farm. These canals, each one named—El Puente (The Bridge), El Medio (The Center), Los Hornos (The Ovens), and La Rueda (The Wheel)—also provide water to run a private power plant that supplies current for the various pieces of electrical machinery about the place as well as for lighting purposes. The farm has first water rights *(primeras aguas)* from the river, and rarely if ever does the flow become so reduced as to cause a shortage. Most of the large properties in the valley and many of the smaller ones have as dependable a water supply.

Immediately below the highest canal the hillside was planted with young deciduous fruit trees. They formed a band a few rods in width and had been set here, where the air drainage was good, to avoid danger of frosts. Don Santiago informed us that he had 28,000 peach trees and 3,000 apple trees. On the lower part of the slope vineyards began and reached completely down to the wall along the road. There were 327 acres (132 hectares) in vines, and Panquehue's greatest wealth consists of the fruitage of these vineyards. Its bodegas, as the wine cellars are called, were two-story buildings, covering nearly an acre, with deep basements capable of holding 2,000,000 liters. Before we left the farm Don Santiago conducted us through these extensive cellars, indicating with pride the great casks, the provision for storing the products of his vineyards for many years, and the carefully worked out system by which the whole stock was cared for. A Belgian, expert in the production and care of wines, was employed for this task. The vintage of this farm, as that of most other Chilean vineyards, finds its market within the country. A little is exported; but the area suitable for vineyards is relatively limited, and domestic consumption is large.

Below the orchards and vineyards the hacienda house and its out-buildings could be seen almost as if from an airplane. Surrounded by gardens and groves of tall trees, the group of buildings covered enough land for a small farm. On the opposite side of the road lay the settlement of inquilinos, occupying an area about equal to the former. It contained fifty-five houses of regular tenants, while six or seven buildings occupied by the foremen or other higher employees adjoined it along the road. It thus constituted a village of some three hundred persons. The arrangement of the tenants' houses was quite different from that commonly seen. In most cases the inquilinos live in a long row of cottages stretching along the highway or the main road of the farm, as in Peñalolén. On Panquehue, however, the settlement was in the form of a square, with streets crossing at right angles, and the cottages were set close together as in a compact village. Looked at from above it appeared less satisfactory (though perhaps more economical of space) than the usual arrangement. It gave something of the character of a town to what in most cases is but a row of peasant cottages. The houses themselves were better built than is common on Chilean farms, where they are frequently miserable huts. This settlement, however, was largely bare of trees, and the dwellings lacked the homely though humble appearance given by the customary wide-spreading grapevine and great fig tree about an inquilino's house.

14 Cafetales and Vegas in Cuba

José García de Arboleya

The Chilean fundo described in the previous reading was one of a type well known in Spanish America, concentrating on the production of staples (particularly grain and meat) for markets which were relatively close. Latin America also possessed more specialized fundos, however, farms which concentrated mainly on the production of certain less essential food products (wine, sugar, tobacco, cacao, and later coffee) for which there was a large demand. Such products could support the costs of transportation for longer distances than grains, and they were thus marketed over wider areas. Some fundos were even able to export part of their produce, though competition and commercial restrictions generally kept them from becoming completely dependent on overseas markets. The following selection is concerned with two types of specialized fundos found in nineteenth century Cuba: the cafetal or coffee hacienda, organized in many respects like a plantation, and the small tobacco vega, which was often more like a family farm than a hacienda.

José García de Arboleya was a Spanish journalist who emigrated to Havana, where he became a newspaper editor and wrote several books before his death in 1876.

The cafetal is the most important farm to be found in the Cuban countryside after the sugar plantation *(ingenio)*, which it often surpasses in charm and beauty. Its area varies from four to twenty *caballerías* of land (roughly 130 to 660 acres), which are dedicated not only to the cultivation of coffee, but also to that of such crops as rice, yuca, bananas, and other fruits and vegetables, which are

Translated by the editor from José García de Arboleya, *Manual de la isla de Cuba* (Havana, Imprenta del Gobierno y Capitanía General, 1852), pp. 136-140.

planted between the coffee trees. The boundary lines, marked by palms and other leafy trees, form magnificent scenic promenades.

The cafetal (like the sugar plantation) also possesses its central compound or *batey,* made up of the main residence, warehouses, drying floors, mills, and sometimes an infirmary. The drying floor (*tendal*) is a square piece of land enclosed by a low wall and has a concrete floor where the coffee beans are placed in the sun to dry, so they do not separate when they are husked. The latter operation is performed in the husking mill (*molino de pilar*), where a large vertical wooden wheel driven by oxen or mules rotates over a circular bin, where the dried coffee beans are thrown to have their shells cracked. The mill is covered by a roof supported on four forked poles, called the octagon because of the number of its sides. From there the coffee beans go to the winnowing mill (*molino de aventar*), a wooden bin with two sieves underneath a pair of revolving arms, which make the shells and dust fly up in the air, letting the fine coffee particles fall through to the ground.

The employees of a cafetal are the administrator, the overseer, and sometimes a physician. At the most it had a hundred slaves, and according to the calculations of Don Tranquilino Sandalio do Noda, a cafetal of eight caballerías (about 272 acres) would have 200,000 coffee trees and would produce 2,500 *arrobas* (about 10,000 pounds) of coffee a year.

In 1846 there were 1,670 cafetales in the whole of Cuba, of which 1,013 were in the eastern part of the island. In 1827 there were 2,067 on the whole island, 1,239 of them in the east. In eighteen years the number of these farms has decreased by 19.2 percent in the east and by more than 20 percent in the west. Since then, far from increasing, their number has continued to diminish, so that today one can say that as many cafetales have failed as are still in production. The present number is perhaps a little less than 1,400; these occupy a total area of 10,000 caballerías, or on the average seven caballerías (231 acres) apiece. The principal cause of this decline is held to be the differential duties in the United States for imports from Cuba, duties which were established in reprisal for the high Spanish duties on American flour, which have forced their merchants to ship it to Brazil. Despite the force of this argument, it is clear that Cuban coffee growers have preferred the cultivation of sugar cane to that of coffee, both because it employs the increasingly limited number of slaves more profitably and because the great fluctuations in coffee prices, which vary from three to thirty pesos a *quintal,* have meant that in bad years they could not cover the expenses of the enterprise, while in average years they received a paltry return (La Sagra estimates it at 1.5 percent a year) and only rarely made a substantial profit.

The cafetales best known for their wealth and the excellence of their product are found in the Sierra Maestra within the jurisdiction of Santiago and in the Vuelta Abajo districts of Alquízar and San Marcos. In the latter district were found many cafetales which were once celebrated for their magnificence; today most of them no longer exist, and their place has been taken by farms raising livestock and provisions. Not counting the value of the coffee trees themselves, the cafetales today represent a total investment of about 40,000,000 pesos divided as follows:

10,000 caballerias of land at 1,500 pesos	15,000,000
15,000 able-bodied slaves at 750 pesos	11,250,000
6,000 young and old slaves at 300 pesos	1,800,000
Buildings, machinery, and tools	12,000,000

At an average price of 3 pesos an arroba, the 1,047,167 arrobas of coffee which are produced annually bring in 3,141,501 pesos, an amount which fails to cover the operating expenses of the cafetales. They manage to make up the difference and sometimes to obtain a small profit from the sale of the secondary crops.

The haciendas dedicated to the growing of tobacco are generally found alongside the rivers, and their average size is less than a cabellería, half of which is used for food crops. They have a house, a drying shed, and a labor force of four to twenty workers, who are not always blacks since this branch of agriculture is the one which depends most heavily on the labor of the white class. In some vegas there is an overseer, but in most cases the *veguero*—who rents his land rather than owning it—lives on his farm and manages it in person. "Guided by the fruits of long experience transmitted to him by his ancestors," as we are told by Don Ramón de la Sagra, "he knows without being able to offer any explanation for it how to increase the strength or mildness of the tobacco; his hand, skilled and guided as if by a prudent instinct, picks the buds from the plant, thus setting a limit to their upward growth, and pulls off the suckers and shoots to provide sap for the leaves in the amount, at the time, and in the circumstances required for the particular kind of tobacco he is trying to grow." But his main preoccupation, one which can even deprive him of his sleep, is that of exterminating the voracious tobacco worms which attack his plants. The veguero may spend whole nights, equipped with a lantern, cleaning off the plants which have been attacked by these destructive insects. And he has a worse plague to struggle with: a voracious breed of indigenous ants called *vivijaguas,* which are to the tobacco plant what the locust is to wheat. These ants have done so much damage that a foreign species of ants, specially imported from France, has been introduced to control them, and public rogations have been held through a special cult of Saint Martial, who figures in our calendar as advocate against the ants.

The best tobacco lands are found in the Vuelta Abajo, a region which owes a certain celebrity throughout the world to the excellence of its tobacco. The vegas of San Juan y Martínez, San Sebastián, Cuyaguateje, Río Hondo, and La Leña are among the most notable. In the Vuelta Arriba, excepting the vegas of Mayarí, Yara, Guisa, and a few others toward the east of the island, the quality of the tobacco is lower, being considered as similar to that of Virginia and Brazil tobacco.

In 1846 there were 9,102 vegas as opposed to 5,534 in 1827; today one can count 10,000. Tobacco is the product which first achieved great importance in our economy. In 1720, 600,000 arrobas a year were already being harvested, but the monopoly established by the government in 1765 and later the royal factory paralyzed its progress, so that in 1811 only 371,560 arrobas were harvested. The end of the monopoly in 1817 and the suppression of the factory in 1821 left exportation and consumption free, and production again began to rise. In 1827 it had already reached 560,000 arrobas, an increase of 101 percent in the space of nineteen years or 5.3 percent a year. Assuming an equal rate of growth in the subsequent years, current tobacco production would be 1,600,000 arrobas yearly. Of this quantity, 400,000 arrobas are consumed internally, and since legal exportation does not go over 450,000 arrobas in the leaf and 100,000 in rolled cigars, some 500,000 arrobas remains unaccounted for, even if we assume a loss of 100,000 arrobas during the process of manufacture and marketing. For each of the preceding years there is a similar excess of production over consumption, and this can be attributed only to the contraband trade provoked by export prohibitions or by the tobacco monopoly in Spain and other countries.

The total investment represented by the vegas, not counting the value of the plants themselves, is about 17.5 million pesos divided as follows:

8,000 caballerías of land at 1,000 pesos	8,000,000
10,000 able-bodied slaves at 750 pesos	7,500,000
30,000 young and old slaves at 300 pesos	900,000
Houses, drying sheds, and tools	900,000
Animals	200,000

Since the average price of tobacco is three pesos an arroba, the annual production of the vegas can be estimated at 4,800,000 pesos.

15   Hacienda Labor in the Valley of Mexico

Charles Gibson

The ability of haciendas to attract free labor depended mainly on whether they could compensate their workers at a level consistent with local conditions of labor supply and demand. This in turn depended on the availability of labor, which determined its market cost, as well as on the size of their profit margins. Manorial haciendas, found in less developed areas where agricultural profits were low and the Indians—possessing considerable land of their own—preferred to remain in the subsistence economy, found some coercion necessary to recruit and hold on to the workers they needed. In the more developed fundo areas, on the other hand, there was generally less need for coercion, since such areas tended to attract a substantial landless population, and this kept the market cost of labor closer to what the haciendas could afford to pay. Thus in the Valley of Mexico, as we see below, most hacienda labor was hired on a short-term basis from the Indian communities nearby, and though workers were often indebted this did not imply their enserfment.

The historian Charles Gibson, who teaches at the University of Michigan, is best known for his immense contribution to our knowledge of how Mexican Indians were affected by Spanish conquest and colonization.

Debt labor, like much else in labor history, received its earliest impetus in the obrajes (textile factories) and spread from them to other employment institutions. Debt could be incurred in many ways.

From Charles Gibson, *The Aztecs under Spanish Rule: A History of the Indians of the Valley of Mexico, 1519-1810* (Stanford: Stanford University Press, 1964), pp. 252-256.

An advance in wages to a "free" obraje laborer placed him immediately in debt. An Indian laborer might be forced to accept money payable in work, or he might be required to purchase, with borrowed funds, the equipment he was to use in obraje labor. Deductions might be made against a worker's account if his finished cloth weighed less than the raw wool with which he started. Forced sales, with price markups and the prohibition of purchases elsewhere, might prolong or increase his debt.

Royal legislation on debt labor in the sixteenth century sometimes forbade loans by employers to their workers and the discharge of debt by labor. But other rules tended to compromise in favor of the employers. As in so many other matters, laws shifted between prohibition and regulation. Loans were to be transacted before judges, but other loans, for tribute or for food or for "necessities," could be transacted privately. Restrictions were placed upon the amount of loans and on the periods for which debts could be effective. Viceregal legislation in 1595 supported the employers even to the point of forbidding payments of debt in money and specifying payments in labor. But labor debts were entirely forbidden again by royal and viceregal legislation in the early seventeenth century. When communities had to perform special Desagüe labor in commutation of tribute arrears, a supervised public debt servitude was established. Limitations on the duration of the debts were attempted, as well as limitations on the amounts, expressed as salary for a given number of months. The law also recognized those employers who paid tributes for their Indian employees, tribute payment sometimes being regarded as a separate transaction, not to be included in computing the maximum legal debt.

No one could argue that the Valley's hacendados absolutely refrained from using the devices of debt employment, for countless records indicate that they did use them. But many other employers used them as well, and one must be cautious in evaluating the special role of debt employment in haciendas. A comparison between the hacienda and the obraje is revealing here, for while both were institutions of debt labor, the obraje was in addition a closed and guarded workshop. Obraje history indicates that debt labor alone was incapable of holding obraje workers, and it may be concluded that it was likewise incapable of holding hacienda workers. In any case, indebtedness was a legal technicality. An Indian worker bent on leaving his hacienda could find occasion to do so despite his indebtedness—just as any Indian could default and escape his tribute debt to a town or his private debt to any creditor. From the viceregal point of view, even the legal technicality could be regarded as inapplicable in the late eighteenth century, for the viceroy was on record in 1784 with the assertion that Indians might freely leave the haciendas regardless of the amount they owed.

// An examination of hacienda records is further revealing. During any agricultural year the working force of a large Valley hacienda might vary from fifty to three hundred or more persons, depending on the seasonal demand for agricultural labor. The nucleus of this labor force consisted of resident workers, the *gañanes radicados* of the hacienda, who might be expected to work regularly six days a week. For the remainder of their workers haciendas relied on a fluid supply from nearby communities. The seasonal operations entailed a continuous influx and departure of workers, under conditions quite different from those of the closed obraje. Records of the late eighteenth and early nineteenth centuries show that by far the larger number of Indians were "de pueblo," only a small percentage being included in the double category of hacienda residents (*laborios*) and homeless persons or vagrants (*vagos*). The finances of the hacienda of Santa Ana Aragón in 1771-72 indicate weekly expenses for wages ranging from under five to over sixty pesos throughout the year. Santa Ana Aragón had at this time forty-two gañanes radicados, of whom fewer than half were in debt to the hacienda, and indeed the largest debts amounted to only a few weeks' wages. All but four of the debtors owed less than a peso apiece. In a great hacienda such as Los Portales, approximately 100 persons owed a total of 367 pesos in 1778, with individual debts ranging from a few reales to 28 pesos. But Los Portales was at this time hiring weekly shifts of more than twice the number of debtors.

// The total indebtedness in these instances appears slight in comparison with the reputation of debt peonage as a controlling and universal hacienda technique. The matter would require documentation through the study of a large number of hacienda records, both in the Valley and elsewhere, and in the nineteenth and twentieth centuries as well as in the colonial era. A document of special interest in this connection is a survey of the economic condition of New Spain written from the point of view of the Spanish employers in 1788. The report speaks of the great shortage of hacienda workers, a shortage that operated to increase the amount of indebtedness in labor peonage. It was impossible, the writer stated, to find Indians who would work with a debt of only five pesos, at this time a legal limit. By "ancient custom" Indians were demanding advances of forty to eighty pesos, and if an employer were to refuse to raise his offer over five pesos, the Indian would desert and move to another hacienda where conditions were more attractive. Here the emphasis is reversed from the conventional interpretation of debt labor, for it assumes relative freedom among the workers, whose objective was not to escape but to enlarge the indebtedness. The writer recognized that regional customs varied in New Spain with respect to the amounts owed, and we may suppose that his comments applied far more to other areas than to the Valley of Mexico, where conditions were less extreme than those described. In any case, the amount of the debt may be considered in some degree as a measure of the bargaining power of the worker. The relatively dense population of the Valley may have reduced this bargaining power, and accordingly reduced the amount of indebtedness and the role of peonage.

Present evidence for the Valley suggests that in late colonial times debt peonage affected fewer than half the workers on haciendas, and that the large majority of these owed debts equal to three weeks' labor or less. But a full explanation for the hold of the hacienda over its workers cannot stop with debt servitude. To Indian workers the hacienda offered solutions to economic conditions not to be found elsewhere. As monetary values came to occupy a large role in Indian society—in tribute, in ecclesiastical charges, in economic exchange— the hacienda offered a regular or irregular income. To Indians who had lost their lands (largely, of course, to haciendas) the hacienda provided a dwelling and a means of livelihood. Under conditions permitting only tiny margins between income and sustenance, the hacienda was an institution of credit, allowing Indians freely to fall behind in their financial obligations without losing their jobs or incurring punishment.

If these conclusions are accurate, we confront the further problem of explaining the evil reputation of the hacienda in Mexican labor history. In part, this reputation may represent an extension, with respect to labor, of a reputation gained in acts of land usurpation. In part, it may relate to areas remote from the Valley or to areas where haciendas were larger and workers less numerous. It may also reflect conditions of the nineteenth century and attitudes of justification relating to the Revolution of 1910, for in the national period

16   Sharecropping on the Peruvian Coast

José Matos Mar

*In much of traditional Latin America, sharecropping was not
a practical way of exploiting large amounts of land because the
demand for agricultural produce was not large enough to induce
subsistence farmers to produce a surplus for the market. Haciendas therefore had to exploit their land directly if they were to
exploit it at all. In areas of higher demand, however, subsistence
farmers often learned to participate in the market economy.
This might lead to more competition for the haciendas, but it
also made it possible for landowners to exploit their land indirectly, letting it out to small farmers who could be counted on
to produce a surplus for sale. We know little about traditional
patterns of sharecropping. The following selection describes the
sharecropping system known as* yanaconaje *as it existed on the
Peruvian Coast during the first half of the present century.
Though this system was somewhat modernized, being used
mainly in the production of cotton, an export crop, many of
its characteristic features seem to have dated from the colonial
period, when it had most likely been used in the production of
maize.*

*José Matos Mar is professor of anthropology at the Univer-
sity of San Marcos in Lima and director of the Instituto de
Estudios Peruanos.*

Yanaconaje is a mechanism for the exploitation of land which
exists entirely within the hacienda system and has antecedents dating
back to the Inca period. During the colonial and republican eras it

Translated by the editor from José Matos Mar, "Las haciendas del valle de
Chancay," in Henri Favre, Claude Collin Delavaud, and José Matos Mar, *La
hacienda en el Perú* (Lima, Instituto de Estudios Peruanos, 1967), pp. 361-364.

has undergone a series of changes and adaptations and is now (1964) regulated by a special law.

A *yanacón* is an individual who works a specific parcel of hacienda land under a kind of rental agreement regulated by written or verbal contract. He is obliged to pay 20 percent of his harvest in kind, with the crop to be grown being determined by the landowner; in the Chancay Valley, as in many others on the Peruvian Coast, it is cotton. The land is exploited in accordance with a set of norms, which in most cases are tacitly agreed upon by the yanacón and the patrón. The hacienda loans money to the yanacón with which he can pay peons if necessary, purchase seed and fertilizer, and rent farm machinery. This is known as *habilitación,* and the sum borrowed has to be repaid with an interest of no less than 15 percent. At the same time, the yanacón is expected to contribute, in proportion to the amount of land he cultivates, to the general expenses of the hacienda (those incurred for administration and the maintenance of irrigation ditches). These obligations are paid in cotton. The nature of the relationship between patrón and yanacón can vary considerably, suggesting in some cases an absolute dependence and in others approximating modern types of agrarian contracts. Yanaconaje thus represents an unequal union between a capitalist system of exploitation which provides land, water, and capital, and a pattern of agricultural labor operating within a pre-capitalist system of land tenure.

The yanaconas usually do not have much capital, though on occasion they have been able to loan money to hacendados. This only happens, however, on haciendas in a state of crisis. The situation of the group is a complicated one, since in many cases the yanacón is also engaged in local commerce, especially in the cotton trade from which he may receive substantial profits. He thus tends to occupy a relatively good economic position in the valley. Comparing his situation with that of the sierra peon (also called a yanacón), one sees important differences. In the sierra, the system follows the rent-labor pattern which is characteristic of serfdom; the yanacón combines work on his individual parcel of land with work on the land which is directly exploited by the hacienda; thus there is a direct relationship of submission and the rent comes to be identified with unpaid labor. In Chancay, on the other hand, the system follows a a rent-product pattern; the hacendado does not directly appropriate surplus labor but rather the surplus product, thus giving the impression of greater individual autonomy for the laborer, since his submission to the owner takes on a social rather than a personal character.

In the Chancay Valley yanaconaje has played a major role in the expansion of the hacienda system and in its increasing productivity. It permitted hacendados to acquire new lands and to maintain possession of those they already had, as well as to perpetuate the absolute control of the estate through the collection of periodic rents, thus guaranteeing the labor needed to exploit the land. The expansion of the sharecropping system has always been related to the cycles of boom and bust. Thus it occurred with the changeover from sugar to cotton production at the beginning of the century and again when cotton prices collapsed during the depression. During these periods many hacienda workers—selected among the most trustworthy and respected members of the labor force—were turned into yanaconas. This may help to explain the conservative attitudes shown by the majority of present-day yanaconas, who have made the interests of the hacendados their own, even to the point of offering strong resistance to any change.

After 1942 the hacendados began to establish direct control over their property, as modernization led to the rapid development of technology and mechanization in the valley. This decreased the utility of the sharecropping system for the haciendas, since it held back their development by depriving them of their less productive land. To displace the yanaconas the hacendados resorted to violence or arranged for them to exchange their holdings for land in newly irrigated zones off the haciendas. This process of displacement was slowed by the passage of the law of yanaconaje (1947) and by the recent agrarian reform law (1964).

The displacement of the yanaconas led to a weakening of their identification with the hacienda and to the appearance of group movements for the defense of their interests. Having lost one of the traditional paths of social and economic mobility, they have turned to commerce and small landholding as substitutes. Yanaconaje is thus being replaced by other forms of indirect exploitation, such as rental and partnership arrangements, which involve fewer commitments for the hacendado.

Until very recently the yanacón always reacted negatively to proposals for reform, behaving like a small landowner and identifying his own interests with those of the hacienda. This conservative attitude reflects the security derived from his of possession of land and a source of capital, which gives him a special status within the hacienda and the society of the valley.

At present there are 787 yanaconas on 17 haciendas in the Chancay Valley; they cultivate 5,048 hectares (1 hectare = 2.47 acres), which represented 32.53 percent of the cultivated hacienda land and 23.53 percent of all the cultivated land in the valley. On the hacienda of Huando, there remain only two yanaconas who have .4 percent of the cultivated area. Jesús del Valle has 18 yanaconas and Caqui 12, working 13 percent of the cultivated area. Yanaconas work 80 percent of Chancayllo and 70.8 percent of Huayán. On the remaining haciendas 50 percent of the land is cultivated by yanaconas.

Under the 1964 agrarian reform law the yanacón is supposed to become a small landowner, receiving ownership of the land he cultivates from the hacienda. This has not yet (as of 1964) been applied in the valley, though the expectation is increasing. Chancayllo and Huayán, the haciendas with the most yanaconas, will soon disappear. Their owners are about to sell out to the yanaconas working the land, creating new small landowners. The more developed modern haciendas have few yanaconas. Their main wish is to free themselves from the burdens of the system.[1]

The existence of the yanaconas has increased social diversity within the valley, creating an intermediate step between the polar groups of the traditional social structure. Socially, the yanaconas have occupied a position between the peons and the owners and administrators, possessing an economic status which is in many ways higher than that of the salaried employees. In addition they have kept a degree of independence within the hacienda organization, establishing direct relations with the owners, to whom they have more access than the peons. Thus they form a distinct group of independent workers or entrepreneurs existing within the hacienda.

Within the hacienda system, the yanacón exhibits a loyalty which at times borders on servility. Perhaps his ties to the land and his chance for relative prosperity—distinguishing him both from peons and salaried employees—has stimulated his spirit of allegiance in exchange for "the patrón's goodness in providing land to work." He appears almost the owner of his land, since his right to exploit it can generally be inherited. To him, the parcel of land he cultivates is his home and the hacienda his community. One should also mention his relationship with the owner or administrator, who has treated him as a person with some responsibility for the integrity of the hacienda and has given him the sensation of belonging to the dominant group, thus awakening a feeling of identification with the hacienda and its owners which is reinforced by spiritual bonds. These circumstances have turned the yanacón into a partisan and defender (directly or indirectly) of the hacienda system and of the landowning class. This makes him appear a conservative or even a reactionary to the other groups within the rural society, since he opposes major changes in the structure of the system or innovations which come from outside, fearing that they will endanger the existing system.

We must also recognize the importance of other relations of dependence, such as those derived from the control of water and capital which are utilized by the hacendados to apply pressure and exercise control over the yanaconas. Some have escaped this control to a certain extent by ceasing to borrow money from the hacienda, either by employing their own capital or else by having recourse to outside moneylenders and banks, particularly the agricultural development bank, thus achieving the status of "free yanaconas."

The Agrarian Reform Law of 1964 has theoretically brought an end to the system of yanaconaje. Now the yanaconas have the opportunity of turning themselves into small landowners by purchasing their parcels of land from the haciendas. In reality they have only managed to become "feudataries" of the latter, identified by little green pieces of paper from the agrarian reform agency which give them the option of buying the land they work. In the final analysis this is the only change. The yanaconas continue to maintain the same relations with the haciendas, which still receive their rent payments and loan them capital, though in some cases this *habilitación* has been cut off.

In conclusion, yanaconaje represented for the hacendado a way of exploiting his land and, for the yanacona, a means of obtaining access to it. By establishing a mechanism by which small farmers could obtain land and capital, it made it possible for part of the lower-class population of the valley to become semi-independent farmers, thus creating an intermediate group within the rural society which helped to guarantee the survival of the hacienda system. Finally it assured an income for both landowners and renters, increasing the value of the property and mobilizing capital which would otherwise have been employed in other sectors of the economy.

17 The North Mexican Ranch

François Chevalier

Though stock raising was a prominent economic activity in all areas of European settlement, the classical Latin American ranch can best be understood as a frontier institution that took its most characteristic form in areas far removed from the major centers of population where the indigenous inhabitants were nomadic and hostile. In such regions, of course, there was seldom much demand for agricultural produce. Thus land had to be used primarily for the grazing of livestock, and its value, as well as the income it could provide, were very low. This meant that it was generally concentrated in fewer hands than elsewhere, giving rise to larger holdings. These tendencies were reinforced by the lack of adequate security in the frontier regions, which led to the rise of feudal patterns—here condoned by governments which were determined to suppress them elsewhere—and to the appearance of the private armies which belonged to so many of the great ranches. The ranches of northern Mexico described here largely conform with this general picture, though the development of silver mining in some areas gave them a somewhat different character than was possessed by the traditional ranches of such regions as the Río de la Plata.

Francois Chevalier was introduced in reading 8.

[During the eighteenth century] the entire northern zone [of Mexico] was exposed to constant incursions on the part of the nomads who, reacting to the Anglo-Saxon advance, infiltrated or migrated southward, on certain occasions even literally besieging such cities as

From François Chevalier, "The North Mexican Hacienda," in Archibald R. Lewis and Thomas F. McGann, eds., *The New World Looks at its History* (Austin, University of Texas Press, 1963), pp. 96–101.

Zacatecas. Many travelers describe these terrible Apaches or other Indian nations, who had become great horsemen, attacking the haciendas and even the small villages which they tried to burn, constantly interrupting communications, and, due to the resulting obstruction of commerce, interfering with the growth of the economy and the population. "Retablitos," *ex voto* paintings from the last century, show us these fearful indigenes: always on horseback, body naked, and sometimes painted in brilliant colors, directing their sure arrows against unwary travelers or herdsmen. Sometimes they had adopted some Mexican traits, such as the broad-brimmed hat or, worst of all, the rifle or the shotgun.

In addition, bands of robbers or outlaws used to wander these lands, even sacking, for example, the village of Sombrerete in 1832.

Therefore the haciendas of the North were always more or less fortified. Such, for example, was the one near Monclova which Padre Morfi described to us in the eighteenth century: "The house, although not comfortable to live in, is well constructed for defense against the Indians; it has a large corral and a patio which is not smaller in which an enormous quantity of livestock would fit in case of attack, which occurs frequently; it is entirely surrounded by a new adobe wall, tall and strong enough; at the north-eastern corner an adobe tower was under construction, from which the artillery can play from under cover and protect the portals of the habitation."

At the middle of the nineteenth century the novelist Payno, who always sticks close to reality, describes for us in the following manner a great northern hacienda:

> The house of the Sauz hacienda was in fact a fortified castle. The façade was made up of a high, broad archway ending on both sides in two tall towers with loopholes, which were matched by two others guarding the back of the house. The *azotea* was surrounded by crenellations behind which a soldier could keep under cover; so that once the massive oak door reinforced with iron bands was closed a siege would be necessary to take that building. Within there were wells of fresh, potable water and supplies for three or four months, arms, munitions and everything necessary for defense. . . . When these country estates were formed from lands belonging to nations never subdued like the Mexicans by the Spaniard, the buildings were constructed like fortifications, sacrificing interior comfort and architectonic proportions to security. In the patio, which was large, three or four coaches, each with its own string of eight mules, could have entered, turned around as in a circus, and passed again through the portal which led to the open country.

Padre Morfi described to us the curious invention of an *hacendado,* whose estate was located still farther to the north, near Santa Rosa, for protection against the constant and sudden attacks of the nomads in the open country: he "conceived of a sort of ambulating castle, constructed on a cart which follows the peons; within are kept some rifles, and at the least sign of attack the workers rush inside and, firing through the loopholes of the little fort, defend themselves against the shots of their enemies until the noise of the contest brings reinforcements to their aid; thus far this invention has freed him from surprise attacks and multiplied his wealth." The good father complains, however, that because of indolence and laziness, few of the neighboring landholders have such initiative.

As is well known, most of these northern haciendas were settled either for the exploitation of silver mines or to furnish these mines with grain and meat, and sometimes with both objects in mind: only precious metals could attract settlers to these arid highlands and severe mountains of northern Mexico. Being often very distant from the principal centers of population, the haciendas formed little worlds capable for the most part of supplying their own needs. In addition to their herds and cultivated fields, they often had mills, workshops, orchards, and vineyards. Accordingly, in northern Durango the hacienda of Santa Catarina, then the property of the Conde de San Pedro del Alamo, contained in the last third of the eighteenth century two thousand inhabitants, whose little huts, along with the church and the main house, formed a vast square plaza. The count possessed 130,000 sheep and 7,000 mares. There were lacking the sedentary Indians of the South, and the workers and servants were of the most varied origins, "from all the castes," at Santa Catarina; and in another place more to the north "Indians, *coyotes,* mulattoes, Pames, Tarahumaras . . . etc.: all are received without distinction, without inquiring who they are, nor whence they proceed." Also, in 1787, the *intendente* of Durango complains that because of the lack of workhands in his immense district, the haciendas and royal mining concessions frequently became "the asylum where bums and bandits may come and go as they please on the pretext of looking for work without anyone inquiring whence and with whose permission they come"; but the excuse for this is that otherwise "it would not be possible to find workers, even bad ones." Thus, peonage based upon retention for unpaid debts does not seem to be so common as in central and southern Mexico. On the haciendas of this same *intendencia* tenant farmers were living on their modest "ranchos"; they were "hard-up" people of various and frequently dubious origins who personally possessed, as did some servants, their own horses and small herds as well as the right to range these animals on the lands of the hacienda.

The great isolated haciendas continued during this period to have their private jails and their own administration of justice, either because the *hacendados* or their henchmen had managed to obtain the offices of the local government, or because they simply exercised a *de facto* power which was not theirs by law. Thus Padre Morfi and a commandant who accompanied him noted near Parras the presence of "a lad in chains," whose master had "punished him by imprisonment" for a misdemeanor; the good Franciscan comments that "his Lordship was surprised by the tyranny and limitless jurisdiction which these *hacendados* appropriate to themselves, and he ordered him set free." In the mid-nineteenth century Payno shows us also the severe Marqués de Valle Alegre having one of his servants whipped without the judge of the village daring to intervene; nonetheless, in the later period such behavior provoked serious resentments among the peons of the hacienda.

And finally, it would be a mistake not to study the private armies of the haciendas, which seem not to have been unusual, above all in the zones most exposed to the attacks of the nomads or of bandits. Sometimes they came into being by authorization or even command of the viceregal government, as in the case of Ciénega de Mata (S.L.P.). In other cases it was a *de facto* situation created in part by necessity and the lack of funds on the part of the government sufficient for such a vast country. Thus, during the period from 1810 to 1818 a henchman of the Conde de San Mateo Valparaíso, "nominated Colonel *ad honorem,* maintained for nearly one year eight hundred men on the northern frontier, whom he paid a peso a day," took part in the struggle for independence on the royalist side, and was routed in the end by the insurgents. In addition, "all the Mexican aristocracy of the viceregal period thought it much to be a captain, and their descendants continued being captains within the home and even outside of it, without the independent government ever concerning itself about them," as Payno writes, who shows us his Conde del Sauz, in the mid-nineteenth century, donning the uniform of a Spanish *capitán de infantería* for a dinner at his hacienda, or before setting out to meet a relative.

These great *hacendados* lived for most of the year in Mexico City or in other cities such as Durango, San Luis Potosí, or Querétaro. But they would go to spend a season at their haciendas, where they gathered together at times many friends and relatives; then, too, they offered a generous hospitality to travelers and hikers, for whom a wing of the main house was generally held in readiness.

When the rich *hacendados* traveled they liked to make a show of their military escort, for "those customs of the wealthy class of colonitial times were preserved many years after the beginning of the republic, as one of so many ordinary things which nobody noticed except those whose business they were." Accordingly, Payno's Marqués de Valle Alegre, wishing to impress his future father-in-law, arrived at the latter's hacienda located in a northern state mounted on a magnificent stallion, dressed as a captain, and accompanied by "twenty-five buckskin knights armed to the teeth." Behind them rolled "the coach of the house, a great spherical machine, the color of the blue sky, with the arms of the Marquis on the doors, supported by two husky gilded springs, enormous rear wheels, and tiny front ones." The canvas cover which had guarded it against the dust of the road had been removed, and the interior brushed so that the lining of velvet, mistreated and worn with use, would show to best advantage. "The coach of the Marquis was followed by that of the servants, of the same style but less luxurious, . . . [with] eight bay mules . . . and eight black mules kept in reserve," and in addition a magnificent "string of white mules, recently purchased, under the care of seven or eight lads well mounted and with their lariats close at hand." Finally, "the rear guard was formed by a squadron of ten mules with their respective muleteers, their new furniture, adorned with little tassels of vari-colored wool, and on their *atarrías* lettering in white fabric upon a red ground which said: 'I serve my master, the Marquis'."

Clearly it was not always that the *hacendados* had such means as this powerful marquis. Certain haciendas were abandoned because of the constant attacks of the nomads. Not a few of the other landowners were debtors who had mortgaged their landholdings and did not have the capital necessary to work their lands. Sometimes their indebtedness was caused by the luxury which they displayed. But above all there were more modest proprietors, who resided throughout the year in the country, living a patriarchal and austere life with their families. Such a man was the landowner near Zacatecas who governed his hacienda by himself and with such good order, composure, and good sense that his dependents enjoyed a much better condition than those in other locales. Padre Morfi notes that "every afternoon the master and the servants gather together in the chapel, pray the rosary, the catechism is explained and, in short, the whole breathes of economy, abundance and piety."

In general, these *hacendados* were religious men who founded chaplaincies and constructed churches where they arranged to have themselves buried. Even the first Conde de San Mateo Valparaíso became a hermit toward the end of his life, living in a grotto of the hills near his principal hacienda.

Among these great landholders not a few had a mentality comparable to that of the nobility of the Old Regime in Europe, showing a certain disregard for money and economic return, carrying their sense of honor to extremes, severe with their wives and daughters, who went abroad infrequently, even though the *hacendados* often fathered many illegitimate children—in sum, the enthusiastic heirs of a whole etiquette inherited from the old Spanish nobility. But at the very time that this nobility seemed to be assuming a set character and to be arriving at its apogee, in the eighteenth century and even later, a wise observer could detect clear symptoms of the great changes which would, a century or more in the future, totally transform traditional Mexican society.

18   The Brazilian Sertanejo

Euclides da Cunha

The position of labor in the frontier stock-raising economies was quite different from what it was elsewhere in Latin America. Ranches could seldom afford to offer high wages or purchase large numbers of slaves like plantations, and the exceptional mobility of men on horseback made it difficult to employ coercion in the manner of the manorial haciendas. The following selection suggests that if cowboys stayed where they were, it was usually not because they were forced to do so, or because of the financial remuneration; rather it was because the life of a cowboy, in spite of its difficulties, allowed them to achieve a degree of independence and self-reliance that the agricultural peon or the urban laborer could seldom aspire to.

Euclides da Cunha (1866–1909) was a Brazilian army officer and engineer who turned later in life to writing. His Os Sertões *(1902), from which the following is taken, is primarily an account of a revolt in the backlands of Bahía led by an enigmatic "messiah" who called himself Antonio Conselheiro.*

The *sertanejo,* or man of the backlands, is above all else a strong individual. He does not exhibit the debilitating rachitic tendencies of the neurasthenic mestizos of the seaboard.

His appearance, it is true, at first glance, would lead one to think that this was not the case. He does not have the flawless features, the graceful bearing, the correct build of the athlete. He is ugly, awkward, stooped. Hercules-Quasimodo reflects in his bearing the typical unprepossessing attributes of the weak. His unsteady, slightly swaying, sinuous gait conveys the impression of loose-jointedness. His normally

From Euclides da Cunha, *Rebellion in the Backlands,* translated by Samuel Putnam (Chicago, University of Chicago Press, 1944), pp. 89–98.

downtrodden mien is aggravated by a dour look which gives him an air of depressing humility. On foot, when not walking, he is invariably to be found leaning against the first doorpost or wall that he encounters; while on horseback, if he reins in his mount to exchange a couple of words with an acquaintance, he braces himself on one stirrup and rests his weight against the saddle. When walking, even at a rapid pace, he does not go forward steadily in a straight line but reels swiftly, as if he were following the geometric outlines of the meandering backland trails. And if in the course of his walk he pauses for the most commonplace of reasons, to roll a *cigarro,* strike a light, or chat with a friend, he falls—"falls" is the word—into a squatting position and will remain for a long time in this unstable state of equilibrium, with the entire weight of his body suspended on his great-toes, as he sits there on his heels with a simplicity that is at once ridiculous and delightful.

He is the man who is always tired. He displays this invincible sluggishness, this muscular atony, in everything that he does: in his slowness of speech, his forced gestures, his unsteady gait, the languorous cadence of his ditties—in brief, in his constant tendency to immobility and rest.

Yet all this apparent weariness is an illusion. Nothing is more surprising than to see the sertanejo's listlessness disappear all of a sudden. In this weakened organism complete transformations are effected in a few seconds. All that is needed is some incident that demands the release of slumbering energies. The fellow is transfigured. He straightens up, becomes a new man, with new lines in his posture and bearing; his head held high now, above his massive shoulders; his gaze straightforward and unflinching. Through an instantaneous discharge of nervous energy, he at once corrects all the faults that come from the habitual relaxation of his organs; and the awkward rustic unexpectedly assumes the dominating aspect of a powerful, copper-hued Titan, an amazingly different being, capable of extraordinary feats of strength and agility.

This contrast becomes evident upon the most superficial examination. It is one that is revealed at every moment, in all the smallest details of back-country life—marked always by an impressive alternation between the extremes of impulse and prolonged periods of apathy.

It is impossible to imagine a more inelegant, ungainly horseman: no carriage, legs glued to the belly of his mount, hunched forward and swaying to the gait of the unshod, mistreated backland ponies, which are sturdy animals and remarkably swift. In this gloomy, indolent posture the lazy cowboy will ride along, over the plains, behind his slow-paced herd, almost transforming his "nag" into the lulling hammock in which he spends two-thirds of his existence. But let some giddy steer up ahead stray into the tangled scrub of the caatinga, or let one of the herd at a distance become entrammeled in the foliage, and he is at once a different being and, digging his broad-roweled spurs into the flanks of his mount, he is off like a dart and plunges at top speed into the labyrinth of jurema thickets.

Let us watch him at this barbarous steeple chase.

Nothing can stop him in his onward rush. Gullies, stone heaps, brush piles, thorny thickets, or riverbanks—nothing can halt his pursuit of the straying steer, for *wherever the cow goes, there the cowboy and his horse go too.* Glued to his horse's back, with his knees dug into its flanks until horse and rider appear to be one, he gives the bizarre impression of a crude sort of centaur: emerging unexpectedly into a clearing, plunging into the tall weeds, leaping ditches and swamps, taking the small hills in his stride, crashing swiftly through the prickly briar patches, and galloping at full speed over the expanse of tablelands.

His robust constitution shows itself at such a moment to best advantage. It is as if the sturdy rider were lending vigor to the frail pony, sustaining it by his improvised reins of caroá fiber, suspending it by his spurs, hurling it onward—springing quickly into the stirrups, legs drawn up, knees well forward and close to the horse's side—"hot on the trail" of the wayward steer; now bending agilely to avoid a bough that threatens to brush him from the saddle; now leaping off quickly like an acrobat, clinging to his horse's mane, to avert collision with a stump sighted at the last moment; then back in the saddle again at a bound—and all the time galloping, galloping, through all obstacles, balancing in his right hand, without ever losing it once, never once dropping it in the liana thickets, the long, iron-pointed, leather-headed goad which in itself, in any other hands, would constitute a serious obstacle to progress.

But once the fracas is over and the unruly steer restored to the herd, the cowboy once more lolls back in the saddle, once more an inert and unprepossessing individual, swaying to his pony's slow gait, with all the disheartening appearance of a languishing invalid.

Disparate Types: The Jagunço and The Gaucho

The southern gaucho, upon meeting the vaqueiro at this moment, would look him over commiseratingly. The northern cowboy is his very antithesis. In the matter of bearing, gesture, mode of speech, character, and habits there is no comparing the two. The former, denizen of the boundless plains, who spends his days in galloping over the pampas, and who finds his environment friendly and fascinating, has, assuredly, a more chivalrous and attractive mien. He does not know the horrors of the drought and those cruel combats with the dry-parched earth. His life is not saddened by periodic scenes of devastation and misery, the grievous sight of a calcined and absolutely impoverished soil, drained dry by the burning suns of the Equator. In his hours of peace and happiness he is not preoccupied with a future which is always a threatening one, rendering his happiness short lived and fleeting. He awakes to life amid a glowing, animating wealth of Nature; and he goes through life adventurous, jovial, eloquent of speech, valiant, and swaggering; he looks upon labor as a diversion which affords him the sport of stampedes; lord of the distances is he, as he rides the broad level-lying pasture lands, while at his shoulders, like a gaily fluttering pennant, is the inevitable scarf, or *pala*.

The clothes that he wears are holiday garb compared to the vaqueiro's rustic garments. His wide breeches are cut to facilitate his movements astride his hard-galloping or wildly rearing bronco and are not torn by the ripping thorns of the caatingas. Nor is his jaunty poncho ever lost by being caught on the boughs of the crooked trees. Tearing like an unleashed whirlwind across the trails, clad in large russet-colored boots with glittering silver spurs, a bright-red silk scarf at his neck, on his head his broad sombrero with its flapping brim, a gleaming pistol and dagger in the girdle about his waist—so accoutered, he is a conquering hero, merry and bold. His horse, inseparable companion of his romantic life, is a near-luxurious object, with its complicated and spectacular trappings. A ragged gaucho on a well-appareled *pingo* is a fitting sight, in perfectly good form, and, without feeling the least out of place, may ride through the town in festive mood.

The Vaqueiro

The vaqueiro, on the other hand, grew up under conditions the opposite of these, amid a seldom varying alternation of good times and bad, of abundance and want; and over his head hung the year-round threat of the sun, bringing with it in the course of the seasons repeated periods of devastation and misfortune. It was amid such a succession of catastrophes that his youth was spent. He grew to manhood almost without ever having been a child; what should have been the merry hours of childhood were embittered by the specter of the backland droughts, and soon enough he had to face the tormented existence that awaited him. He was one damned to life. He understood well enough that he was engaged in a conflict that knew no truce, one that imperiously demanded of him the utilization of every last drop of his energies. And so he became strong, expert, resigned, and practical. He was fitting himself for the struggle.

His appearance at first sight makes one think, vaguely, of some ancient warrior weary of the fray. His clothes are a suit of armor. Clad in his tanned leather doublet, made of goatskin or cowhide, in a leather vest, and in skintight leggings of the same material that come up to his crotch and which are fitted with knee pads, and with his hands and feet protected by calfskin gloves and shinguards, he presents the crude aspect of some medieval knight who has strayed into modern times.

This armor of his, however, reddish-gray in hue, as if it were made of flexible bronze, does not give off any scintillations; it does not gleam when the sun's rays strike it. It is dead and dusty-looking, as befits a warrior who brings back no victories from the fight.

His homemade saddle is an imitation of the one used in the Rio Grande region but is shorter and hollowed out, without the luxurious trappings of the other. Its accessories consist of a weatherproof goatskin blanket covering the animal's haunches, of a breast covering, or pectorals, and of pads attached to the mount's knees. This equipment of man and beast is adapted to the environment. Without it, they would not be able to gallop through the caatingas and over the beds of jagged rock in safety.

Nothing, to tell the truth, is more monotonous and ugly than this highly original garb of one color only, the russet-gray of tanned leather, without the slightest variation, without so much as a strip or band of any other hue. Only at rare intervals, when a "shindig" is held to the strains of the guitar, and the backwoodsman relaxes from his long hours of toil, does he add a touch of novelty to his appearance in the form of a striking vest made of jungle cat or puma skin with the spots turned out—or else he may stick a bright red bromelia in his leather cap. This, however, is no more than a passing incident and occurs but rarely.

Once the hours of merrymaking are over, the sertanejo loses his bold and frolicsome air. Not long before he had been letting himself go in the dance, the *sapateado,* as the sharp clack of sandals on the ground mingled with the jingling of spurs and the tinkling of tambourine bells, to the vibrant rhythms, the "rip-snortings" of the guitars; but now once more he falls back into his old habitual posture, loutish, awkward, gawky, exhibiting at the same time a strange lack of nervous energy and an extraordinary degree of fatigue.

Now, nothing is more easily to be explained than this permanent state of contrast between extreme manifestations of strength and agility and prolonged intervals of apathy. A perfect reflection of the physical forces at work about him, the man of the northern backlands has served an arduous apprenticeship in the school of adversity, and he has quickly learned to face his troubles squarely and to react to them promptly. He goes through life ambushed on all sides by sudden, incomprehensible surprises on the part of Nature, and he never knows a moment's respite. He is a combatant who all the year round is weakened and exhausted, and all the year round is strong and daring, preparing himself always for an encounter in which he will not be the victor, but in which he will not let himself be vanquished; passing from a maximum of repose to a maximum of movement, from his comfortable, slothful hammock to the hard saddle, to dart, like a streak of lightning, along the narrow trails in search of his herds. His contradictory appearance, accordingly, is a reflection of Nature herself in this region—passive before the play of the elements and passing without perceptible transition from one season to another, from a major exuberance to the penury of the parched desert, beneath the refracted glow of blazing suns. He is as inconstant as Nature. And it is natural that he should be. To live is to adapt one's self. And she has fashioned him in her own likeness: barbarous, impetuous, abrupt.

The Gaucho

The gaucho, valiant "cowpuncher" that he is, is surely without an equal when it comes to any warlike undertaking. To the shrill and vibrant sound of trumpets, he will gallop across the pampas, the butt of his lance firmly couched in his stirrup; like a madman, he will plunge into the thick of the fight; with a shout of triumph, he is swallowed up from sight in the swirl of combat, where nothing is to be seen but the flashing of sword on sword; transforming his horse into a projectile, he will rout squadrons and trample his adversaries, or he will fall in the struggle which he entered with so supreme a disregard for his life.

The Jagunço

The jagunço is less theatrically heroic; he is more tenacious; he holds out better; he is stronger and more dangerous, made of sterner stuff. He rarely assumes this romantic and vainglorious pose. Rather, he seeks out his adversary with the firm purpose of destroying him by whatever means he may. He is accustomed to prolonged and obscure conflicts, without any expansive display of enthusiasm. His life is one long arduously achieved conquest in the course of his daily task. He does not indulge in the slightest muscular contraction, the slightest expenditure of nervous energy, without being certain of the result. He coldly calculates his enemy. At dagger-play he does no feinting. In aiming the long rifle or the heavy *trabuco,* he "sleeps upon the sights."

Should his missile fail to reach its mark and his enemy not fall, the gaucho, beaten or done in, is a very weak individual in the grip of a situation in which he is placed at a disadvantage or of the outcome of which he is uncertain. This is not the case with the jagunço. He bides his time. He is a demon when it comes to leading his enemy on; and the latter has before him, from this hour forth, sighting him down his musket barrel, a man who hates him with an inextinguishable hatred and who lies hidden there in the shade of the thicket.

The Vaqueiros

These contrasting characteristics are prominent in normal times.

Thus, every sertanejo is a vaqueiro. Aside from the rudimentary agriculture of the bottom plantations on the edge of the rivers, for the growing of those cereals which are a prime necessity, cattle-breeding is in these parts the kind of labor that is least unsuited to the inhabitants and to the soil. On these backland ranches, however, one does not meet with the festive bustle of the southern *estancias.*

"Making the roundup" is for the gaucho a daily festival, of which the showy cavalcades on special occasions are little more than an elaboration. Within the narrow confines of the mango groves or out on the open plain, cowpunchers, foremen, and peons may be seen rounding up the herd, through the brooks and gullies, pursuing intractable steers, lassoing the wild pony, or felling the rearing bull with the boleador, as if they were playing a game of rings; their movements are executed with incredible swiftness, and they all gallop after one another, yelling lustily at the top of their lungs and creating a great tumult, as if having the best time in the world. In the course of their less strenuous labors, on the other hand, when they come to brand the cattle, treating their wounds, leading away those destined for the slaughter, separating the tame steers, and picking out the broncos condemned to the horsebreaker's spurs—at times like these, the same fire that heats the branding iron provides the embers with which to prepare the roast, cooked with the skin on, for their rude feasts, or serves to boil the water for their strong and bitter-tasting Paraguayan tea, or *mate*. And so their days go by, well filled and varied.

Unconscious Servitude

The same thing does not happen in the north. Unlike the *estancieiro*, the *fazendeiro* of the backlands lives on the seaboard, at a distance from his extensive properties, which he sometimes never sees. He is heir to an old historic vice. Like the landed proprietor of colonial days, he parasitically enjoys the revenues from vast domains without fixed boundaries, and the cowboys are his submissive servants. As the result of a contract in accordance with which they receive a certain percentage of what is produced, the latter remain attached to the same plot of ground; they are born, they live and die, these beings whom no one ever hears of, lost to sight in the backland trails and their poverty-stricken huts; and they spend their entire lives in faithfully caring for herds that do not belong to them. Their real employer, an absentee one, well knows how loyal they are and does not oversee them; at best, he barely knows their names.

Clad, then, in their characteristic leathern garb, the sertanejos throw up their cottages, built of thatch and wooden stakes, on the very edge of the water pits, as rapidly as if they were pitching tents, and enter with resignation upon a servitude that holds out no attractions for them. The first thing that they do is to learn the *ABC*'s, all that there is to be known, of an art in which they end by becoming past masters—that of being able to distinguish the "irons" of their own and neighboring ranches. This is the term applied to all the various signs, markings, letters, capriciously wrought initials, and the like which are branded with fire on the animal's haunches, and which are supplemented by small notches cut in its ears. By this branding the ownership of the steer is established. He may break through boundaries and roam at will, but he bears an indelible imprint which will restore him to the *solta*[1] to which he belongs. For the cowboy is not content with knowing by heart the brands for his own ranch; he learns those of other ranches as well; and sometimes, by an extraordinary feat of memory, he comes to know, one by one, not only the animals that are in his charge but those of his neighbors also, along with their genealogy, characteristic habits, their names, ages, etc. Accordingly, should a strange animal, but one whose brand he knows, show up in his *logrador*, he will restore it promptly. Otherwise he will keep the intruder and care for it as he does for the others, but he will not take it to the annual fair, nor will he use it for any labor, for it does not belong to him; he will let it die of old age.

When a cow gives birth to a calf, he brands the latter with the same private mark, displaying a perfection of artistry in doing so; and he will repeat the process with all its descendants. One out of every four calves he sets aside as his own; that is his pay. He has the same understanding with his boss, whom he does not know, that he has with his neighbor, and, without judges or witnesses, he adheres strictly to this unusual contract, which no one has worded or drawn up.

It often happens that, after long years, he will succeed in deciphering the brand on a strayed bullock, and the fortunate owner will then receive, in place of the single animal that had wandered from his herd, and which he has long since forgotten, all the progeny for which it has been responsible. This seems fantastic, but it is nonetheless a well-known fact in the backlands. We mention it as a fascinating illustration of the probity of these backwoodsmen. The great landed proprietors, the owners of the herds, know it well. They all have the same partnership agreement with the vaqueiro, summed up in the single clause which gives him, in exchange for the care that he bestows upon the herd, one-fourth of the products of the ranch; and they are assured that he will never filch on the percentage.

The settlement of accounts is made at the end of winter and ordinarily takes place without the presence of the party who is chiefly interested. That is a formality that may be dispensed with.

The vaqueiro will scrupulously separate the large majority of the new cattle (on which he puts the brand of the ranch) as belonging to the boss, while keeping for himself only the one out of every four that falls to him by lot. These he will brand with his own private mark, and will either keep them or sell them. He writes to the boss, giving him a minute account of everything that has happened on the place, going into the most trivial details; and then he will get on with his never interrupted task.[2]

That task, although on occasion it can be tiring enough, is an extremely rudimentary one. There does not exist in the north a cattle-raising industry. The herds live and multiply in haphazard fashion. Branded in June, the new steers proceed to lose themselves in the caatingas along with the rest. Here their ranks are thinned by intense epizootic infections, chief among them *rengue*, a form of lameness, and the disease known as the *mal triste*. The cowboys are able to do little to halt the ravages of these infections, their activities being confined to riding the long, endless trails. Should the herd develop an epidemic of worms, they know a better specific than mercury: prayer. The cowboy does not need to see the suffering animal. It is enough for him to turn his face in its direction and say a prayer, tracing on the ground as he does so a maze of cabalistic lines. And, what is more amazing still, he will cure it by some such means as this.

Thus their days are spent, full of movement, but with little to show for it all. Rarely does any incident, some slight variation, come to break the monotony of their life.

Bound together by a spirit of solidarity, they unconditionally aid one another at every turn. Let a giddy steer flee the herd, and the vaqueiro will snatch up his *guiada*,[3] put spurs to his nag, and gallop after it in hot haste. If his efforts do not meet with success, he has recourse to his neighboring companions and asks them to "take the field," a phrase that is characteristic of these rustic knights; and his hard-riding, lusty-yelling friends by the dozen and the score will then follow him, scouring the countryside, riding over the slopes and searching the caatingas, until the beast, in the language of the cattle-men, has been "taken down a peg" and "turns up his nose" or else is thrown by main force when his horns are grasped in the cowboys' powerful hands.

19 Frontier Society on the Argentine Pampas

Domingo F. Sarmiento

Most of the frontier ranching zones of Latin America were neither productive nor populous enough to support much of a landed aristocracy. There the typical figure was not the great hacendado surrounded by servile dependents—the few land-owners wealthy enough to live this way were generally found in the cities and seldom saw their estates—but rather the small rancher, the gaucho proprietor as he was known in Argentina, who had more in common with the cowboys who worked for him than with the wealthy and educated elite of the cities. But if social relations tended to be more egalitarian, political relations often took on a strongly feudal character, with local leaders or sometimes bandit chieftains building up their own private armies and carving out spheres of influence, which the urban authorities were then forced to recognize in order to maintain some control over the situation. The implications of this particular combination of tendencies can be clearly observed in this classic description of the traditional rural society of the Argentine plains.

Domingo F. Sarmiento (1811-1888) was one of nineteenth-century Argentina's notable political figures. Exiled to Chile for his opposition to the dictator Rosas, he there made a name for himself as an author and educator before returning to enter politics after the latter's fall in 1852. He served as president of the republic from 1868 to 1874.

The Argentine rustic, at the moment of his arrival at maturity is in possession of such a character as has resulted from the natural

From Domingo F. Sarmiento, *Life in the Argentine Republic in the Days of the Tyrants, or Civilization and Barbarism,* translated by Mrs. Horace Mann (New York, 1868), pp. 46-55.

circumstances about him, and from his want of any true society. He is a man independent of every want, under no control, with no notion of government, all regular and systematic order being wholly impossible among such people. With these habits of heedlessness and independence he enters on another step of rural life, which, commonplace as it is, is the starting point of all the great events which we are shortly to describe.

It is to be remembered that I am speaking of the essentially pastoral part of the people, and that I select for consideration only their fundamental characteristics, neglecting the accidental modifications they receive, the partial effects of which will be indicated separately. I am speaking of the combination of landed proprietaries which cover the surface of a province, four leagues, more or less, being occupied by each.

The society of the agricultural districts is also much subdivided and dispersed, but on a smaller scale. One laborer assists another, and the implements of tillage, the numerous tools, stores, and animals employed, the variety of products and the various arts which agriculture calls to its aid, establish necessary relations between the inhabitants of a valley and make it indispensable for them to have a rudiment of a town to serve as a center. Moreover, the cares and occupations of agriculture require such a number of hands that idleness becomes impossible, and the men of an estate are compelled to remain within its limits. The exact contrary takes place in the singular society we are describing. The bounds of ownership are unmarked; the more numerous the flocks and herds the fewer hands are required; upon the women devolve all the domestic duties and manufactures; the men are left without occupations, pleasures, ideas, or the necessity of application. Home life is wearisome and even repulsive to them. They need, then, factitious society to remedy this radical want of association. Their early acquired habit of riding gives them an additional incentive to leave their houses.

It is the children's business to drive the horses to the corral before the sun has quite risen; and all the men, even the lads, saddle their horses, even when they have no object in view. The horse is an integral part of the Argentine rustic; it is for him what the cravat is to an inhabitant of the city. In 1841, El Chacho, a chieftain of the Llanos, emigrated to Chile. "How are you getting on, friend? " somebody asked him. "How should I be getting on? " returned he, in tones of distress and melancholy. "Bound to Chile, and on foot!" Only an

Argentine gaucho can appreciate all the misfortune and distress which these two phrases express.

Here again we have the life of the Arab or Tartar. The following words of Victor Hugo (*Le Rhin*) might have been written in the pampas: "He cannot fight on foot; he and his horse are but one person. He lives on horseback; he trades, buys, and sells on horseback; drinks, eats, sleeps, and dreams on horseback."

The men then set forth without exactly knowing where they are going. A turn around the herds, a visit to a breeding pen or to the haunt of a favorite horse, takes up a small part of the day; the rest is consumed in a rendezvous at a tavern or grocery store. There assemble inhabitants of the neighboring parishes; there are given and received bits of information about animals that have gone astray; the traces of the cattle are described upon the ground; intelligence of the hunting-ground of the tiger or of the place where the tiger's tracks have been seen, is communicated. There, in short, is the cantor; there the men fraternize while the glass goes round at the expense of those who have the means as well as the disposition to pay for it.

In a life so void of emotion, gambling exercises the enervated mind, and liquor arouses the dormant imagination. This accidental reunion becomes by its daily repetition a society more contracted than that from which each of its individual members came; yet in this assembly, without public aim, without social interest, are first formed the elements of those characters which are to appear later on the political stage. We shall see how. The gaucho esteems skill in horsemanship and physical strength, and especially courage, above all other things, as we have said before. This meeting, this daily club, is a real Olympic circus where each man's merit is tested and assayed.

The gaucho is always armed with the knife inherited from the Spaniard. More fully even than in Spain is here realized that peninsular peculiarity, that cry, characteristic of Saragossa—*war to the knife.* The knife, besides being a weapon, is a tool used for all purposes; without it, life cannot go on. It is like the elephant's trunk, arm, hand, finger, and all. The gaucho boasts of his valor like a trooper, and every little while his knife glitters through the air in circles, upon the least provocation, or with none at all, for the simple purpose of comparing a stranger's prowess with his own; he plays at stabbing as he would play at dice. So deeply and intimately have these pugnacious habits entered the life of the Argentine gaucho that custom has created a code of honor and a fencing system which protect life. The rowdy of other lands takes to his knife for the purpose of killing, and he kills; the Argentine gaucho unsheathes his to fight, and he only wounds. To attempt the life of his adversary he must be very drunk, or his instincts must be really wicked, or his rancor very deep. His aim is only to *mark* his opponent, to give him a slash in the face, to leave an indelible token upon him. The numerous scars to be seen upon these gauchos, accordingly, are seldom deep. A fight is begun, then, for the sake of shining, for the glory of victory, for the love of fame. A close ring is made around the combatants, and excited and eager eyes follow the glitter of the knives which do not cease to move. When blood flows in torrents the spectators feel obliged to stop the fight. If a *misfortune* has resulted, the sympathies are with the survivor; the best horse is available for his escape to a distant place where he is received with respect or pity. If the law overtakes him he often shows fight, and if he rushes through soldiers and escapes, he has from that time a wide-spread renown. Time passes, the judge in place has been succeeded by another, and he may again show himself in the township without further molestation: he has a full discharge.

Homicide is but a misfortune, unless the deed has been so often repeated that the perpetrator has gained the reputation of an assassin. The landed proprietor, Don Juan Manuel Rosas, before being a public man, had made his residence a sort of asylum for homicides without ever extending his protection to robbers; a preference which would easily be explained by his character of gaucho proprietor, if his subsequent conduct had not disclosed affinities with evil which have filled the world with terror.

With respect to equestrian sports, it will suffice to point out one of the many which are practiced, that the reader may judge what daring is required of those who engage in them. A gaucho rides at full speed before his comrades. One of them flings a set of *bolas* at him so as to shackle the horse in the midst of his career. Issuing from the whirlwind of dust raised by his fall, appears the rider at a run, followed by the horse, the latter carried on by the impulse of his interrupted career according to the laws of physics. In this pastime, life is staked, and sometimes lost.

Will it be believed that these displays of valor or skill and boldness in horsemanship are the basis of the great exploits which have filled the Argentine Republic with their name and changed the face of the country? Nothing is more certain. However, I do not mean to assert that assassination and crime have always been a ladder by which men have risen. Thousands of daring men have remained in the position of obscure bandits; but those who owe their position to such deeds are to be counted by larger numbers than hundreds. In all despotic societies, great natural gifts tend to lose themselves in crime; the Roman *genius* which could conquer the world is today the terror of the Pontine Marshes, and the Spanish Zumalacarreguis and Minas are to be met by hundreds in Sierra Morena. Man's need of developing his strength, capacity, and ambition, requires him, upon the failure of legitimate means, to frame a world, with its own morality and laws, where he shows complacently that he was born to be a Napoleon or a Caesar.

In this society, then, where mental culture is useless or impossible, where no municipal affairs exist, where, as there is no public, the public good is a meaningless word, the man of unusual gifts, striving to exert his faculties, takes with that design the means and the paths which are at hand. The gaucho will be a malefactor or a military chief, according to the course which things are taking at the moment when he attains celebrity.

Such customs need vigorous methods of repression, and to restrain hardened men, judges still more hardened are required. What I said at the outset, of the captain of the freight-carts, is exactly applicable to the country justice. He wants bravery more than anything else; the terror of his name is more powerful than the punishments he inflicts. The justice is naturally someone of former notoriety recalled to orderly life by old age and his family ties. Of course, the law he administers is altogether arbitrary; his conscience or his passions determine it, and his decrees are final. Sometimes justices officiate during their whole lives, and are remembered with respect. But the consciousness of these methods of administration and the arbitrary nature of the attendant penalties, produce among the people ideas of judicial authority which will have their effects hereafter. The justice secures obedience by his reputation for formidable boldness, by his force of character, his informal decisions, his decree, the announcement "such are my commands," and the forms of punishment which he invents himself. From this disorder, perhaps long since inevitable, it follows that the military commander who reaches distinction during rebellions possesses a sway, undisputed and unquestioned by his followers, equal to the wide and terrible power now only to be found among the nations of Asia. The Argentine chieftain is a Mohammed who might change the prevailing religion, if such were his whim, and contrive another. He has power in all its forms; his injustice is a misfortune for his victim, but no abuse on his part; for he may be unjust—still more, he must be unjust—for he has been a lawless man all his life.

These remarks are also applicable to the country commandant. This personage is of more importance than the former, and requires in a higher degree the combination of the reputation and antecedents which distinguish him. Far from being lessened, the evil is even aggravated by an additional circumstance. The title of country commandant is conferred by the rulers of the cities; but as the city is destitute of power, influence, and supporters in the country, the administration lays hold of the men it most fears, and confers this office upon them in order to retain their obedience—a well known procedure of all weak governments, which put off the evil of the moment only to allow it to appear later in colossal dimensions. Thus the Papal government has dealings with banditti, to whom it gives offices in Rome, encouraging brigandage by this means, and making its continuance certain; thus did the Sultan grant Mehemet Ali the rank of Pacha of Egypt, having afterwards to purchase the continuance of his own reign by recognizing his vassal's title to an hereditary throne. It is singular that all the chieftains of the Argentine revolutionary movement were country commandants: Lopez and Ibarra, Artigas and Guemes, Facundo and Rosas. This is the constant starting point of ambition. When Rosas had made himself master of the city, he exterminated all the commandants to whom he owed his elevation, intrusting with this influential position commonplace men, who could only follow the path he had traced. Pajarito, Celarragan, Arbolito, Pancho el ñato, Molina, were among the commandants of whom Rosas cleared the country.

I assign so much importance to these lesser points, because they will serve to explain all our social phenomena, and the revolution which has been taking place in the Argentine Republic. The features of this revolution are distorted because described in words from the political dictionary, which disguise and hide them by the mistaken ideas they call up. In the same way that the Spaniards gave familiar European names to the new animals they encountered upon landing in America; saluting with the terrible name of lion, which calls up the notion of the magnanimity and strength of the king of beasts, a wretched cat called the puma, which runs at the sight of the dogs, and naming the jaguar of our woods the tiger. Evidence will soon be brought to show the firm and indestructible nature of the foundations upon which I assert the civil war to be based, however unstable and ignoble they may appear. The life of the Argentine country people as I have exhibited it is not a mere accident; it is the order of things, a characteristic, normal, and in my judgment unparalleled system of association, and in itself affords a full explanation of our revolution.

Before 1810, two distinct, rival, and incompatible forms of society, two differing kinds of civilization existed in the Argentine Republic: one being Spanish, European, and cultivated, the other barbarous, American, and almost wholly of native growth. The revolution which occured in the cities acted only as the cause, the impulse, which set these two distinct forms of national existence face to face, and gave occasion for a contest between them, to be ended, after lasting many years, by the absorption of one into the other.

I have pointed out the normal form of association, or want of association, of the country people, a form worse, a thousand times, than that of the nomad tribe. I have described the artificial associations formed in idleness, and the sources of fame among the gauchos—bravery, daring, violence, and opposition to regular law, to the civil law, that is, of the city. These phenomena of social organization existed in 1810, and still exist, modified in many points, slowly changing in others, and yet untouched in several more. These foci, about which were gathered the brave, ignorant, free, and unemployed peasantry, were found by thousands through the country. The revolution of 1810 carried everywhere commotion and the sound of arms. Public life, previously wanting in this Arabic-Roman society, made its appearance in all the taverns, and the revolutionary movement finally brought about provincial, warlike associations, called *montoneras,* legitimate offspring of the tavern and the field, hostile to the city and to the army of revolutionary patriots. As events succeed each other, we shall see the provincial *montoneras* headed by their chiefs; the final triumph, in Facundo Quiroga, of the country over the cities throughout the land; and by their subjugation in spirit, government, and civilization, the final formation of the central consolidated despotic government of the landed proprietor, Don Juan Manuel Rosas, who applied the knife of the gaucho to the culture of Buenos Ayres, and destroyed the work of centuries—of civilization, law, and liberty.

Notes

The editor's notes are enclosed in brackets. All other notes are by the authors of the individual readings.

Introduction

1. Murdo J. MacLeod, *Spanish Central America: A Socioeconomic History* (Berkeley and Los Angeles: University of California Press, 1973), p. 291. A similar point can be made about the Argentine plains, where a true landed aristocracy established itself only in the nineteenth century, after it became possible to sell meat as well as hides.
2. Eric R. Wolf and Sidney W. Mintz, "Haciendas and Plantations in Middle America and the Antilles," *Social and Economic Studies* 6 (1957): 380.
3. The best introduction is Rodolfo Stavenhagen, ed., *Agrarian Problems and Peasant Movements in Latin America* (Garden City, N.Y.: Anchor Books, 1970).
4. See V. S. Naipaul's perceptive account of the early history of Trinidad in his *The Loss of El Dorado: A History* (New York: Knopf, 1970), part I.
5. Alvaro Jara speaks of an early "gold cycle" which is followed by a "silver cycle" in his *Tres ensayos sobre enconomía minera hispanoamericana* (Santiago, Centro de Investigaciones de Historia Americana, Universidad de Chile, 1966), pp. 24–26, 52.
6. See Sherburne F. Cook and Woodrow Borah, *Essays in Population History: Mexico and the Caribbean* (2 vols. Berkeley and Los Angeles: University of California Press, 1971-1974), I, pp. 376-410. For a general account of the depopulation, see Nicolás Sánchez-Albornoz, *The Population of Latin America: A History* (Berkeley and Los Angeles: University of California Press, 1974), pp. 39-66.
7. See, for instance, Arnold J. Bauer, *Chilean Rural Society from the Spanish Conquest to 1930* (Cambridge, England: Cambridge University Press, 1975), pp. 180-181; and Robert G. Keith, *Conquest and Agrarian Change:*

The Emergence of the Hacienda System on the Peruvian Coast (Cambridge, Mass.: Harvard University Press, 1976), pp. 110-111.

8. On the difficulties of being an absentee sugar planter, see Richard Pares, *A West-India Fortune* (London: Longmans, Green & Co., 1950), pp. 141-159.

9. The consolidation of landholdings in Barbados is described by Richard Dunn, *Sugar and Slaves: The Rise of the Planter Class in the English West Indies, 1624-1713* (Chapel Hill: University of North Carolina Press, 1972), pp. 66-67. For Brazil, see Harry W. Hutchinson, *Village and Plantation Life in Northeastern Brazil* (Seattle: University of Washington Press, 1957), pp. 25-26, 33-36.

10. Dunn, *Sugar and Slaves,* p. 69, 89.

11. Ibid., pp. 95-96.

12. See Keith, *Conquest and Agrarian Change,* pp. 80-92, 111-122.

13. Wakefield's argument, which is mainly concerned with Australia, was originally presented in his *A Letter from Sydney* (1829; reprint, London: Dent, 1929).

14. Keith, *Conquest and Agrarian Change,* pp. 98-105. /

15. Horacio Giberti, *Historia económica de la ganadería argentina* (2nd ed. Buenos Aires: Ediciones Solar/Libería Hachette, 1961), pp. 31-34.

16. François Chevalier, *Land and Society in Colonial Mexico: The Great Hacienda* (Berkeley and Los Angeles: University of California Press, 1963), pp. 220-226 and "The North Mexican Hacienda," in Archibald R. Lewis and Thomas F. McGann, eds., *The New World Looks at its History* (Austin: University of Texas Press, 1963), pp. 101-106.

17. The fact that such a stable population was already coming into existence helps to explain why slaves in the Northeast could be easily transformed into service tenants. See J. H. Galloway, "The Last Years of Slavery on the Sugar Plantations of Northeastern Brazil," *Hispanic American Historical Review* 51 (1971): 586-605; and Peter Eisenberg, "Abolishing Slavery: The Process on Pernambuco's Sugar Plantations," *Hispanic American Historical Review* 52 (1972): 580-597.

18. This conclusion has recently received additional support from John Tutino, "Hacienda Social Relations in Mexico: The Chalco Region in the Era of Independence," *Hispanic American Historical Review* 55, no. 3 (1975): 496-528.

19. See José Matos Mar, "Las haciendas del valle de Chancay," in Henri Favre, Claud Collin Delavaud, and José Matos Mar, *La hacienda en el Perú* (Lima: Instituto de Estudios Peruanos, 1967), pp. 348-352.

20. On northern Mexico, see Charles H. Harris, *A Mexican Family Empire: The Latifundio of the Sánchez-Navarros, 1765-1867* (Austin: University of Texas Press, 1975).

1. Haciendas and Plantations

1. These secondary psychological gratifications have often been used to defend the hacienda system, or have been denied validity by its opponents. At various points in history, every social system which provided personal gratification of this sort has been defended as productive of security by some, and attacked as destructive of personal liberties by others. The present discussion attempts to describe and analyze these characteristics as derivatives of a functioning social system.
2. In recent years, there has been a tendency for plantations in some parts of the world to develop secondary cash crops which could take the place of the major cash crop in case of unfavorable changes in the market. Also to be noted is a tendency of "underdeveloped" countries to force plantations to pay greater attention to the subsistence needs of their laborers. Such changes may eventually lead to major changes in the plantation type.
3. Some have defended the rationalization of production under the plantation system as an aspect of the liberation of the worker from ties of submission to a personal overlord, controlling his very life. Others have criticized the plantation system for its supposed destruction of a highly integrated way of life, be it that of the hacienda or of some traditional village group. It would seem to us that these forms of organization take shape in response to cultural forces which are not dependent primarily on the personalities or personal philosophies of the organizers of production. They represent instead answers to problems posed by differing kinds and sizes of markets, differing amounts of available investment capital, and differing political situations.

2. The Early Brazilian Sugar Economy

1. Although long-term comparisons of monetary incomes—based on gold value—are practically meaningless, for the sake of curiosity we would mention that the annual per capita income (of the population of European origin) at the turn of the sixteenth century amounted to about $350 in terms of today's values. This income per capita was evidently far higher· than that prevailing in Europe at the time, and at no other period of its history—even at the height of the gold cycle—did Brazil regain this level of income.
2. A salary of £15 a year would be considered very high at the time, inasmuch as the actual cost of slave labor would not be much more than £4 a year—assuming a price of £25, a useful life of eight years, and that one-third of the slave's time was absorbed in producing food for his own sustenance. As a basis for comparison it might be mentioned that farm wages in the

Northern United States in the second half of the eighteenth century were about £12, and about half as much in England.

3. Starting with a gross income of £1.5 million in the sugar sector, and assuming 10 percent of this income went for payment of wages, purchases of livestock, lumber, and so on, and that the cost of replacement of imported factors was of the order of £120,000, it may be deduced that the net income of the sector was about £1.2 million. Deducting £600,000 for the cost of imported consumer goods, this would leave £600,000, which represented the investment potentialities of the sector. Since tied-up capital amounted to £1.8 million and at least one-third of the latter was in buildings and facilities erected by the slaves themselves, it may be deduced that over a period of two years the capital could be doubled.

4. The Brazilian Sugar Plantation

[1.   In Brazil there were traditionally two types of sugar planters, the senhores de engenho, whose plantations had their own mills, and the lavradores, smaller planters who lacked their own mills and therefore had to take their cane to one of the large plantations to be turned into sugar. Some lavradores were independent and took their cane to the engenho of their choice; others were obliged to take it to a particular engenho, either because their land had originally been granted on that condition, or because the senhor had given them money in return for a commitment to bring their cane to his engenho, or because they were sharecroppers on land owned by the engenho.]

[2.   The mestre de açucar (sugar master), barqueiro, and contra-barqueiro supervised the boiling down of the cane syrup. The purgador was in charge of the process of draining the molasses from the sugar. The caixeiros were responsible for drying and packing the sugar and for distributing it to the lavradores and the merchants in the city. The feitores were the overseers and the feitor-mor the chief overseer. Roças were plots of land used for growing food crops.]

[3.   Messapés were fertile black soils, the best for growing cane. Salões were soils of mixed sand and clay, used for cane but less fertile than the massapés. Apicús were sandy areas at the edge of the sea subject to inundation by tidewater.]

[4.   Caldeireiros and tacheiros were specialized workers employed in boiling down the cane syrup.]

6. Masters and Slaves in Southern Brazil

1. Slaves played skillfully upon planter paternalism to escape or mitigate punishment for minor transgressions. A slave might ward off a lashing by fleeing immediately upon committing an offense to the proprietor of a neighboring plantation. On arrival, the slave would request the planter to "adopt" him (*tomar padrinho*). If the planter accepted, the slave returned to his master with a note or else the planter personally escorted him back. Then the slave would be admonished not to repeat his offense lest he suffer the consequences.

7. Masters and Slaves in the Brazilian Northeast

[1. Freyre believes that many of the distinctive characteristics of Brazilian civilization can be attributed to Moslem influences on Portuguese culture and society; see his *New World in the Tropics: The Culture of Modern Brazil* (New York: Knopf, 1945), pp. 39-66.]

10. The Problem of Hacienda Markets

1. In comparison with the other figures, this one seems exaggerated; nevertheless the others all come from years of bad or mediocre harvests which produced crises.
2. These figures, taken from inventories, include maize which had been stored from earlier years and do not therefore give the exact size of the harvest for the particular years to which they refer.

12. Patrón and Peon on an Andean Hacienda

[1. Huasipungueros: Indians who had *huasipungos*, or small plots of land given them by the hacienda on which to grow their food.]
[2. Pes: dialect form of the Spanish *pues* (well, then).]
[3. Taita: Quechua word for father; taita cura: the parish priest.]
[4. Cholito: diminutive form of *cholo*, meaning a person of mixed white and Indian blood. The use of dimunitives is one way in which Icaza tries to replicate Indian patterns of speech, the other being the substitution of u for o at the end of words. Thus socorro becomes socorrito or socorritu, patrón becomes patroncitu, taita becomes taiticu or taitiquitu (a double diminutive).]

16. Sharecropping on the Peruvian Coast

[1.   The situation described here has of course changed since the more radical agrarian reforms carried out by the military government which seized power in 1968.]

18. The Brazilian Sertanejo

1.   An uninclosed pasture, sometimes at quite a distance from the farmhouse.
2.   In writing letters, he eschews the common formula, "Your humble servant," and naively substitutes for it "Your cowboy friend F." Occasionally, in conveying word of a disaster, a straying of the herd, for instance, his conciseness is startling: "Dear Boss. This is to let you know that your herd is *under control.* Only four steers lost their hides in the brush. The rest are still *alive and stamping.*"
3.   Name given to the elongated, sharpened prong.

Bibliographical Note

For those wishing to read more on the subject, there is an immense literature concerned with landed estates and estate agriculture in Latin America. The present listing is intended to help orient the reader and makes no pretence of completeness.

For more complete bibliographies the reader is referred to *The Economic Literature of Latin America: A Tentative Bibliography* (2 vols; Cambridge, Mass., 1936) and to the bibliographies in volume II of *La historia económica en América Latina* (Mexico, 1972), as well as to Magnus Mörner's excellent historiographical article, "The Spanish American Hacienda: A Survey of Recent Research and Debate," *Hispanic American Historical Review* 53 (1973): 183–216.

The agrarian systems of Latin America have been intensively studied by social scientists since the 1920s. For an overall view, one may begin with Solon L. Barraclough and Arthur L. Domike, "Agrarian Structure in Seven Latin American Countries," *Land Economics* 42 (1966): 391–424, which summarizes a series of reports issued by the Inter-American Committee for Agricultural Development (ICAD) or with Ernest Feder, *The Rape of the Peasantry: Latin America's Landholding System* (Anchor Books, 1971), written by an economist who collaborated on the ICAD reports. The special characteristics of the plantation are dealt with in *Plantation Systems of the New World* (Washington, U.S. Government Printing Office, 1959). Among works dealing with the agrarian systems of individual countries or regions may be mentioned: George M. McBride. *The Land Systems of Mexico* (New York, 1927) and his later *Chile: Land and Society* (New York, 1936); Nathan L. Whetten, *Rural Mexico* (Chicago, 1948); Lowry Nelson, *Rural Cuba* (Minneapolis, 1950); Carl Taylor, *Rural Life in Argentina* (Baton Rouge, La., 1954); Thomas R. Ford, *Man and the Land in Peru* (Gainesville, Fla., 1955); and Orlando Fals-Borda, *El hombre y la tierra en Boyacá: bases sociológicas y históricas para una reforma agraria* (Bogotá, 1957).

For the colonial period, one should begin with François Chevalier's study of the origins of the Mexican hacienda system, *Land and Society in Colonial Mexico: The Great Hacienda,* ed. by Lesley B. Simpson (Berkeley, 1963). The argument that the growth of the hacienda reflected the Indian demographic collapse was first made by Woodrow Borah in *New Spain's Century of Depression* (Berkeley,

1951) and the relations between the Indian communities and the developing haciendas were clearly delineated by Eric R. Wolf in his *Sons of the Shaking Earth* (Chicago, 1959). The general picture outlined in these works has been filled in and clarified by the work of Charles Gibson, whose *The Aztecs under Spanish Rule: A History of the Indians of the Valley of Mexico, 1519-1810* (Stanford, 1964) contains much information on colonial haciendas. As research has been extended to areas not previously studied, it has become clear that there was a great deal of regional variation in the way hacienda systems developed. Alvaro Jara, ed., *Tierras nuevas: Expansión territorial y ocupación del suelo en América (siglos XVI-XIX)* (Mexico, 1969) contains papers concerned with how land tenure systems developed in a number of different areas. William B. Taylor describes the distinctive land tenure system found in southern Mexico in *Landlord and Peasant in Colonial Oaxaca* (Stanford, 1972). Murdo J. MacLeod provides a broad interpretation of the changes which led to the rise of the hacienda system in his *Spanish Central America: A Socioeconomic History, 1520-1720* (Berkeley, 1973). Robert G. Keith, *Conquest and Agrarian Change: The Emergence of the Hacienda System on the Peruvian Coast* (Cambridge, Mass., 1976) describes the patterns of change found in an area which was totally dependent on irrigation. Mario Góngora has written three books dealing with the evolution of landed estates in Chile: *Evolución de la propriedad rural en el valle del Puangue*, written with Jean Borde (2 vols; Santiago, 1956); *Origen de los "inquilinos" de Chile central* (Santiago, 1960); and *Encomenderos y estancieros* (Santiago, 1970). The highland area north of Bogotá in Columbia has been studied by Germán Colmenares, *La provincia de Tunja en el nuevo reino de Granada. Ensayo de historia social (1539-1800)* (Bogotá, 1970); Colmenares has also written a *Historia económica y social de Colombia* (Bogotá, 1973). Finally, the development of the Argentine cattle economy and its large ranches or *estancias* is well described in Horacio C. E. Giberti, *Historia económica de la ganadería argentina* (2nd. ed.; Buenos Aires, 1961).

The changes in the rural economies and societies of Latin America associated with the growth of exports in the nineteenth century have been studied by a number of scholars. Arnold Bauer examines the case of Chile in his *Chilean Rural Society from the Spanish Conquest to 1930* (Cambridge, England, 1975), which in spite of its title is primarily concerned with the second half of the nineteenth century. James R. Scobie describes the change from a stock-raising to an agricultural economy and its social consequences in *Revolution on the Pampas: A Social History of Argentine Wheat, 1860-1910* (Austin, 1964). Peter F. Klaren examines the modernization of the traditional sugar haciendas of the northern coast of Peru in the initial chapters of his *Modernization, Dislocation and Aprismo: Origins of the Peruvian Aprista Party, 1870-1932* (Austin, 1973). A more detailed study of Peruvian agriculture is Jean Piel's *Capitalisme agraire au Pérou*, of which only the first volume has yet appeared (Paris, 1975). Finally William P. McGreevey examines commercial agriculture and its role in the economic development of Colombia in *An Economic History of Colombia, 1845–1930* (Cambridge, England, 1971).

Studies of how haciendas operated, based primarily on estate records, are a comparatively recent phenomenon. An interesting collection of papers, originally presented at a conference on Latin American economic history, has been published in Enrique Florescano, ed., *Haciendas, latifundios y plantaciones en América Latina* (Mexico, 1975). The geographer Ward Barrett has studied the hacienda of Atlacomulco in Morelos (Mexico), which belonged to the descendants of Cortés in *The Sugar Hacienda of the Marqueses del Valle* (Minneapolis, 1970); and Charles H. Harris III has studied a huge Coahuila estate, built up through the consolidation of numerous haciendas, in his *A Mexican Family Empire: The Latifundio of the Sánchez-Navarros, 1765–1867* (Austin, 1975). In this context one should also mention Enrique Florescano's suggestive study of price fluctuations and their consequences in eighteenth-century Mexico, *Precios del maíz y crisis agricolas en México (1708–1810). Ensayo sobre el movimento de los precios y sus consecuencias económicas y sociales* (Mexico, 1969).

Turning to the plantation, we begin with Brazil. Here, the best general treatment, both of the sugar economy of the Northeast and the later coffee economy of the South, can be found in Celso Furtado's *The Economic Growth of Brazil* (Berkeley, 1963), Frédéric Mauro, *Le Portugal et l'Atlantique au XVIIe siecle, 1570–1670* (Paris, 1960) is primarily concerned with Portuguese-Brazilian trade but contains much valuable information on the organization of plantations and the production of sugar. Peter Eisenberg examines how economic change and the abolition of slavery affected northeastern sugar plantations in *The Sugar Industry in Pernambuco, 1840–1919: Modernization Without Change* (Berkeley, 1963). The coffee plantation system of the South is dealt with in two excellent local studies: Stanley Stein, *Vassouras, a Brazilian Coffee County, 1850–1900* (Cambridge, Mass., 1957), which is concerned with an older coffee area near Rio de Janeiro, and Warren Dean, *Rio Claro: A Brazilian Plantation System, 1820–1920* (Stanford, 1975), which examines a county in the state of São Paulo.

The plantation systems of Spanish America have been less well studied, though for Cuba Ramiro Guerra y Sánchez has studied the development of the sugar economy in *Sugar and Society in the Caribbean: An Economic History of Cuban Agriculture* (New Haven, 1964) and Fernando Ortiz has compared the social and economic patterns associated with the cultivation of sugar and tobacco in *Cuban Counterpoint: Tobacco and Sugar* (New York, 1947). The cacao plantations of colonial Venezuela are also discussed by Federico Brito Figueroa in his *La estructura económica de Venezuela colonial* (Caracas, 1963). The plantation economy of the British West Indies, on the other hand, has been intensively studied and there are a number of books which are relevant to the study of Latin American plantation systems. Among these may be mentioned Richard B. Sheridan, *Sugar and Slavery: An Economic History of the British West Indies, 1623–1775* (Baltimore, 1975); Richard S. Dunn, *Sugar and Slaves:*

The Rise of the Planter Class in the English West Indies, 1624–1713 (Chapel Hill, 1972); and Lowell J. Ragatz, *The Fall of the Planter Class in the British Caribbean, 1763–1833: A Study in Social and Economic History* (New York, 1928).

There is a considerable literature dealing with the comparative study of slave labor systems, interest in this subject being stimulated originally by Gilberto Freyre's *The Masters and the Slaves: A Study in the Development of Brazilian Civilization* (2nd ed.; New York, 1956). The different arguments which this subject has evoked are well represented in Laura Foner and Eugene D. Genovese, eds., *Slavery in the New World: A Reader in Comparative History* (Englewood Cliffs, N. J., 1969). Cuban slavery, in particular, has received a great deal of attention. Herbert S. Klein found it to be relatively mild in *Slavery in the Americas: A Comparative Study of Virginia and Cuba* (Chicago, 1967) while Franklin W. Knight, *Slave Society in Cuba During the Nineteenth Century* (Madison, Wisconsin, 1970) takes the opposite point of view. Cuba has also provided us with one of the few first-hand accounts of slavery in Esteban Montejo's *The Autobiography of a Runaway Slave,* edited by Miguel Barnet (London, 1968).

There are few studies concerned with the history and operation of individual Latin American plantations, though Jose Wanderley de Araujo Pinho has written a history of a large sugar plantation near Bahia in his *Historia de um engenho do Reconcavo, 1552–1944* (Rio de Janeiro, 1944) and Gabriel Debien has studied two eighteenth-century Haitian plantations in *Plantations et esclaves à Saint-Domingue* (Dakar, 1962). Again, the presence of some excellent studies on the British West Indies partly compensates for this deficiency; Richard Pares, *A West-India Fortune* (London, 1950), follows the activities of a family of planters on the island of Nevis, and Michael Craton and James Walvin's *A Jamaica Plantation: The History of Worthy Park* (Toronto, 1970) traces the history of a large sugar estate from the seventeenth century down to the present.